Our Houseless Home

A Colourful Bush Childhood During the Great Depression

Lyle Courtney

MICHELLE ANDERSON PUBLISHING
MELBOURNE

First published in Australia 2010
by Michelle Anderson Publishing Pty Ltd
PO Box 6032, Chapel Street North
South Yarra 3141 Melbourne
www.michelleandersonpublishing.com
mapubl@bigpond.net.au

Designed and typeset by
Ironbark Graphics, Maryborough
Printed by McPherson's Printing, Maryborough

National Library of Australia Cataloguing-in-Publication entry

Author: Courtney, Lyle.

Title: Our houseless home : a colourful bush childhood during the great depression / Lyle Courtney.

ISBN: 9780855724030 (pbk.)

Subjects: Courtney, Lyle—Childhood and youth.
Depressions—1929—Victoria—Biography.
Country life—Victoria—Biography.
Victoria—Social conditions—1901-1945.
Victoria—History—1901-1945.

Dewey Number: 994.504092

Dedicated to:

That remarkable woman Auntie Mag, for her unselfishness and loving care. My unorthodox father, my siblings who accompanied me on the journey and my mother, the person I never got to know. My darling wife, Eileen, for being an integral part of my life for over 44 years, always devotedly caring for me in health and during several potentially serious illnesses. Without her encouragement and advice, I could never have completed this infinitesimal part of Australian social history. I especially appreciate the countless hours she spent repeatedly reading its seemingly never ending drafts, guiding me through my frequent bouts of "waffling on" and convincing me to delete most (not all) of the insignificant memories. Had they been included, little would have been added to the story, and the memoir would have been thrice as long.

Conversions

Money and measurements have been expressed in the terms appropriate to the period.

1 inch	2.54 centimetres	1 ton	1.01 tonnes
1 foot	0.30 metre	1 gallon	4.54 litres
1 yard	0.91 metre	1 bushel	36.32 litres
1 mile	1.60 kilometres	6 pence	5 cents
1 acre	0.40 hectare	12 pence	1 shilling
1 ounce	28.3 grams	1 "bob"	1 shilling
1 pound	0.45 kilogram	10 shillings	1 dollar
1 hundredweight	50.8 kilograms	£1 (one pound)	2 dollars

Family of Hugh and Anne McCully

	Born
William	1880
John	1882
Elizabeth (Auntie Liz)	1883
Mary (Auntie Tot)	1885
James	1886
David	1888
Margaret (Auntie Mag)	1889
Florence (my mother)	1891
Annie	1893
Andrew	1896
Deborah (Auntie Deb)	1898
Alice	1901

Family of Thomas and Florence Courtney

	Born
Louis	1917
Keith	1920
Lloyd	1922
Yvonne (Vonnie)	1924
Valma	1925
June	1926
John (Jack)	1927
Lyle	1930

We did not get to know any of Dad's family – three brothers and three sisters – until after the war, therefore they did not play any role during our time of hardship.

Contents

Introduction

It is my hope that readers will focus on the story and not the way it is written. Along the way, after reading the then available copy, friends generously gave me asked-for advice and help, but when I attempted a more formal and up to date style, the story lost its simplicity.

While I did make some of the changes suggested, I decided that even though I was well aware of its shortcomings, the work should reflect my unsophisticated line of thought.

Lyle

* * *

Around twenty-five years ago, out of the blue, Lyle told me he was going to write about his experiences growing up in the bush during the Great Depression. I enthusiastically embraced his decision and was very disappointed when the project just seemed to fade away.

A chance comment from a teenage great niece caused me to ask Lyle to resume writing.

When I made reference to Auntie Mag, she inquired, "Who's Auntie Mag?"

Perplexed, I realised that memories of dear self-sacrificing Auntie Mag could fade into oblivion, after just one generation.

On returning home I said, "Lyle, you must write your story. You owe it to Auntie Mag".

It was just the incentive that was needed and the words started to flow, albeit spasmodically, for another ten years.

The story isn't something that was being remembered as it was being written. It was constantly being relived at family gatherings and when friends from the past dropped in, thus ensuring the memories stayed alive.

It was just intended to be a family history, but as I read it I thought other people could be interested too. Lyle was less enthusiastic and procrastinated for years; proving his father's gene of finding a reason to prolong a decision was alive and well.

In an inspirational moment I decided to publish a limited number of copies to celebrate his eightieth birthday.

Eileen

1

Our Retreat to the Bush

Expecting a chilly night, I kindled the wood fire in our lounge room. As the crackles and murmurs of the gum leaves and sticks increased with the updraught and the flames grew higher, I slumped into a comfortable chair in front of the window next to the fireplace.

A glorious autumn day was drawing to a close. Pensively my eyes wander to the southeast, across the 40 odd yards of partially cleared shallow gully to where ironbarks, grey box and un-culled undergrowth of the state forest ascends the opposite slope. The forest actually comes to our fence, no more than 12 yards from where I sit, but each year I reluctantly clear the undergrowth from that strip for fire protection. As my eyes rest on a little reedy waterhole with a weathered red-clay bank half way across the firebreak, suddenly I feel a deep swell of nostalgia.

In the enchantment of the moment, the present fades and I see that pool as I first saw it on an autumn evening such as this more than 50 years ago. Driven by the urgency of approaching night, two young brothers and their maiden aunt in charge of a goat and her two kids, paused there uncertainly as the mother goat drank, to plot their course to the bush camp, set up that day by older males of the family.

It was the 14th of March 1935. The boys Jack and I, aged seven and five, the youngest of eight siblings, had stayed with Auntie Mag in the empty house that had been our family home since long before I was born on the 7th of January 1930. Soon after my mother's death at the age of 39, three weeks after my birth, my father struck another patch of bad luck that sent us heading for destitution as the severity of the Great Depression increased. By 1935 the position was desperate and under unpleasant circumstances, Dad lost our house and its 11 acres of land, leaving us virtually penniless.

Yet, even in the pathos and bitterness of that moment, Auntie Mag insisted on staying behind to clean up the soot and mortar, from where in a defiant claim of ownership, the sturdy cast iron stove had been torn from its brick surrounds by my father. It was impossible for Auntie Mag's nature to allow her to leave the house though now stove-less and empty in an untidy state for its new occupants.

My father was basically a kindly dreamer, but a thorough education in the school of experience enabled him to accept the realities of life and, in his own unorthodox way, cope with ever-changing fortune. He was a scrupulously honest man, with courage to speak his mind and then bear the consequences. He was born in Melbourne in 1881, the son of a sailor and the licensee of a Collingwood hotel.

He left home at the age of 13 and spent the next 17 years among the big timber of the Strzelecki Ranges in Gippsland, where with large families of stoic Catholics and Presbyterians, he helped destroy for farmland perhaps the best hardwood forest the world has ever seen. The guilt of being a partner in that crime haunted him for the rest of his life and instilled in him a deep repentant understanding and mateship with nature.

Those years in the wilds of Gippsland, amid the fellowship of kindly people in common hardship, was a major factor in his decision to take the remaining members of his young family into the bush instead of seeking compromising charity.

Fearless loyalty and compassion for her late sister's children, especially Jack and me, left Auntie Mag no choice but to turn her back on the comfortable life style of her family and accompany us.

The night was closing in fast as we left the waterhole and walked up the eastern slope of the wooded range of hills that cradled the town behind us. White quartz gravel, muted in the twilight, was liberally strewn among the leaves and sparse undergrowth that covered the ground beneath the black-trunked ironbarks which stood unchallenged on the highest points of the hard Ordovician sandstone ridges.

Some 15 minutes later we crested a hill and looked over the miles of forest declining eastward, to the cleared farmland of the volcanic plains beyond and the distant range of mountains indistinctly blending into the far horizon. But best of all, just before the forest thickened and became more diverse a few hundred yards down the slope, like a beacon of hope, a glorious campfire illuminated Dad, my three brothers, Louis, 17, Keith, 14, Lloyd, 12 and my 11-year-old sister Yvonne, all busy with the chores of the occasion, amid the calico tents and other meagre chattels of our new home.

Sharp, our stately old German collie dog, bounded up the hill to make first contact and for some moments lost his usual dignity as he jumped around us with delight. Moments later with mutual relief my tribe, except for my two youngest sisters, was reunited. At last I felt secure in the unknown "wilderness". Lloyd relieved us of the mother goat, known as the old goat, and led her with the two kids – Donk and Sarah – close at heel, a short distance from the camp, where she was tethered with our other goats for the night.

Not far from the goats, a persistent plaintive sighing sound, of "carr carr carr . . ." with intermittent heavy fluttering of wings, indicated that our poor disoriented chooks, unceremoniously plucked from the perches in their cosy hen house the night before and tipped into the bush at nightfall this evening, were desperately trying to find roosting spots in the scrub beside the camp. Thankfully, they all survived the night and soon became well-adapted bush chooks, and continued to enrich our diet with their eggs, and produce enough chickens to maintain our flock.

The autumn day, which had been so warm, was quickly turning into a cloudless chilly night. Above the close western tree-topped horizon, the waxing moon hung on its side, nursing the ghostly promise of the next full moon, while a few stars were becoming visible in the fading twilight.

With the ordeal of the race against time behind us and happy to be with my family again, the strange situation in which I found myself began to be an adventure. With my fear now abated I became aware of an appetising smell coming from an unfamiliar large saucepan sitting on some loosely stacked bricks at the edge of the campfire. Suddenly I was hungry. None of us had eaten since that final meal in our old home over seven hours before, but during the afternoon, Dad and the older boys had made a cup of tea from the familiar large black cast-iron kettle now pleasantly humming as it simmered on more stacked bricks near the big saucepan.

From the conversation it was obvious we were all hungry. Soon there was the clink of china being unpacked, as eight plates were spread on the ground in the light of the fire. With words of caution from Dad, Keith lifted the saucepan from the bricks. When the lid was removed with a burst of appetising aroma, about two gallons of choice stew was revealed. "Where did that come from?" Auntie Mag inquired with surprise. "Mrs Hovey," came a chorus of shouts. Yes, shouts they were, for Auntie Mag was deaf. Thoughtful Mrs Hovey was the mother of Keith's best friend, Reg. Rightly suspecting that we would neither have the time or ingredients to prepare a good meal on our first night in the bush, she had sent Reg and his father in the late afternoon, on a mission of mercy with that heavy saucepan and its welcome contents.

Even at my tender age I realised the generosity and thoughtfulness of that seemingly humble offering. Times were very hard for our entire neighbourhood during the Great Depression. Little did we know we would never have the chance to return Mrs Hovey's kind deed, for little more than a month later, on the 24th of April, she died suddenly.

The last rays of the sun had gone, as we sat around on makeshift seats – for we were chairless – and scoffed our meal of stew with scrumptious campfire toast spread liberally with soft brown seasoned dripping, followed by goats' milk tea. Dad said, "You wouldn't get better than this at Menzies". Even though we youngsters did not know that Menzies was an up-market Melbourne hotel, no one had cause to argue. Over the years I have come to realise that atmosphere and circumstance are often more important than the cuisine, for that simple meal remains one of the most memorable of my life.

My recollections of that eventful day ended as the moon dropped below the treetops and the Milky Way with the gems of the Southern Cross in the south was a glorious blaze. Overcome by sleep, I vaguely remember being put to bed by Dad, and hearing repeated requests for the presence of our lone hurricane lantern which, dull as it was, seemed to be in great demand.

Suddenly it was a bright new day. I had spent my first night in a tent. Did I dream? I wonder. Certainly not that more than 2500 nights would pass before I next slept in a house.

Nor did I have the slightest notion that by a quaint coincidence, less than two miles away, Eileen, who would become my wife and soul mate, was seeing the light of her second day in the maternity ward of the local hospital. She was born on the very day we retreated to our bush camp.

Overcome with the nostalgia of reliving that far-off evening, I sat in the quiet comfort of my chair for some time and pondered over the series of unusual circumstances that led to that event so long ago.

My thoughts wandered to how my poverty-stricken family fared in the following years of the Great Depression. Yet, during those years, I did not feel deprived. This was no doubt due to the loving closeness of my siblings; my loyal self-sacrificing aunt; the complexity of my father's unorthodox philosophy; the caring community in which we lived and our glorious bush playground. Thus leaving me with memories of a strange but wonderful childhood.

As I sat, I felt a compelling urge to record an infinitesimal snippet of Australia's social history.

2

Dad's Wonder Wheel

Having just reached the age of five I had little understanding of the drastic upheavals that had befallen my family in the short time since my birth. Perhaps that was just as well, for being a sensitive child I may have seen my birth as a bad omen.

When I appeared Dad was the managing director of a company that had been formed in the early 1920s, to develop, and eventually produce for sale, his invention the "Goeben Suspension Wheel" for cars. This aim resulted in the building of what was one of the first electrified engineering workshops in the country town of Maryborough where my family lived.

The selling point of Dad's wheels was that they had solid rubber tyres, thus avoiding punctures, the main curse of inflated tyres of that era. A quite complicated series of mechanisms transferred the hammering from the predominantly unsealed, rutty and corrugated roads to the top of the wheel, causing it to be cancelled out so that only the rim and tyre of the wheel was unsprung. This greatly increased the comfort for the occupants of the vehicle and reduced considerably the petrol necessary to drive the car.

Strangely, these seemingly exaggerated claims were completely verified by the numerous newspaper cuttings stored away in the family treasure chest, "the old tin box". They were reports of various independent trials with cars fitted with sets of Dad's wheels. Many times over the next few years I pondered over those glowing reports, until over-handling and the hard conditions of our camp caused the paper – then brittle and yellow – to crumble and mix with fragments of other saved documents into an unreadable "rat's-nest" in the bottom of the old seafarer's trunk.

In its heyday the Goeben Wheel Company had a vast amount of capital for those days. Why then, you may ask, did the wheel fail? The simple concept, and rapid improvements in the design and manufacturing methods of the pneumatic tyre, along with the surge in road construction technology, rang the final death knell for my father's "Wonder Wheel". But there seems to have been a time before the Depression, when the world sought such an innovation. That was when the other directors of the company were eager to start mass production of the wheels. However, the evidence indicates that my strong willed father was – metaphorically speaking – the spanner in the wheel.

Always a perfectionist, Dad was not satisfied that the ultimate design had been achieved. His hapless business associates stood by in utter frustration, as my father procrastinated while the time slot for the "Goeben Suspension Wheel" passed.

Another document which has long since crumbled in the old tin box graphically placed a value on the extent of their frustration. It was a formal letter from the other directors of the company, offering Dad 80,000 pounds to relinquish all rights (51 percent) to the wheel patents and the company – again an enormous amount at that time. Dad refused the offer. Not because he wanted more, but for the same reason he rejected the offers from mostly well meaning relations and friends, to relieve him of his eight young children when they were left motherless. He had a strong desire to oversee the development of his creations.

Strictly speaking, in the case of us kids, that sentiment was not the only consideration. Mum had made Dad promise just before she died that he would keep the family together.

At the gathering after Mum's funeral, without any consultation with Dad, the eight of us had been selected by various relations and friends, in some cases with considerable competition.

Our would-be benefactors were a diverse lot, with motives ranging from sublime to suspect. One very wealthy childless couple – long standing friends of our parents – had ambitions for Keith. They pledged to give him the best of everything that money could buy, including an education that would make him worthy to inherit their extensive grazing properties and elegant old family homestead. In later years Dad often said they were fine people, but his refusal to let my sibling go must have ended that close friendship, for my only knowledge of them came from family conversation.

Some of my soft-hearted aunties were motivated by sheer compassion, others by a sense of duty or a mixture of both those emotions, while an uncle it was suspected could have used an extra pair of hands to help him with the work around the farm and house.

However it seems I was not in demand, due perhaps – as I was constantly reminded throughout the rest of my childhood, and beyond – to the fact that from the very start I was a dreadful howler. Apparently for my first six months my inconsolable howling was only broken by sleep, and I was given to understand that no one would ever have called me sleepyhead.

Even though that marathon effort of mine – possibly worthy of a place in the *Guinness Book of Records* – often arose during reminiscences by older family members and friends, it was more than 20 years before I heard anyone attempt to explain the reason for my sorry state.

The announcement was publicly made on a most unlikely occasion – the wedding of my sister Valma. Except for the marriage itself, which proved to be a fairy-tale affair for over 50 years, things didn't go right that day. It started with pageboy trouble. Our four-year-old nephew, who had been assigned the task of delivering the ring on a decorative cushion to the best man, suddenly flung those items across the church floor.

But it was at the reception where things really began to get a bit iffy. It started with the Loyal Toast. Keith decided it was time to go public with his republican feelings. When the dour Presbyterian minister, now acting as master of ceremonies, asked the gathering in his strong Scottish accent to "Be upstanding for the Loyal Toast", Keith stuck to his seat. Although all of my family shared his sentiments and eagerly debated the subject in the company of like minds, we were taken aback by this public display. Admittedly it was a family tradition, though not an obligation, not to stand for *God Save the King* at the pictures, but that was in the dark. This seemed to be going just a bit too far for most of us, especially in front of the very respectable and royalist family of our newest in-law. However – like the conservative minister and his wife – they were magnanimous in the face of such an affront. They ignored the event with admirable dignity, and appeared to give us instant absolution for the transgression of our "rebel" brother. The only indication that the reverend had even noticed the royal insult was, "I am sure we will ALL stand for the next toast – to the Bride and Groom".

With that little hiccup out of the way, things progressed more or less normally for the remainder of the formal part of the reception. Later however, as we mingled and chatted, Lloyd, who had imbibed a few too many pre-wedding drinks, (the reception was non-alcoholic) was particularly talkative and eager to make Valma's new in-laws feel accepted as part of the family. To substantiate his expressions of goodwill and kinship, he passed on a few family secrets – not that we had any secrets of consequence – and obligingly explained some alleged idiosyncrasies of various members of our family. Possibly so they wouldn't feel out of it, this goodwill was extended to include our strait-laced preacher and his seemingly-more-so wife.

At that time I was 21, six foot two and a half inches tall and incredibly thin. I could hardly throw a shadow when I stood sideways to the sun. About that time a radiologist referred to me as being two-dimensional. I had celebrated my eighteenth birthday during a seven-week stay in hospital with rheumatic fever. That illness left me with an allegedly damaged heart, and medical advice forbade any strenuous exercise. Ten years after Valma's wedding, my condition was correctly diagnosed as a harmless congenital variation of the heart. These physical features, added to the yet to be told experiences of my childhood, were not the kind of things to build up my confidence, or take me to the top of my peer group.

While I had plenty of confidence in the confines of my family and close friends, I was embarrassingly shy in public. I was especially uncomfortable in the company of those around my own age. The males made me feel inferior and though I secretly craved the company of girls, my mental attitude robbed me of that pleasure. This self analysis was necessary to explain why I looked so pitiful that memorable afternoon, when Lloyd called me over and formally introduced me to the dignified "parsonic" pair, amid the small group of disciples gathered around chatting or more correctly, listening to him. After the introductions were completed, my brother evidently decided some explanation for my humble demeanour should be offered.

It was then I learned the reason for my unhappy babyhood: I was very conscious of the sympathetic looks, as I stood transfixed listening to Lloyd relate that my mother had not recovered from my birth. How three weeks after that event, Mum died of septicaemia after being contaminated through the later-acknowledged careless habit of a local midwife, of not scrubbing up after attending to the needs of her horse. Solemnly he explained how several other mothers had died under similar circumstances within a short time, so ending the popularity of home births in our town. I hung my head and blushed during this recital of the story I had heard so often. But the punch line was yet to come: "So Lyle wasn't fed on breast milk, he didn't stop howling for six months, because cow's milk made him constipated".

My flush of excruciating embarrassment turned to anger. This was beyond the limit. I exploded with a burst of oratory totally unsuitable for the company and occasion. In something akin to shell shock, Lloyd stood speechless, as all eyes looked our way except those of our little group, who turned away and dispersed. I was certainly no advertisement for the virtues of cow's milk as a baby food.

But I digress:

Dad's resolve to keep us together presented no real problems for a time. The nurse Dad had employed to look after Mum and myself had stayed until Mum's death. Then relatives, friends and neighbours rallied to assist, but this sympathy-engendered desire to help quickly waned under the pressures of their own obligations. It soon became obvious that a live-in nursemaid/housekeeper was required. Since before Valma was born, Mum's second cousin Sis Severino began boarding with my family when she obtained a job at the local knitting mill at the age of seventeen. Over almost five years, Sis had virtually become part of the family and when she was not at work, she often helped Mum care for my numerous young siblings and no doubt she also helped with the general household chores as well. I suppose it was therefore a natural progression that Dad approached Sis to take on the job. Even though it must have been a daunting challenge, she agreed. To compensate for leaving her job at the mill she would be paid, for then, an acceptable sum of ten shillings a week.

In spite of her willingness, caring for eight children – ranging in age from one month to twelve years – and keeping house, was too big of a task for one so young. It soon became obvious that more help would have to be found.

Auntie Mag, who was two years older than my mother and had often helped ease Mum's workload, volunteered to come and assist for a few months. The few months lasted until her death forty-six years later. No mother could have been more caring and loving to her charges or more loved and respected in return throughout her long life.

With two women in the house to share the work all went well for nine months, until Dad began to quickly lose control of his financial affairs. Dissent within the Goeben Company ensured its inevitable collapse. Finally the company went into recess and Dad was out of a job. Soon there was no money to pay Sis, so for financial reasons she had to leave us. Fortunately she was able to reclaim her former job at the knitting mill – a stroke of luck in those hard times.

Dad never lost faith in his "Wonder Wheel". More than another decade passed before he finally agreed to deregister the company. Even then, he still unrealistically believed the realisation of his visualisations would bring joy to the motoring world, and wealth to his family. In order to achieve that end he persistently talked of his dream to form a new company.

3

Awakening to the World

As well as being tattered, the first page of my memory is not dated, but I believe the year to be 1933. That year the Pioneer Memorial Tower on Bristol Hill was opened. The architect of the tower had incorporated recycled parts from Maryborough's recently demolished old gaol the most obvious of these was the fine bluestone circular staircase. Being taken to see this new edifice was my first big adventure into the outside world.

One afternoon, Auntie Annie and Sis Severino arrived at our house to accompany Auntie Mag in taking me to see the new tower. With long blond sausage curls and in rompers, I remember setting off with Auntie Mag and our visitors. I am sure they walked the two miles; although I have few memories of the journey in either direction. I presume I was conveyed in my cumbersome cane-hooded three-ply-bodied pram which with its small wheels must have been hard to push. It wasn't until years later, that I first saw a light pusher.

I did not cry, but I recall feeling my first pangs of terror, as I looked over the town below, from the lofty wire cage at the top of the tower. Then, like a scene change in a film, I was safely home again, being endearingly quizzed about my great adventure. I responded with gusto, but I have had an unreasonable fear of heights ever since.

Somewhere around that time, I also discovered embarrassment while I was being bathed in a big tin tub in front of the sitting room fire, surrounded by a gaggle of onlookers. I also discovered the pride of ownership when Jack renounced all claims to his fine trike in my favour, which was still virtually in the same condition as it was when he obtained it spanking new, in the afternoon of our prosperity, before Mum died.

The next few pages of my memory are crowded with happiness and wonder.

Each morning I patiently waited as Auntie Mag brushed and combed the glossy black hair that almost reached her waist, then watched completely fascinated as she swiftly plaited it into two long braids, then deftly fashioned them into a bun behind her head.

Often we would stroll across our paddock into the nearby bush, where each time I would know the sheer rapture of some new event. When there was a heavy fog, I wondered at how within a short distance, the trees of the forest became ghostly images against the light grey wall that seemed to enclose us in a little dome-world of our own, in which the contents constantly changed as we walked. Enthralled I saw each hanging gum leaf tipped with a glistening dewdrop. While amid the scanty foliage of suitable shrubs, or strung in rows between the wires of our paddock fence, the small orb-webs of myriad anonymous spiders, were whitened by a cover of tiny dewdrops. I saw these as dainty, delicate "fairy" versions of Auntie Mag's beautifully crocheted doilies.

It was while I strolled hand in hand with Auntie Mag – or at times of boldness, running on ahead – that I saw my first butterflies; watched the dragonflies skimming over the two dams near our home; crouched to watch the black ants that were almost too tiny to see and jumped back as hordes of the formidable meat ants rushed out to defend their mounds. Mounds that were beautifully adorned with tiny colourful stones to form an abstract mosaic that often extended over several square yards.

Filled with nostalgia, I remember the delight of seeing my first gleaming buttercup, and picking my first early nancys on those short walks from our house with my favourite aunt. My first robin sitting on our paddock fence, far outshone the sad little English bird mid snow and leafless trees in my picture book.

At times on blissful cloudless days, we watched wedge-tailed eagles slowly circling on resting wings, ever rising in the thermals, until, as intermittent specks, we lost them in a blink. I learned to name the spectrum colours from glorious rainbows, and chuckled to a sense of "catching-out" the moon, when we found its ghostly form in the daytime sky. She also showed me the simple wonders of the night. With a tinge of fear I clasped her hand tightly when the huge reddish full moon breached the eastern horizon, but I soon relaxed as it ascended, and became a seemingly smaller glorious golden disk. Its vague images stirred my imagination, as they surely have done to young minds since the dawn of humanity.

When the nights were dark and clear, we would gaze at the brilliant dome above, as Auntie Mag taught me the names of the Milky Way, the Pot, the Seven Sisters and the Southern Cross. I learned to know the brighter planets with their constant "stare", and how they nightly changed their position against the background of the twinkling "fixed" stars. On those occasions, the lesson often included a duet of *Twinkle Twinkle Little Star*. At times on pleasant misty nights, we would stroll the 100 yards or so along the narrow foot track that skirted the Prisoners' Dam behind the school, to see the delightful "fairy" lights of numerous glowworms, shining through the short dewy grass.

In our garden, I would giggle with delight as Auntie Mag manipulated the snapdragons by squeezing the tube behind the head to make them open their "mouths" to "bite" my fingers. I called them puppy dogs. I half expected some response, when I returned the stares of the wide-faced pansies, while the sight of my first fuchsia extended my knowledge of beauty to horizons I had not dreamed of. My teacher had opened my eyes to the beauty of nature and instilled in me a lifelong thirst to explore and protect its wonders.

My aroused curiosity, on rare occasions, did bring mild rebuke from my mentor. Auntie Mag could not understand the sheer delight I gained from catching in the snow-white lace curtains, as they buzzed against the windowpane, any odd blowfly that strayed into the sitting room. With disgust she would tell me they were dirty, but they always looked immaculately groomed to me. My other fall from grace concerned African marigolds. I was so hopelessly intrigued by their intricate structure, that I could not resist uncurling and removing their petals. Auntie Mag never ever gave me even the lightest smack, instead she would tell me that I was a "tinker" or a "scallywag". She did not realise that it was just a thoughtful child beginning to explore the wonders of creation.

On Auntie Mag's knee, I found another world through the *Weekly Times*. With patient affection as we turned the pages together, she explained the things that excited my interest.

The *Nature Notes* by Charles Barrett was my favourite page. Eagerly we would wait for what seemed an eternity to me, for the glossy colour insert each week that depicted some aspect of the world's wildlife. Even by today's standards they possessed a classic quality.

I coveted the pocket watches depicted in an advertisement which sparked in me an obsession with both watches and clocks. I absolutely refused to spend the pitiful few pennies I received, in the hope I would one day reach the 15 shillings needed to buy one. I would draw clock faces at every opportunity. If cardboard was available, I would cut them out and then pin on movable hands.

The crochet page was also the subject of close scrutiny. Auntie Mag had been an avid crocheter, but even if the price of cotton had not been a restricting factor, she would never have been able to produce all the patterns I urged her to make. However, she could not resist my desperate pleadings for one particular item. Intently I followed each stitch of its creation. I can still recall the ecstasy of the moment when I at last held the materialisation of that printed pattern. That milk jug cover with a splendid rampant reindeer, and a surround of sparkling green glass beads, became my most treasured possession. The reindeer was my choice of two patterns: the other depicted a kangaroo. Overwhelmed by my delight in the finished article, Auntie Mag immediately began work on the kangaroo cover. I left her in no doubt that I also loved that finished article with its 24 pink glass beads, but she must have noticed that I mostly selected the reindeer to cover our brown crockery milk jug. That is why the kangaroo cover still remains in excellent condition, while that glorious reindeer remains only in my memory.

Auntie Mag was a splendid cook and I never wandered far from her when she was baking. Even though by now it was hard to get the necessary ingredients required for some of her more delicious recipes, by improvising, she was still able to bake a few tasty items for us. She always seemed to keep up the supply of homemade biscuits, my favourite was her bran biscuits and often she would answer my plaintive pleas by producing a batch. At this time though, the thing I regarded as the greatest culinary delight – probably more for their looks than taste – were her rainbow cakes. These were frequently produced, but always at intervals that ensured they would always be considered a special treat.

Often we would stand on the footpath and watch the unhurried activities of a country town in the early 1930s. Long before Tommy Harper's dainty ice-cream cart with its fringed canopy came into view, we would hear its spring mounted bell tinkling to the uneven movements of his dreamy horse as it plodded the streets of our neighbourhood. We knew that the random punctuation of silence indicated a sale: a treat for a child and a halfpenny, penny, or maybe even threepence, for Tommy. But alas, only on rare occasions was even the lowest denomination available for us to procure a taste of the delicious homemade frozen delight that Tommy packed into a cone with a wooden spoon.

In stark contrast to Tommy's delightful little cart and the atmosphere it created, were the local sanitary wagons. Aesthetics had not been a consideration in the design of these ponderous contraptions that seemed to cast indignity on the two sturdy draught horses that gave them locomotion. They had rectangular sheet-iron-clad cabinets, with sliding doors on the sides and back to give easy access to the eight-gallon cans that lined the floor and sturdy shelves. The seat for the driver and his assistant was covered with an equally ungainly square-section sheet-metal hood which extended above the height of the can cabinet behind.

Although commonly called night carts, that was not strictly correct, for they were diurnal. Outside school hours or during holidays, they were often followed by an ever changing relay of young louts engaged in the pastime of scurrilous banter, which in spite of their zeal, seemed to rate very low on the list of the occupational hazards to the operators of this essential service. Because of the offensive odour the cart exuded, plus the desire to distance themselves from such unpleasantness, sensitive souls avoided them. Ladies, engaged in gardening or other outdoor activities, would discreetly vanish indoors during the weekly visit. The fear of the ultimate social embarrassment of being caught on the W.C., while the pan was being changed, incited dedicated vigilance on the appointed day. Children were often posted to keep nit, especially when an emergency sitting was expected to be of an extended duration. I loved the tarry smell of the "new" cans; they smelt so clean and refreshing. It was a smell that could penetrate through one's clothes and linger for quite a while after going to the dunny.

I was well aware that staring at the night cart and its operators was unacceptable in polite society, but I was nevertheless intrigued and loved to watch the intricacies of the operation. With dignity born of nonchalance, these worthy professionals would lift the tailgate of the outhouse and extract the often-overflowing can. After being closed with the clamping lid from the freshly tarred exchange can, the heavy container was hoisted to a leather protection patch on the night-man's shoulder, before a usually long haul to the conveyance in the street. Those lock-on lids with a rubber sealing ring were the cause of considerable community pride: it was not allowed to be forgotten, that its inventor was "Grandfather Green", the venerable founder of the enduring tinsmith establishment that flourished in Tuaggra Street.

As a child I imagined the Greens had cornered this busy part of town, for under a big chestnut tree across the street, was Green's blacksmith shop. Tuaggra, appears to have been a token gesture of belated goodwill towards the long gone Jaarra tribe of Aborigines, who had known the Maryborough area by that name.

I was introduced to the marvels of machinery as I watched from our gate: no triumph of space-age technology could cause greater elation in an imaginative pre-school boy than did the council's steam road roller, that roamed our town. The entwined emotions of fascination and fear bound me to the spot, as wide eyed I watched the large whirling flywheels and huge crunching roller, as the steam hissing monster lumbered up and down Waterloo Road. I cannot help but think that name was the work of someone with a distorted sense of humour, for Waterloo Road was the road to the cemetery.

While I was too young to realise the significance of the events taking place, I was also fascinated by funerals. Often we would solemnly stand and watch the assorted processions of cars, horse drawn vehicles and even men on horseback, go past. Sometimes magnificent black horses would draw the hearse, with big black plumes on their heads. Auntie Mag told me they had white plumes for children's funerals, but happily, that was something I never witnessed.

I can still visualise strange looking men walking one behind the other, carrying an assortment of items towards the cemetery. They were the last of the once substantial population of Chinese, who had been lured to the district by the discovery of gold. I was often told that they were on their way to the cemetery to perform a ceremony which included the roasting of pork, and placing it on the graves of their departed countrymen.

Quite often when Auntie Annie – mostly with Sis – visited us, if the day was pleasant I would accompany them and Auntie Mag, on the one-mile stroll to the cemetery. For me these walks were always a joyous adventure into the bush. I was too young to understand the significance of Mum's untimely death, but I was always appropriately moved during the solemn ritual of cleaning the vases, and then replacing them, filled with fresh water and flowers, on the earth mound of Mum's grave.

4

From Soap to Susso

When I really got to know Dad, he was no longer prosperous, but his inventiveness had not diminished. In order to make some sort of living at a time when jobs were impossible to obtain, he had turned his hand to making soap for sale.

I remember being shooed away from the four-gallon kerosene tin buckets of hot fat that simmered on the makeshift grate in the back yard. Dad was always alert to the degree of danger associated with any activity. The cauldrons of boiling fat and the presence of nasties such as caustic soda, meant that I was never permitted to go too close. It was not until some years later, when Auntie Mag was making soap for our own use, that I watched the chemical fury, as the caustic soda turned the clarified fat into soap. Even then it seemed nothing short of magic.

Dad's fertile imagination ran wild with the basic soap recipes, which resulted, in due course, in some excellent grades of toilet soap. But as with the wheel, his goal always exceeded his achievements, so the quality of the soap varied from batch to batch.

To a large degree – especially with laundry soap – the home product had to be supplemented with factory made "imports" to meet the demand. This was not because Dad's production line was stretched to capacity: the problem was that the chief ingredient, fat, in that time of little money, was also the most popular spread for bread.

"Yankee Magic" and "Butterfly" were two bar-soap brands my family "doctored" and passed off as their own product. As this process presented little chance of physical injury to bystanders, I was permitted to watch at close quarters. Evidently no consideration was given to the likelihood of psychological damage from watching this unethical action. Intently, I would watch the wafers of soap being shaved off to remove the moulded brand names and other marks of identification, before the soap was cut into the single cakes that were moulded along the bar. Economically, this was a wise exercise. Being able to buy one cake at a time was the equivalent of buying a bar on time payment. I eagerly collected the discarded gaudy wrappers that depicted butterflies and monkeys. The possession of such "treasures" filled my young mind with enchantment.

Louis seemed to be the chief salesman and Lloyd his worthy assistant. I especially remember them setting out to "do the town", with the soap packed in a large cane basket. In those days before pre-packaging and supermarkets, for a while, the operation teetered on the brink of being a viable business, but in spite of hope and hard work our financial situation daily became worse.

When Auntie Mag came to live with us, she had a nest egg of some 300 pounds. It was an interim part payment, pending the sale of farm livestock and other assets, which she had inherited equally with two younger siblings, Andrew and Alice, from their mother. Sadly, this amount was the only payment she ever received. Since coming to help us out, Auntie Mag had been delving into her savings to meet the shortfall in our family's finances. Dad insisted they were only loans, which would be generously redeemed when things improved. Within a year or two, Auntie Mag's inheritance was virtually gone.

Mum had bought an exquisite "Richard Lipp" rosewood piano, mainly so my older siblings could practise their lessons, but as well I believe she loved playing it herself, as she did the violin.

One of Auntie Mag's great pleasures was to sit at the piano and play and sing the hymns she had learnt as a girl, before she became deaf. Perhaps it was because of this, that when Dad finally faced the reality of our hopeless financial situation, he offered her the ownership of the piano in exchange for the loans. Auntie Mag accepted the proposition and everyone thought the deal was quite equitable. Henceforth, it was always referred to as "Auntie Mag's piano".

Evidence indicates it was on the 23rd of March 1933, when Dad was first forced to swallow his pride and seek sustenance from the "Labour Bureau Relief Committee". From the tales of those who shared the queue, Dad executed this indignity with a colourful proclamation. The story goes, that the bumptious official was somewhat perplexed when Dad announced, "I have come to surrender". Then gracious in victory, the official – on behalf of G. L. Goudie, Minister for Labour, bestowed on Dad a voucher to the value of 29 shillings, for the purchase of listed basic essentials to sustain us for a fortnight. Had they been able to rake up another shilling, we could have had three bob each.

Dad was now a susso worker. For that pittance susso workers were obliged to perform any work nominated by the Council. The designated work was mostly pretty menial, the major job consisted of chipping vegetation from the system of unmortared sandstone-slab-lined spoon gutters and the main drain that disposed of the town's domestic waste-water. Grass and other weeds thrived in the spaces between the slabs of sandstone and hindered the flow of the household slops. If left unchipped they created a series of stagnated mini-reservoirs along the drains. During dry periods when there was insufficient run off of fresh rainwater from the roofs and roads to flush them out, the drains would become putrid, especially in warm weather.

Thanks to the cheap labour of the susso workers, that situation was greatly reduced during the 1930s. Even though the nauseating fetid air permeated the clothes and skin of the humbled workers, due to their efforts the town in general smelt much sweeter. These gutters provided an ideal habitat for black-fronted dotterels. The town's drainage system must have supported thousands of these birds. Almost every street supported a family party, which were mostly left unmolested and with a hint of affection, were universally called guttersnipes by the locals. Fortunately for Dad, he was one of the lucky ones who from time to time were selected to assist in maintaining the grounds and splendid floral displays in the more salubrious atmosphere of either our fine public park or Phillips Gardens – known at that time as "The Reserve".

The following year, the entire local "susso workers" had the privilege of working for a while in those idyllic conditions at beautiful Princes Park and the Reserve – but not for long. They were assembled and equipped with three-bushel bags and other weapons, in an attempt to protect the floral displays and lawns, by beating off the unbelievable hordes of flying grasshoppers. Sadly, in spite of the valiant endeavours of the poverty stricken workforce, they were no match for the persistent waves of the hungry marauders, which stripped the whole town of all but its toughest greenery. There was one fortunate spin-off, the hoppers did a marvellous job of clearing the weeds from the gutters.

That grasshopper plague was awesome: the birds seemed to enjoy the feast, but many cats that gorged themselves died. By day the insects crowded the sky, and a constant shower of their broken bodies fell from the north-facing fly-wire screen of a few square feet, that my older brothers had suspended between two poles in our front garden. At night as they rested, my brothers collected them in bucketfuls from around the butts of trees.

5

Memorable Moments and Medical Marvels

By the time we retreated into the bush, my two youngest sisters were becoming blurred in my memory. About eighteen months before, they had been whisked away by Mum's eldest sister Liz, to join her family of six boys and two girls on their remote mallee selection near Lake Cargelligo in New South Wales.

On one of that family's frequent visits to see their numerous Victorian relations and friends, Auntie Liz, a kindly but forthright soul, suggested that Valma, eight, and June, seven, would benefit from a holiday on their farm. Dad reluctantly consented on the understanding that they would be returned on the next trip to Victoria. No one suspected it would be three years before we saw them again. Yvonne had been left behind to help with the household chores and to be a companion for Auntie Mag. Missing out on what was then thought to be an adventurous holiday of a few months and being parted from her two sisters, must have been a sad blow for Yvonne.

Apart from missing the girls and keenly awaiting their return, for a while things went on much the same in our diminished household. Our house seemed to be the rallying point for many of the neighbourhood kids. Louis and Yvonne seemed to always have plenty of friends, Keith had one special friend – Reg – while Lloyd joined any combination that suited him at the time. Unlike me, Jack was always in demand: apparently he had never caused anyone the slightest bother since conception. He never cried and was universally admired and loved for his "manly demeanour". Of all my siblings' friends, only tall, good-hearted, easygoing Reg – whose boundless imagination often subsidised his memory – seemed to enjoy my presence: that was why I liked him so much.

Although Jack was only two and a quarter years older than me, my brothers and Yvonne were happy to have him tag along on most of their excursions into the bush or town, while their preferred choice in my case was that I stay at home. Although I do remember that on rare occasions Yvonne was conscripted to take me on messages, or on a visit to one of her friends.

Mabel – a few months older than me – lived on the corner across the road, and was the only playmate I had. She spent a lot of time at our place, but I ungallantly regarded her as a bit of a nuisance, because she stopped me from doing more interesting things with Auntie Mag. Even so, we got on pretty well together.

When I reached the age of four and a half, Yvonne, Jack and Mabel escorted me across the road to school. I was installed in the prep grade, which was popularly known – much to my indignation – as the "Bubs". On that first day, I shared a desk with Mabel, who being an old hand of six months, was appointed to guide me over the first few bumpy weeks. I immediately fell in love with the blunt round-nosed scissors and the squares of shiny paper that were brightly coloured on one side, and handed out with diligent thrift, but apart from that school did not live up to my expectations.

Only a few months before, with visions of the exciting event to come, I arrogantly strutted before an assortment of kids in our yard, with a pencil in my mouth, bumptiously proclaiming "I'm a big school boy". Unfortunately, no one had bothered to tell me the old proverb about pride having its fall. My pride did fall that day and it took me with it. There I was, flat on my face with a pencil stuck down my throat and a mouth full of blood. My family's concern was not lessened by our family doctor gravely elaborating on the dire injuries such a folly could cause – with special reference to the jugular vein. Thankfully, the pencil had missed my jugular vein, but that wooden stake went straight through the heart of my ego, my self-confidence was gone and the painful recovery ensured I never again so much as even nibbled the end of a pencil.

That was not the most serious health problem that befell us youngsters while we were still living in the house by the school. Keith and Valma almost died from double pneumonia. After the doctor had given up all hope, Dad attended them day and night, constantly applying mustard plasters to their already burning chests, until the crisis had passed. Dad's mustard plasters were simply a paste made with powdered mustard and spread on a hot damp cloth, which was applied to the chest and covered with flannel or other woollen material to help retain the heat. I gather the plaster could be repeatedly reheated and reapplied. Dad's faith in that – even then – old-fashioned remedy was justified. The amazed doctor gave Dad full credit for saving their lives. Dad had gained this faith in the curative powers of mustard, from the isolated bush settlers of his youth who revered it as a lifesaver. They used it in the form of plasters for any serious respiratory problems, and as an additive to a hot bath for childhood convulsions. Dad was a devout believer in the curing powers of a number of different poultices: any minor infection was promptly treated with a bread poultice. This version was made by soaking bread in boiling water. After as much water as possible was squeezed out in a cloth, it was bound to the affected part in the same manner as the mustard variety. More serious or stubborn infections, were subjected to a most abominable concoction – the onion poultice. This too was simplicity itself, just boiled onions applied in the same way as the other poultices, but the disgusting smell of stale onions lingered around one's person for hours – or even days – and in our imaginations for long after the wound had healed. All of these poultices were expertly applied, hot enough to cause discomfort, yet cool enough to not burn our tender skin. At times Dad would blow on the surface that was to be applied to the skin until it was cooled to the optimum temperature. We also had great faith in poultices. They seemed to work wonders.

We were often subjected to various other "cures" of those days: kerosene was used for "drawing out" splinters and as an antiseptic for the numerous punctures to our feet, due either to them being bare or because the soles of our shoes had worn thin. Standing on old nails and bits of wire, which seemed to be everywhere, caused most of the "enspikements". At times they would penetrate quite deeply, which made them hard to pull out. Dad's dread of tetanus caused him to view these injuries with great concern. After the initial treatment of repeatedly bathing the wound in a hot solution of Condy's crystals (potassium permanganate), they received the extra treatment of being held in the smoke of burning flannel. Though mystical as this seemed, we submitted ourselves to the process without question, for as with mustard, the health-giving powers of flannel were far beyond our understanding. Finally, raw Condy's crystals were sprinkled onto the wound and lightly rubbed as an extra precaution.

Like so many people of his generation, Dad was always wary of constipation. His perceived dire consequences of this condition were imparted to us by implication rather than explanation. Only Lloyd seemed to grasp the gravity of Dad's concern – possibly due to his vivid memory of my babyhood problem. For the rest of us, the subject would have been irrelevant had it not been for the weekly precautionary dose of senna leaves. Each Saturday morning it was mandatory to chew then swallow a small quantity of this nauseating substance which though much smaller resembled in toughness and shape – though not the taste or smell – dried gum leaves. Many of our young acquaintances were subjected to a weekly drench of a brew made from those same terrible leaves which they referred to – I always thought with a hint of snobbery – as "Senna Tea".

But the vilest of all medicines was castor oil. Fortunately we were only expected to take it for severe stomach upsets which it usually aggravated. Years after the last dose, the mere thought of this purgative, caused the face to distort. Unfortunately its repulsiveness blinded its victims to the beauty of the elegant long-necked cobalt blue bottles that contained it. Most youngsters who had suffered their contents would revengefully smash these bottles on sight.

A meagre supply of Aspros in their pink packet and fascinating white-waxed concertina packaging was our only available painkiller. On rare occasions depending on our financial resources, other patent medicines were introduced, but overall Dad managed our well being with considerable skill and thrift. In spite of this, however, one thing had him stumped – my navel. In my case, this normally unobtrusive part of the human anatomy was a prominent symmetrical dome. It was reminiscent of a starter button, indeed so much so, that it incited a desire to push it. When it was pressed it offered little resistance and on being released, it would promptly pop out again to its usual shape. There was general agreement about the cause of this affliction: it was the result of the incessant howling during my early months of life – another minus for cow's milk as baby food.

Dad viewed this malformation with considerable concern. He

wrongly believed that it was a serious rupture, which would give me problems in the future. For that reason he persevered with simple ingenuity to effect a cure. The main component of the treatment was a cross of adhesive tape, with its intersection strategically placed where it could firmly press a ball of cotton wool or other rounded object (when we were really flush, a halfpenny) onto the offending bulge. Looking back I realise the high priority placed on this treatment, for though money was scarce, there was always sufficient tape to enable me to bear my cross. The plaster would stay on for about a week, and failure to report that it had fallen off, was one of the few things that caused Dad to growl at us. However in spite of his dedication, it was all to no avail. By the time I was 12 there was still no improvement, so without any fuss, or declaration of defeat, the battle was abandoned. I still have that harmless "starter button".

In these times of miraculous scientific medical procedures and drugs, such treatments may seem bizarre, but in those times when often a doctor's bedside manner was more helpful than the concoctions at his disposal, anything that hadn't actually proved to be fatal, was worth another try.

6

Tragedy and its Consequences

In my earliest memories, recommissioned kerosene lamps became our source of illumination. The electric lights that hung from the ceiling and the white crockery brass-capped switches only served to remind my elders of brighter times. Though I must have been only about four, I was vaguely aware of the shadowy gloom that suddenly came over our house during the hours of darkness.

The events of one particular night are still undiminished in my mind. I awoke to the sound of bustling activity. Instinctively I knew that something was wrong. I opened my bedroom door to a nightmarish scene. In the gloom, the dull lamplight cast monstrous shadows on the walls and ceiling. At first the silhouettes were reminiscent of weird beings, but as my eyes adjusted, I recognised the familiar faces of the men and boys, who in the dim light blended with the furniture they were carrying out of the house.

The answers to my anxiously repeated query, "What are they doing?" were unsatisfactory evasions that did nothing to allay my feeling of distress. The furtive operation continued until virtually the only furniture remaining in the house were our beds, a large cedar chest of drawers, a kitchen dresser, meat safe, two cedar tables and a cabinet sewing machine that didn't work. That same night, to avoid a dispute about ownership if the bailiff moved in, Auntie Mag's piano found a new home at Auntie Annie's place. It did not return to us until almost 10 years later. Our fine handcrafted furniture was spirited off to a neighbour's place. About four years later, our gramophone was returned and installed in Lloyd's fastidiously tidy brick floored tent, making it the music centre of our second camp. Apart from those two retrievals, the traumatic midnight manoeuvre was all to no avail, for we ended up losing the rest of our furniture without recompense.

Poverty stricken though we were the chances were that Dad could have retained the house and land, had it not been for a tragic event that happened early in 1934, some 15 miles away at a settlement called Dunach.

With our changed circumstances, the Studebaker car that had conveyed our family in style was sitting on blocks, gathering cobwebs and dust. It had been replaced by a dogcart, which was pulled by a flighty unreliable mare named Doll. Dad's friend Harry, a wealthy bachelor farmer and company friend, had raised her on the fertile pastures that surrounded the treeless domes of geologically ancient volcanoes at Dunach. This, naturally, made the poor pastures and gravelly ironbark clad hills of Maryborough an abomination to Doll. That and her incredible aptitude for jumping fences ensured that she was more often roaming the network of roads around her luscious birthplace, than pulling our dogcart. On one particular occasion her period of freedom was somewhat extended because Dad had not been able to ascertain her whereabouts. In view of this, generous Harry told Dad he would try to find her on the following Sunday. On that Sunday, as Harry was riding his horse along one of the picturesque roads not far from home, his mentally disturbed brother, stalking from behind a hedge, shot him dead as he rode past. A newspaper report proclaimed he was listening to the beckoning bells, as he rode to church in Talbot – some six miles away. But knowing Harry well, Dad scoffed at that suggestion. He was convinced that "good hearted Harry" was setting out in search of the errant Doll. Dad mourned the loss of his good and faithful friend, but did not realise the full consequence of the event for many months.

The first hint that something was amiss came by way of Keith. Keith and the headmaster of the school, Mr George, had an affinity founded on their mutual love of art – a field in which the teacher thought Keith had significant potential – and gardening. The school garden was a showpiece, due in no small part to Keith's industrious assistance. He not only helped grow and tend the plants like some of the other children; their vigorous growth was testimony to the incessant offerings of fertiliser from our crafty house cow Gipp and cows from the nearby dairy that Dad had agreed to allow to graze on his property – and a spasmodic supply from Doll – which Keith diligently collected.

One day while Keith was bagging up manure, he was approached by the son of a neighbour and asked if he had permission to do so. When bewildered Keith replied that Dad didn't mind, he was told, "It has nothing to do with your father." When Keith reported the incident to Dad, he was equally mystified but saw no reason to follow it up. Shortly after, with a traumatic impact, Dad received legal notice to vacate the house.

Dad arranged to buy the house and land in 1926 for 550 pounds, to be paid off in instalments. He paid a deposit, followed by another payment of 100 pounds. Harry entered into a somewhat complicated business deal with Dad involving company shares, which included him paying off our house, and the deeds ended up in Harry's name. Because of their close friendship and apathy born of mutual trust, the legalities to correct the matter were never finalised.

The beneficiaries of Harry's will found the deeds and sold the house, without even informing Dad of their intention. Dad's protests and explanations were in vain.

A court case for vacant possession followed and as Dad had no documentation to prove the deal was ever completed, Dad lost the case. We were ordered to vacate the house and land, and at that time further legal appeal was far beyond Dad's means.

7

Bailiffs and Goats

The debt collectors were moving in. I learned later, that an inventory of our possessions had already been posted at the police station, and that there was the threat of their imminent seizure for debt. Dad had already been sentenced to a day's gaol for being unable to pay a minor fine, but as the nearest gaol used for this purpose was at Castlemaine, some thirty miles away, it caused a bit of a transport problem. Getting him there for the police, and hard-up Dad getting back home again. Both problems were solved when the compassionate and practical police sergeant arranged for Dad to spend the day working in the police station garden.

A bailiff earned my first pangs of hate and life lasting contempt from Dad, when he kicked over my trike proclaiming, "This is the cause of your trouble, wasting money on rubbish". It would have served no purpose to explain that when Mum bought it for Jack, because of our better financial position, it was not considered to be a luxury.

Dad tried to retrieve two steers that Mum's brother Will had offered to agist on his square-mile farm, when our paddock was eaten out, but my financially secure bachelor uncle would not release them until previously unmentioned agistment fees were paid. We lost the steers, and the relief the money from their sale would have brought.

Gipp, our house cow, who had gained affection and respect for having learned to turn the garden tap on when she wanted a drink, and resentment for not having learned to turn it off again, was sold to Pascoe's. Pascoe's owned the bigger and most prosperous of the two dairies that adjoined our twenty-acre property. They ran two horse-drawn milk carts.

The second dairy owned by Mr Souter was a one-man operation. He would ride his bike past our place morning and night, on his way to milk his few cows. He delivered the milk around the town on the same pushbike, with milk cans attached to its sides.

The sale of Gipp was the reason why we got the goats: thrifty Lloyd earned a few shillings a week, cleaning out Pascoe's milking sheds and filling the feed boxes of the bails each evening. One of the proprietors always rewarded him with sixpence a time, but when his brother was acting paymaster, the recompense was only threepence. In spite of this discrepancy, when a new source of milk was required, Lloyd was in the best position to finance the new venture. Generously he willingly agreed for the good of his family to invest 15 shillings of his hard earned savings in three "nannies" and one "billy" – as female and male goats were commonly referred to in those days.

I was familiar with goats before this: an old lady who lived on the far back corner of the school had a small flock. I had often been warned about McDonald's disreputable old billy goat, he was accused of having charged a number of boys from the school in response to provocation. Our goats however, were quite placid. Shortly after buying the goats, there was some excitement when the "Old Goat" produced twin kids, which after considerable deliberation were named Sarah and Donk. Donk had big long ears, Sarah's ears were almost non-existent. Someone told us "she must have desert goat blood in her", so without question, we henceforth referred to this variety as "desert goats". Unknown to me Donk was neutered, which caused him to grow into a good-natured giant.

Both Donk and Sarah became family pets and lived to roam the stoney hills and gullies of the bush around our home for many years – in Sarah's case, almost 20. Those goats and their descendants were to play a major part in our lives.

* * *

The time at the house was quickly running out, by now Dad had decided his best option was to take us into the bush. My brothers were always wandering around the bush, so as the time for our move drew near, Dad asked if they had any suggestions about a suitable campsite. They were eager to oblige. Several sites were inspected before the one on the eastern slope of a big hill was chosen. Everyone except Auntie Mag and I had a preview of the campsite and in varying degrees approved.

Our impending evacuation of the house stirred Reg's memory. During a foray into our ceiling with Keith, in search of sparrow eggs during the previous spring, he had noticed the abundance of copper wire that once serviced the aforementioned switches and lights, of our now defunct electrical system. Copper wire was always at a premium, the uses that an imaginative lad can put the soft pliable metal to is amazing, and Reg was renowned for his imagination – not least when narrating his adventures.

"Gawd! Look at that wire," he enthused as he coveted the prize. "Let's get some pliers and rip 'er out, it's no use here." "Like hell!" Keith responded, "Dad would kill us". Keith stood his ground, until somewhat aggrieved and with great reluctance, Reg had to be content to bide his time as he lusted for the treasure in the roof. But now on the brink of our departure, he persisted: "You won't need that wire any more, you'll be gone in a few days". His will prevailed.

Things were pretty quiet around the house that afternoon, so Reg slipped home to fetch a pair of pliers, then the pair ascended the manhole in the passage. The vents in the steep gable roof, with the beams of light streaming through the odd nail hole in the corrugated iron and through the various cracks, provided enough light for their keen young eyes to follow and strip the booty. Once it was rolled up in its various categories, it wasn't hard to smuggle it out of the house.

Did Dad go crook? Certainly not in this life, for although he lived another thirty-three years, he died with no reason to doubt that when the fuses were replaced on the pole from which the cables were slung to the house, a mere click of the switches would restore the house to its former luminosity for the new owners.

We will never know what the new occupants thought: probably poor innocent Dad got the blame.

We were all up early the day we had to leave the house. Amid all our misfortune, we had a stroke of good luck – Doll was at home in the paddock, so she would be available to transport our belongings to our retreat. Except for viewing the proposed campsite many times, nothing was moved until this day. This was not due to indolence: it was because we needed all our remaining worldly goods and besides we could not leave them unprotected in the bush.

From the crack of dawn on the fateful day, there was great activity: the things from the yard went first. There were two near-new 10-foot sheets of corrugated iron and the sides of the case that had protected the piano on its journey from Germany. In combination, these would later constitute a considerable part of the three walled shack, which for quite a few years served as the kitchen, family room and after our sisters came home, that was where Dad bunked down on one of our handouts – a leather-upholstered Edwardian couch. All day the dogcart, with mostly Louis at the reins, shuttled to and fro, until only the fixtures remained in the house. One of these fixtures, the impressive stove, had been my mother's pride and joy over her last couple of years and it was still in mint condition. Dad realised such an asset would be invaluable in our new situation, and it was indisputable, the stove was his. It was late afternoon when Doll hauled the cart with the last load from the house. On board was the still warm stove, freshly extracted from its brick surrounds. That same stove continued to serve my two bachelor brothers for some 60 years.

With the empty house spick and span, Auntie Mag closed the back door for the last time then, with Jack and I, turned in the red rays of the setting sun towards the bush.

8

Our First Bush Camp

As I awoke on that first morning in our bush camp, an awareness of the unfamiliar preceded my consciousness. For a moment, I was mystified by the strange sounds and atmosphere around me, the like of which I had never known before. Suddenly it all became clear, I remembered the events of the previous day.

To my ears – now tingling close to numbness from the chill of the crisp autumn morning – came birdcalls from all around the tent. I heard the raucous shouts of the red wattlebird, the melodious notes of the grey thrush, the wistful piping of the yellow robin and the loud assertive proclamations from the tiny weebills and the less distinctive calls of an assortment of honeyeaters and thornbills. Those sounds with the carolling of magpies and the lilting song of a crested bellbird some distance away, blended in a glorious dawn chorus. Of course, I only knew the names of a few of the cast, but in a short time I would know them all, sometimes by their official common names, but mostly by the more colourful titles bestowed on them by the local bush workers and wanderers.

Added to those sounds were hushed voices, the sound of footsteps, the occasional sound from the goats and chooks, the crack of a stick being broken for the fire and the metallic clink from the lid of the kettle or porridge saucepan. The blaze of the campfire appeared as a yellow blur through the thin walls of the tent, varying in intensity as it was eclipsed by the early risers, while the brilliant rays of the rising sun filtering through the gently moving gum leaves caused mottled shadows to dance on the sunny side of the tent.

Suddenly I felt a surge of indignation at the implications of being alone. Chances were I was the only one missing the action around the fire. Even the cocoon of thin blankets that snugly enclosed my body was powerless against such thoughts.

Getting up was simply a matter of addition. Out of economic necessity, the males of my family had long since abandoned pyjamas, so the only night attire we wore was a flannel. These undershirts took their name from the woollen material from which they were made. This year when we were particularly – as Auntie Mag always said – "hard up", she had made by hand, a basic sleeveless version for us, but out of the best "Doctors Flannel", which in spite of its high quality seemed to be within the range of our finances. We only ever had one good flannel each: a few well-worn spares were shuffled among us when our own needed washing. I suspect that was the reason why mine were always too big. For health reasons, Dad insisted we wear our flannels both day and night, in all seasons.

I was completely oblivious to the existence of underpants for men or boys, for in contrast to the importance of flannels, they had long since passed into the category of dispensable luxuries in our household. So apart from the crotch length tail and front flaps of my flannel, my tender skin had no protection from the hard abrasive low-grade tweed of my "susso" pants. Suspended on elastic braces, they extended to just above my knees, causing painful chafing on the legs. The chafing was particularly severe if one was unlucky enough to be caught in a shower of rain and they became wet. Perhaps time has caused my memory to exaggerate their harshness, yet over the years, any contact with the scouring material Scotch Brite has stirred old memories of those torturous pants. "Susso" footwear for children, for all seasons, was mainly rubber-soled canvas sandshoes, which stunk to the high heavens in summer and quickly became soggy in winter. Socks were considered to be desirable, especially during the winter, but although Auntie Mag skilfully knitted some to augment the meagre "susso" supply and was forever darning socks, their availability was never really assured. Jack and I however, seemed to have some priority with socks, for which we were grateful for they certainly improved the comfort of our government footwear. I loved to watch Auntie Mag manipulating the four needles required to knit socks, but Jack went much further and acquired the nimble art himself.

Having dressed in the aforementioned garments, I joined the others at the breakfast fire, where my appetite was soon appeased with porridge, toast and several cups of sweetened white tea.

The chill of the night began to dissipate in the brilliant rays of the new day's sun; the atmosphere of adventure, which raised our spirits last evening, began to reappear as plans were discussed to secure our tenuous position while the good weather prevailed. Even so, there was no great sense of urgency. As the sun rose the dawn chorus diminished, while the sounds of wing beats increased as the birds eagerly sought their morning meal and the honeyeaters, especially the wattlebirds, engaged in seemingly unprovoked scuffles among themselves, or with other species.

Our shifting had given Lloyd, Yvonne, Jack and I a respite from school, yesterday of necessity; and today being Friday, Dad suggested it might be better if we spent the day settling in, and get off to a fresh start with the new week. There was a lot of rivalry between Yvonne and Jack about their school attendance – unlike me, always seeking excuses to stay at home, and a declaration of a stomach ache was mostly an acceptable reason – they were loath to miss a single day. But on this occasion, neither would have an advantage, so they accepted Dad's offer.

In this restful atmosphere, for the first time, I began to assess the scattered layout of the camp. The three ten by eight foot tents were erected to perfection on freshly cut bush saplings of the required dimensions. From memory, the walls were about three feet high, and the gable roof tapered up to the lower of the twin ridgepoles, while guy ropes and steel pegs strategically placed secured the main body of the tent. The top ridgepole supported the fly, which covered an area slightly bigger than the tent proper, and was held stretched out several inches above the tent roof, by separate guy ropes. I soon learned that the fly and the air gap are most important in keeping the inside of the tent dry.

I had slept in the tent a dozen yards west of the campfire. Auntie Mag, Yvonne, and Jack had not only shared the tent with me, they also shared the big wooden double bed. Four to a bed was not considered unduly crowded in those days of few beds and many children. The common practice of head and tailing it (the way sardines are packed in tins) did help ease the situation. Auntie Mag and Yvonne at the head of the bed, while Jack and I rested our heads at the foot. In spite of this deplorable situation, we were strongly imbued with the code of polite society: we were all fully-fledged prudes. Personal privacy was a cherished and unquestionable right. To maintain this goal, when we were getting up or going to bed, it was usually necessary to dress and undress under the blankets. About 50 yards further west, another tent stood. It soon became known as Lloyd's tent, for Louis who was to share it, seemed to have an uncanny knack of finding a more comfortable bed at Auntie Annie's, or in the home of one of his many friends. The third tent, some 20 yards along the reef outcrop to the south of the fire, would become known as Keith's tent, even though he shared it with Dad.

Close to the third tent, a small roughly built shed, to serve as a store for the remnants of our chattels had been constructed from bush poles and scrap material. With notable foresight and fortitude, just before we left the house by the school, Louis, Keith and Reg had manhandled a cumbersome discarded 10-foot by 10-foot cyanide tank lid, of riveted heavy sheet-metal, almost two miles from behind the old gold mining settlement of Bluchers. They foresaw that it could serve as a roof for this store-shed they knew we would need.

The camp was close to a wire fence on the town side of the camp. On reflection, I remembered that on our flight last night, we had entered a big farm gate some time after leaving the waterhole, and we had to get through this fence to enter the camp. I later discovered the camp was situated within the right angle "V" of two more or less square government paddocks, which joined to form a stylised letter "L". It was the larger of the two paddocks that we had crossed. The smaller paddock adjoined this fence about a hundred yards past Lloyd's tent. It was not much more than three acres and consisted entirely of a partially cleared steep gully. This paddock which was reserved for a rubbish tip, was either leased or just used, by a colourful local character, Noah (pronounced "Noor" by most locals) Davies, who used it to retain the horses he needed to run his nearby eucalyptus distillery plant. Consequently this paddock was locally known as "Noor's Gully".

Until later that morning, I had never seen Noor's Gully, but it was not unknown to me, for it was reputed to be haunted. Some of the stories dated back to the mining days, when a shanty (a small rough bush pub) defiled the head of this pretty sloping gully. I was later told that such shanties were the only refuge for the lost souls of the bush, who sought solace in the cheap low-grade grog, only to find further damnation in the horrors of the d.t.'s. It was believed by the enlightened, that those jim-jams were the birthplace of the ghosts that had thrived and diversified in the eagerly gullible imaginative minds of the local youngsters, through to my own generation.

It even went a bit further with Keith and Reg. A year or so before, they were passing there while returning home from the bush on a bright moonlight night, when they noticed what they presumed were a couple of white horses peacefully grazing in the paddock. One of Reg's fantasies was that he had a special affinity with horses, which nourished his hopes of one day being a Queensland drover. On their way home Reg decided he would get a bridle and return to the paddock to ride the horses. Of course, out of a sense of mateship, Keith agreed to accompany him. Soon after they returned home scared out of their wits: there were no horses in the paddock. Henceforth they were believers.

The larger paddock was known as "The Park Reserve". It did not seem to be leased, although cattle did appear in it from time to time, this could have been authorised agistment, but it was more likely they were there without consent. My reason for this conclusion is that the "park", as we called it, at once became Doll's home paddock during her periods of enforced exile, yet no fee was ever asked for or paid. It soon became apparent that the convenience of this paddock would have been a big factor in Dad's choice of the site.

Setting up the stove was to be the first priority of the day. During discussions over breakfast, it was decided the best place for it would be backed up against a clump of healthy greybox suckers. These trees would be large enough to support some kind of roof – the design of which would depend on whatever materials became available. As soon as breakfast was over Dad and the older boys moved to the chosen spot. They had some second-hand bricks, but not sufficient to build the base and the back and sides up to the required height.

Again I scanned the camp: something was amiss – there was no lavatory. "Where's the dunny?" I asked timidly. "We haven't got one," came the reply. "You have to use the quarry." The answer left me bamboozled, for quarry meant nothing to me. Jack volunteered to further my education. "Come with me," he coaxed, as he collected a short-handled shovel and made for the head of a narrow little gully that sloped away to the east of the camp. As a consequence of eons of weathering, hard vertical sandstone plates – reminiscent of those on the back of a stegosaur – up to several feet high, ran in a north-south direction along the shoulder of the hill to our right, giving the area a timeless quality. It later became our favourite playground. Soon on the other side, some hundred and fifty yards from the campfire, we approached two gorges amid a dense covering of applejack (the local common name for long leaved box) coppice of a uniform height of five or six feet. I later learned the uniform height was the result of harvesting every two or three years for eucalyptus distilling.

"There are two quarries," Jack informed me, "this one for the girls", then pointing to a smaller one further on, but really an extension of the first, "and that one for the boys". The use of these quarries as lavatories was not due to indolence; times were so hard, that not even the nearby local tip could furnish the material to build a dunny. The applejack coppice and other undergrowth provided considerable privacy for the purpose for which they would be used. Even so, within a couple of days Keith had updated the facilities in the larger quarry with a dunny-sized enclosure constructed from four sapling poles and old 3-bushel hemp wheat bags.

"You'll have to be careful though, it's a really snaky place among these rocks," Jack warned. That statement was soon confirmed when Dad killed a big red-bellied black snake, between the quarries and the camp. Strange to say, that is the only member of that species I have ever heard of being seen anywhere close to our town.

The more deadly eastern brown snake was fairly common and knowledge of their presence kept us vigilant in warm weather, but the danger of moving around the camp at night without lights, proved to be far less than what we had assumed. For in spite of walking the bush on countless occasions over the years at night, only on two occasions did I see a brown snake, and on both occasions it was just shortly after dark.

I later learned that these quarries were two of four in the area, where sandstone slabs had been extracted – substantially with prison-labour – to pave the gutters of our town. The gutters that Dad, as a "susso" worker, had been chipping and sweeping since his "surrender".

When we returned to camp, the stove had been moved to the chosen position, and was sitting on a base of unmortared bricks. It was to be used in that state until sufficient bricks could be obtained to finish the job. It was all right for cooking things in saucepans on top, but the oven was completely useless. It would be some weeks before enough bricks were available to finish the job, but finally it had double brick hobs, and a naked sheet metal flue extending a few feet above where it was secured to the tree trunks with wire. We could not afford the luxury of mortar, but strange to say, the lack of mortar proved to be a great boon to our comfort on the cold nights that were to come.

Enough pieces of old sheet metal, round bush-timber (trimmed and barked straight saplings of the desired size) and wire were collected to enable a flat roof of a few square feet to be erected just above head height, over the stove. Auntie Mag was relieved to be able to again get the stove hot enough for baking, although she often remarked how hard it was to control the temperature. In spite of that understated drawback, this set-up served as our kitchen for the next 11 or so months.

On that first morning as we stood around with cups of tea in our hands, a man and a youth approached. I had not seen them before and I gathered they were not even acquaintances of any member of my family. They were father and son, and their name was Chapman. They lived half a mile or so through the bush, on the other side of the cemetery road. Being our new neighbours, they had come to welcome us and to see if they could be of any assistance. They too, were in poor circumstances, but had been lucky enough to have selected a few acres of land, on which they were now in the process of building a house that had reached the stage where part of it provided shelter; so one of their tents could be dispensed with. Mr Chapman suggested it might ease the situation for us. We later learned it was not really surplus, but this good man thought our need was greater than theirs. Unselfishness and compassion seemed to thrive in those hard times.

Later that afternoon, the Chapman tent was erected between the tent where I had slept and the fire. It was more than twice the size of the new white tents and seemed huge to me, but it did nothing to improve the aesthetics of our camp, age had changed it to a dirty brownish grey. Nevertheless, it proved to be a godsend, and when our two ten foot sheets of black corrugated roofing iron, with a few other bits and pieces, were placed on bush poles in the manner of a carport on the campfire side of the tent, our undercover area was greatly increased. It also provided a roof for our cedar extension dining table.

It was a time of calmness and reflection, as we settled in over the weekend. From the conversation and preparations, I gathered that our shift had coincided with what was – from a social point at least – a promotion for my father. Thanks to the intervention of our Member of State Parliament, George Frost, Dad would no longer earn our pitiful Sustenance in the slate and bluestone gutters of our town. He was now one of those chosen to seek the gold which the government hoped would restore the State of Victoria to the prosperity it had enjoyed in the golden years of the eighteen hundreds. Had it not been for this timely "promotion" to the Mining Sustenance, our flight to the bush would have been more difficult. As part of the deal, a tent, pick, shovel and panning dish – all marked with numerous broad arrows, to signify government ownership – were supplied free, to enable the aspirant to wander at will in the "wilderness" in the hope of fulfilling his quest. It seems the other two kits of tent and tools were supplied so that Louis and Keith could help Dad in this new "enterprise", but I gathered that because of their age they were to be just his helpers and lacked the status of being on the Mining Sustenance.

The following Monday, Lloyd, Yvonne, Jack and – reluctantly – I returned to school, while Dad and his "mates" sallied forth into the bush on a prospecting mission, where they found others engaged in the same pursuit, most of whom, in varying degrees were known to them.

One of Louis' best friends and peers, Sid Murray, was already an experienced gold seeker. With his father and brothers, he worked in their family's deep reef mine, or helped operate their horse-drawn puddling machine at Bluchers. It was from such friends, my family learned the rudiments of fossicking, friends who would unselfishly show them the spots where a little surface gold could be had without too much trouble. A few specks of gold would make desperate men gamble their energy recklessly.

After school, we enthused over the few grains of gold that glistened at the bottom of a small essence of lemon bottle half filled with clear water. As we twisted the bottle, the gold tumbled, so at times the uneven thickness of the glass would greatly stretch and magnify the image of the small specks, to a size that would have made the hours of toil worthwhile. But there were no illusions when the pittance was tipped into a saucer: the day's work had left us – and our sovereign state – as far as ever from financial salvation. But it was a thrill to be shown how to pick up the specks of gold on the tips of our wet fingers, then how to firmly hold that finger over the bottle opening and gently rinse the gold back into the water.

Each night we were eager to see how much the contents of the bottle had increased. The increase was ever so slow, although soon a few small chunky pieces accompanied the much finer majority. One piece had been deemed by the old hands to be about half a pennyweight. After a week or so, it was estimated the yield exceeded two pennyweights. Everyone agreed it was time for a sale, so it was taken to the bank and sold for four shillings and a few pence. Gold was only about four pounds an ounce at that time, even so, it gave us quite a lift. Over the next few months, there would be a number of such sales and at odd times, they included little mini-nuggets of around a pennyweight, but my family's wager of hard work was never on a real winner.

* * *

Water was a bit of a problem at the home site. A small excavation about 200 yards down the gully, left long ago by prospectors, collected enough run-off from rain, to provide us with a limited supply of blackish gum leaf-stained liquid. The goats and chooks found this water quite agreeable and we grudgingly found it acceptable for washing our clothes and ourselves. Carrying this water up the long incline to the camp was a big incentive for water conservation. This factor was instrumental in "spinning out" its meagre supply for the duration of our stay at that camp.

Our drinking and cooking water was obtained from the town supply. In spite of the stove and wire incidents, the new owners of our old property graciously opened their taps to our needs. Because we only had two 4-gallon kerosene tins, carting water was virtually a daily routine. At times it was a bit of a nuisance having to catch and harness Doll to the dogcart solely for such a short errand, but overall things worked out all right – well it did up until just before Christmas, when a circus came to town.

The circus set up camp about a mile away, beside our magnificent railway station. Of course we couldn't afford to go, in fact the thought of going didn't even cross our minds, but from mid afternoon, we could hear the noises of unfamiliar animals. The commonest sound was a muffled moan, which at times would rise to a roar. Dad confirmed my suspicion it was the sound of lions. I had never seen a lion, but I knew all about them! I had seen illustrations of them springing on white-pith-helmeted hunters and heard how the hunters were often dispatched even as they fired their elephant guns. I had also heard tales of how they often caused hunters inconvenience by gobbling up their beaters and bearers, and sneakingly removed helpless black children from their beds. Yes, I knew all about lions!

I was terrified by the sound. What would our chances be if one escaped? We would have no more hope than those poor kids had in those African camps. Even Dad's reassurances were to no avail, I wished we were back in our old lion-proof house. It was there amid the tents as the day ebbed away, that I first felt the need to devise some form of self-defence, in case I came face to face with an escaped man-eater. I looked around for inspiration: one of the short-handled round-mouthed mining-shovels leaning against a tent seemed like a god sent solution to my predicament. I decided that a good swift clout on the head with the back of the shovel would be my salvation. I kept this plan to myself, but maintained close proximity to one of those three shovels until the circus left town next morning.

Evidently Doll instinctively sensed that the lions were a threat, for at the first sound of them, she became quite agitated, and as the roars became louder in the still night air, she became frantic. The sound of her snorting and whinnying, as she recklessly galloped around the "park", kept us awake late into the night. Then suddenly, except for the occasional roar, and the sound of shunting in the railway yards, there was silence. In horror I wondered if a lion had got Doll. However, next morning it was undramatically accepted that Doll had merely jumped the fence, and was once again on her way back to the more peaceful pastures around Mount Greenock.

Doll's sudden departure left us with a water problem for the next few days. Then Louis, who was always a trier, came to the rescue: he managed to obtain a pair of bike wheels from somewhere, and constructed a handcart suitable for the job. Although carting the water was still a persistent burden of slow manual drudgery for Dad or my older brothers, it was a lot better than having to actually carry it. Lloyd, whose standards of perfection greatly exceeded his ability to achieve them, repeatedly said the cart's construction was rough; but we were still very grateful.

For a couple of years I felt quite secure and smug about my secret strategy for dealing with lions – then another circus came to town, and set up in front of the railway station. So like most of the kids around, we decided to go down after school, to see the animals being fed. I hadn't seen any of these exotic animals in the flesh before, so it was quite an event. I was very impressed by the size of the elephants, but with my rebel attitude towards authoritarianism, I couldn't understand why they allowed themselves to be bullied by their puny keepers – the camels seemed to have much more self esteem. Suddenly I spotted a couple of lions in a four-wheeled cage: they were enormous, and looked ferocious. With a shudder, I realised that a shovel was inadequate insurance for my lion problem.

* * *

Our local eucalyptus oil industry was based on coppice growth – mostly referred to as suckers – from the stumps of mainly long leaved box and to a lesser degree on ironbark, yellow gum, and red box. The "euky" cutters spared grey box, because its oil was unsuitable for the trade.

In a loose sequence, consecutive areas of suckers were harvested about every two or three years, when they could be up to 10 feet high. Harvesting was a very work-intensive process: a sharp blow to the inside base of the sucker with the back of the axe, would cause it to cleave off as cleanly as if it had been a separate entity just glued to the living stump. After harvesting a small area, the cutter – either male or female – would carry or drag each sucker to a central point. They would then proceed with the somewhat dangerous process of removing the branchlets from each stalk, with a sharp sickle, until a rounded heap of leaves, several cubic yards in bulk was formed. The cutter would repeat the tiresome process of knocking and sickling, until there were sufficient heaps to fill the vats (usually two) at the bush distilleries, which – with a touch of reverence – were referred to as "eucalyptus plants". Ideally, the leaves were pitchforked on to a conveyance as soon as possible after cutting, but at times the distilleries could not keep up with the cutters and the leaves would remain on site for many weeks. When this occurred, the heaps would often become permeated with the silk of unidentified caterpillars, which feasted and thrived in the enhanced environment of the heaps.

After stripping, the denuded stalks were tossed into a loosely stacked heap of a similar size to the leaf stacks. From the cutters, point of view, these sticks were valueless, but for scroungers like us, they were a valuable resource, that could be put to a wide range of uses, the most obvious two being for firewood and stick-fence construction. Being loosely stacked, the euky-sticks soon dried. Then the tops could easily be broken into suitable lengths for the stove, while the thicker ends, though often several feet long were fed into the open doors of the stove's firebox as they burnt, thus dispensing with the need to expend further energy with our old blunt axe. This also applied to the wood obtained from old dead stumps, which, especially after years of white-ant infestation, could be knocked from the ground with moderate exertion.

Treatment of a batch of leaves occupied a whole day for the distillers: the huge boilers pushed the steam through the leaves in the large underground vats, then through the condenser. The condenser consisted of a large concrete trough set in the ground, which was filled with water, and contained a system of two-inch metal pipes. As the eucalyptus bearing steam passed through these pipes, the steam that carried the eucalyptus vapour was turned into a liquid. Because the pipes sloped towards the outlet, which protruded from a specially constructed shallow embankment at the far end of the cooling trough, the resulting liquid trickled from the open end of the pipe, where it was collected in a container. After the mixture was allowed to settle for a while, the pure eucalyptus oil would rise to the top, where it could be easily skimmed off.

In the 1930s, the eucalyptus plant closest to us transported the leaves in wagons, which were mostly drawn by old worn out and underfed draught horses – it was a pitiful sight. On a number of occasions one of these forlorn beasts died in the paddock and its carcass would be dragged behind a dray to some deserted digger's-hole in the bush. Thankfully, within a few years of my first contact with this eucalyptus plant, it changed hands and an equally decrepit truck relieved the horses of their invariably terminal burden.

9

A Time of Anguish

The news of us "going bush" spread quickly through Mum's large and widely scattered family.

Dad had already earned some notoriety from the members of that family who were more conscious of social status for his often-unorthodox ideas and actions, but they were totally unprepared and somewhat outraged by this latest affront to their respectability. None more so than Auntie Tot.

On first hearing from Louis about the exploits of Boadicea, my formidable Auntie Tot instantly became the basis for my visualisation of that warrior queen. At other times I imagined a wooden bust of her likeness, riding the bow of some ancient galleon in the fury of battle. Yet in spite of these impressions, it seems that in her own way, Auntie Tot was a well-meaning soul who, in her Gippsland hometown of Leongatha, was a prominent and highly respected citizen. So perhaps we wrongly saw her as an interfering busybody, when on hearing of our situation, she penned the following letter dated 9/4/35 to Auntie Mag. I did not read this letter until some 50 years later:

My Dear Maggie

It is quite a long time since I have written to you. Do you know I bought a present at Xmas for you & I never got it sent, so I said to Ivy the other day I think I will get something and send it now. And now I hear you are out of the house, (I don't know your address) & living in a tent. Well Maggie I don't think you are doing the right thing it is no life for you or

Vonnie. Now Will and Mona are coming down next week & if you will let Vonnie come down, I will keep her & look after her & treat her the same as Mavis for a while anyway, until things look up a bit & Tom gets work & can get his home together again. And until then you should take the two little ones & go out to Will. I think this is your duty out of fairness to yourself & the little children. Tom can well look after himself & the three older boys, he is as good as a woman in the house. What does Louis do, does he try to get work.

Now Maggie I am not writing a long letter but if you answer this, I will write again I have just written to Will to ask him to bring Vonnie down. She may be short of clothes. But I will fix her up when she gets here. And now Maggie you think over what I have said. If you take the two little children & look after them & the three girls [go] *away the others will be all right without you, a tent is no place for a woman to live in & you must get out of it. Hoping that you will do this, we only want to do what is best for you & the children. Mavis is twelve today Vonnie is about her age I think & they should be good pals Mavis is easy to get on with.*

I am still keeping Colin & Eric at school, but am looking out for jobs for them Ivy is still at Williams the Shoeman. Now Maggie dear I will close hoping to hear from you soon & that you are going to do what we ask. Fondest love from your loving sister.

Tot.

(PS) When Will goes in for Vonnie you be ready with the two little ones & go out & stay at Evansford while they are away.

Tot.

Tot's husband George Brown was a self-employed carpenter and builder, who in spite of the Depression, was earning an income adequate to provide for his four dependents and there seemed to be no hassle about taking on another. Even so, I now realise it was an act of compassion and considerable generosity, that moved Auntie Tot to deprive us of our eldest sister.

Thankfully, for the time being, I remained oblivious to the pressure being put on Auntie Mag by Auntie Tot and – without consulting Dad – her plans for Jack's and my future. I can only imagine the anguish that letter must have caused to both Auntie Mag and Dad, before Dad agreed that Yvonne would go to Auntie Tot's place for a holiday, ". . . until things picked up".

One afternoon a few days after the letter arrived, gentle Auntie

Annie guided her eldest brother, our Uncle Will – who much to the consternation of some of his siblings and their offspring had recently taken a new bride – to our lowly bush camp. The swiftness of the operation was really a mercy. It didn't take long to gather up Yvonne's few possessions, then she was gone, without prolonged farewells and before she, or we, realised the extent of our mutual loss.

Although Auntie Tot – often with other members of her family – would visit Maryborough several times a year, Yvonne was never with them. We did not see our eldest sister again for five years.

I cannot recall ever hearing any talk about Jack and I going to live at Evansford, presumably that suggestion was promptly vetoed by either Dad or Uncle Will. Possibly Uncle Will – who was not renowned for his generosity – would have seen no short term economic sense in keeping two extra who were too young to be of much use around the farm. Although a nicer explanation for me, would be that Dad just decided that his family had been depleted enough, and it was time to say no. Whichever was the case, dear reliable Auntie Mag stayed put.

We did miss Yvonne. A letter from Yvonne dated 27/4/35 – only eighteen days after the date on Auntie Tot's letter – indicates that in spite of the comfort and adventure of her new surroundings, she was concerned about our welfare and missing us just as much as we were missing her:

> *Dear Auntie all*
>
> *Just a few lines to let you know that I am well. Will you please send me my books for I can do nothing. I am going to school down here. Mavis has a bike & goes for all the messages. Did Jack and Lyle go to the display. Did Lyle go in it I wish I could have been home to go to it. Uncle George has a wireless. I suppose Auntie Maggie is very lonely on Saturday when she is doing the washing. Keith and Lloyd you try and help her to wash up on Saturday. Eric and Colin have gone to the pictures the name is Tarzan and His Mate, Mavis, Auntie Tot and I are going on Tuesday. Jack & Lyle will you write and tell me what the display was like. Did you go in the dovet & did Lyle go in the march. I don't like up here on Saturday I would like to be at home. I don't like the school either. I go to Sunday School and church every Sunday morning, I don't go at night . . . have you missed a day at school since I left Jack I bet Lyle has, I have not . . .*

Auntie Tot bought me a pair of shoes & slippers. The ones Dad bought I keep for my best ones. The shoes Auntie Tot bought me were fours. Dad when you buy me shoes, size 4.

If the boys don't help Auntie Maggie I won't be here very long. Auntie Maggie did you write to Valma and June I am going to write tomorrow if I get the time. I've got to go to Sunday school & Church and set the table for dinner . . .

As I read those words, written by my eldest sister so long ago, they impart the uncertainty and sadness she felt at being plucked from her loved ones and the world that was hers. However, from another letter we received soon after, it was evident that Yvonne was becoming more attuned with the Brown household. The letter proudly reported that she and her contemporary cousin, Mavis, had received a reward of one shilling each from Auntie Tot, for walking all the way to and from church with their toes turned out. The reward was in accordance with the prevalent assumption of many status conscious citizens of that era, that walking with feet turned out – together with holding the little finger turned out while drinking from a cup – were the genteel "hallmarks" of a higher social class. In accordance with the philosophy of my family, such pretentiousness was considered hilarious.

It seems that Auntie Tot was not happy with Auntie Mag's decision to stay with us, so she decided it required face-to-face intervention. It seems that she persuaded her sister Deb's husband, who lived and worked on the metropolitan sewage farm at Little River, not far from Werribee, to assist her intervention. A few weeks later, unannounced, with Auntie Annie again as guide, Auntie Tot, Auntie Deb and Uncle Jim arrived among us. Well, that's not strictly right, for as soon as the matriarch of the Brown family and her retinue were sighted, Keith, Jack and I retreated into the bush. But as Tot's voice had to be raised to the level required to penetrate Auntie Mag's deafness, Jack and I were close enough to know that the visit was not a happy one. Auntie Tot's voice was by far the loudest and most prominent.

After a tirade of accusations that Dad's inept handling of his company's affairs was the cause of our plight, it became clear there was a genuine concern for the welfare of Auntie Mag. She relentlessly cajoled and bullied "Maggie" to forsake us and return to the comfort of the family at Evansford. "I have Yvonne, Tom and the boys will manage", she pressed again and again, to support the many sound reasons why she should go. My heart was heavy with despair. Gentle Auntie Mag was no match for her overpowering sister, and being intelligent she must have seen the folly of casting her lot with us. There was no mention of Jack and I also going to Evansford, it seems that option was non-negotiable.

After the best part of an hour, Auntie Tot's voice from the camp became more subdued, as blustering and bullying gave way to reasoning and gentle persuasion. It was then that Jack and I timidly emerged from the bush, to face a kind of genetic "Scramble", as our ears, eyes, noses, hair and other personal features were likened to those of various family members, of several generations.

They didn't accept the offer of a cup of tea, probably the abundance of bush-flies and, for those who liked it white the thought of goats' milk was a consideration in making that decision. However things were quite pleasant by the time they were ready to depart, but as they arranged themselves in the car, Auntie Tot's parting words left me with a heavy heart: "Think about what I've said Maggie, go back home". Then our tormentor, with her pleasant uncritical companions, departed to the exchange of farewell waves that continued until their car crested the hill. We all felt it was time for a cup of tea.

As soon as they had gone, Keith rejoined the rest of the family. He had avoided hearing how terrible it was, the boys not having proper jobs. The blame for which was apportioned between themselves and Dad, even though finding work was virtually impossible. Louis was not at home, so he also missed the unfair accusations of laziness. To varying degrees, the visitation had traumatised us all and left an atmosphere of uncertainty. Auntie Mag made no comment – nor was she asked about her attitude to Tot's proposal. This was not due to lack of interest or concern, it was a case of while uncertainty prevailed, there was still hope. After a while, there seemed to be nothing new to say about the visit and the teapot was empty, so gradually the group dispersed. I think Dad went on some errand and probably Lloyd adjourned to continue reading a Western in the comfort of his tent. Keith, Jack and I went into the nearby bush to collect some sucker-sticks for our fire. We had not gone far when Keith, who at that stage was a would-be hunter who longed to own a rifle, decided to go and see if there were any hares in Jukes' paddock, which was situated just behind the cemetery. He alleged that as it was getting late I would be too slow, so I was directed to return home.

There was a slight breeze and the air was chilly, as I neared the seemingly deserted camp. Despite the sound of wing beats and the rustling of leaves from the birds eagerly feeding as evening approached, there was an eerie kind of silence around the place. As I drew closer, I saw Auntie Mag amid the long evening shadows; sitting huddled before the open firebox doors of the stove. I timidly approached with an uncertainty that was out of place with us, and climbed onto her knee. Apart from having to straighten up, she hardly seemed to notice me as we sat for minutes in silence. Then, with a heavy pounding heart, I put my face close to her "good" ear and mustered the courage to plaintively ask, "Are you really going to leave us?" In contrast to my mere presence, the poignancy of my question swiftly shattered her deep thought, and evoked the answer that it begged. She wistfully smiled and kissed my temple, "Good heavens no!" she reassured, "Why on earth would I want to leave you?"

There can be no doubt that Auntie Mag would have seriously considered the contents of her sister's tirade. The arguments that her welfare would be better served elsewhere were solid, but there was really no decision to be made, Auntie Mag's very nature deprived her of options.

10

Simple but Ample Fare

Surely my memory exaggerates the weeks and weeks of crisp dewy mornings and glorious autumn days, broken by just a few pleasant showers that followed our move to the bush. Nevertheless, we did have a particularly gentle introduction to camp life, and soon the unfamiliar became the normal.

I can't remember having any longing to be back at the house that had been the only home I had known. Our poverty was no worse than it had been, and my growing love affair with the rocky terrain and wonderful bush around our camp more than compensated for the loss of the house that in many ways epitomised the gloom of the Great Depression.

We were still enjoying the novelty of spending most nights around a glorious campfire in the spot where it was that first night. Even when the nights were a bit misty, it was beautiful to shelter beneath old coats and folded-sugarbag hoods, listening to the light raindrops hissing as they hit the gleaming coals that flushed a range of hues and formed a gallery of fantastic pictures in our imaginative minds.

On some of those misty nights in autumn, every now and then, a huge moth would appear out of the dark, and make a suicidal plunge into the campfire, where it would sizzle and burn like a spilled barbecue sausage. I was told they were goat moths, and when one was captured before it could commit self-immolation, the reason for the name became clear when I was instructed to look directly into its dark face. To anyone with the slightest imagination, the antennae and gaunt face is a superb caricature of a large-horned billy goat. The larvae of these large greyish-brown moths can live for years below ground, before emerging during the first rainy nights in autumn. In the light of day their discarded 4- or 5-inch-long bloated pupa cases, with their detached delightfully ornate headpieces, were to be seen scattered throughout the surrounding bush. Over the years I collected those fascinating crown-like headpieces, in the hope I could some day put them to a use worthy of their beauty, but alas, the task exceeded my ingenuity.

One afternoon, we had a bit of a windfall: only Auntie Mag, Lloyd, Jack and I were home, so I felt quite vulnerable as I watched the horse and what seemed a particularly high cart, advancing towards our camp along the track through the "park". Auntie Mag would not have heard the slow plod of the horse and the iron tyres of the cartwheels crunching the quartz gravel, so she remained in her tent. But Lloyd appeared, and with Jack and I stringing behind, he approached the vehicle as it stopped on the other side of the fence.

The driver, dressed in a three-piece suit and felt hat, seemed to be a person of some importance. He was a stranger to me but Lloyd addressed him as Mr Frost. Instantly my trepidation was allayed, for although I didn't have much idea what it meant, I knew George Frost was our local member. Even at my tender age, the flood of anecdotes I had heard about his "good works" in helping the poor and other unfortunates, allowed him to share the same niche in my mind as Christ.

In fact one of the anecdotes did seem to have Biblical connotations. It concerned "feeding the masses" with bread. Many times I had heard the inspiring story that when he was a baker during a particularly nasty flood, when raging water that was too rough for any available boat covered the bridge across McCallums Creek, isolating the small town of Majorca for several days, he played a major role in securing a rope to trees at both ends of the disintegrating bridge. Then alone he made the necessary number of trips through the chest-high torrent, with a basket full of bread and other essentials on his head, to relieve the besieged and hungry citizens.

As the Mayor of the time he was the force behind the tenacious endeavours to bring industry to our dying town. The Progress Association persuaded people of good will – including those who could only spare a few shillings – to invest in struggling companies, on the condition that they would shift to Maryborough. Its success ensured our town's survival. It was no wonder that George Frost retained his seat in the Legislative Assembly, until his death in 1942.

With few words, Mr Frost unloaded a three-bushel wheatbag of apples onto our side of the fence and departed: I saw him more as a real life Santa Claus.

I later learned, that he owned one of the many small orchards that were scattered around our district. I was told that in earlier days, those orchards had supplied most of the fruit sold in our town. A few in fact were still commercial ventures, but our benefactor gave most of his fruit to the needy.

That was the first of a number of occasions over the next few years, on which that good man would deliver an unexpected bag of fruit, with the same inimitable humility, which allowed no hint of charity.

Those apples were a joyous gift: for some weeks apple pies and those delicious baked-batter apple puddings replaced pancakes and pan scones, and our teeth sparkled from slicing through the crisp white flesh of fresh raw apples. Each time we partook of those glorious puddings – descriptively called "elephant-hide puddings" by us kids – and pies, which we liberally garnished with goats' milk, Auntie Mag would invariably say, "I miss the cream, we always had lashings of cream with our puddings at home – before Grandma died".

When Auntie Mag referred to her mother while talking to us, it was always Grandma, especially in the realms of cooking, where to Auntie Mag, Grandma's teachings were gospel. Perhaps her faith was justified, for although handicapped by lack of ingredients and with her stove out in the open, Auntie Mag proved to be a highly skilled cook. Yet any praise of her culinary creations would bring forth a self-denigrating comparison with her mother and to a lesser extent her oldest sister Liz: "Grandma was the one who could cook," she'd say. And if the praise persisted, she would reinforce her case with the damning evidence: "I never even learned how to cure a pig – Grandma or Liz always did that, they would never let me have a pig to try".

Over time, many new innovations were introduced to our menus. Keith had managed to scrape up the 30 shillings to buy the new Canadian-made pea-rifle he had long desired, so rabbit and hare appeared on our table more often. I loved roast rabbit, but could barely stomach hare, except when it was minced and heavily disguised in a mixture of homemade macaroni, with plenty of fried onions, a packet of mixed spice, homemade sauce and – when it was available – some grated cheese. Mixed spice – which I considered a most important ingredient – must have been very cheap, for it always seemed to be on hand. But I liked this dish much better when it didn't contain any minced hare. It was delicious that way – and it still is.

That galvanised cast-iron mincer was another thing that fortunately came with us from our old home. Over the next few years, it played a more important role in sustaining us, than just mincing hares.

We had been accustomed to having rolled oats or "Digestive" (a brand name for a wheat meal) porridge for breakfast but, even though I'm sure it would have been quite cheap, because of the large quantity needed for seven healthy appetites, it became a burden on our finances. Some of our neighbours had replaced porridge with boiled wheat. We tried it too, but only once, it was a bit too rough for us. When the boiled wheat was chewed, it attained the texture of chewing gum – we were far too genteel for food like that.

The ability to innovate was the dominating talent of my family, so it wasn't long before someone decided to put the raw wheat through the mincer, with the bread-crumbing cutter attached – it was a great success. One pass through the mincer would produce a product just acceptable to our delicate palates, but repeatedly putting the grindings through our old flour sieve, and re-mincing the coarse portion could produce a high-grade meal. Lloyd soon achieved the undisputed recognition of producing the finest grade. We all shared the job of producing the meal. If the mincer was even a quarter full, it was virtually impossible for even the men to turn. Jack and I could only succeed by dribbling a few grains through in a continuous stream, it was a very slow process, and seemed more so, when the breakfast pot was waiting. Jack and I mostly produced a pretty gritty product. I didn't like it at all, even though Jack insisted he liked it best that way. I suspected his claim was a sort of corruption of the moral behind the fable about the fox and the grapes – it wasn't a case of what you can't get is no good, but the best you can do is tops.

Despite the varying grades of our wheat meal, it was accepted with gusto, especially with honey – which for us was always more easily obtained than sugar, which cost four pence a pound – and plenty of cold goats' milk. However it was not its popularity that often made it the main item on our menu for both breakfast and tea, and on occasions – when things were really crook – we would even have it for our midday dinner. But I don't remember ever having it three times in the one day.

Regrettably, in that first year, on a few occasions other "forbidden game" filled the crusts of a "special" pie: we cannot forget our transgressions, but remorsefully mollify our shame, by blaming the "rotten system", that in a land of plenty, made us stoop to such depths for a meal. The winter of 1935 was a year when unusually large flocks of lorikeets came to feast on the nectar that was literally dripping from the brimming cups of the blossom that festooned the red ironbarks of our forest. In later years they came in similar numbers, but by then necessity's tyranny had waned.

Around this time we also had another winner: each morning Keith, and on occasions Lloyd, would walk more than a mile through the bush to Bluchers, to receive the generous handout of a bucket of skim milk. In those days skim milk was not held in very high regard as human food. It was a common belief that if one drank more than a meagre amount, "It gives you the scours". We all had a healthy sense of self-preservation, so we heeded the warning. In spite of its poor image we found it handy for making custards, scones, pancakes and – when it was available – a good cup of cocoa. However, through ignorance, we were unaware of its full blessing. Those of us who lived for another 50 years, were to see the slick TV-ad merchants promote that once-maligned product, under new and catchy brand names, as a symbol of health and youthful vitality. That and the more sobering statistics from the Heart Foundation are good reasons for us to belatedly reassess the value of that once thought lowly gift.

When the weather was good during weekends or holidays, Jack would mostly accompany Keith on those pleasant morning strolls. I always looked forward to the occasional time when I was allowed to accompany them. It was always an adventure, with lots of exciting things to see on the way. There was Bluchers Hill – an old mine dump of blue slate that ranged in size from dust to large chunks, strewn throughout with an assortment of quartz and igneous oddities, that could quickly capture the interest of my curious mind. Although the slate hill protruded high above the extensive sand heaps from the quartz crusher that surrounded it, the hill's volume was much less.

I soon learned that the sand – ranging from pockets of clean free flowing white sand, often with a bluish hue, to a compacting brownish grade – had been produced by a huge stamper that had crushed the quartz from the mine. The remains of that massive construction of hard red bricks, because of its strong cement mortar had defied persistent attempts to demolish it. Defiantly it still stands as a monument to its builders.

It seems that Bluchers Mine was a hive of activity up until the first years of the "Great War", as it was called, and often, it seemed to me, with a sense of affection. More than twenty years later, in spite of the large unprotected gaping hole, that reputedly plunged almost 900 feet into the sandstone that carried the quartz reef, the area was one of the most popular playgrounds of the local bush-roaming youngsters. One of their delights was to fetch a rock from the slate hill, and hurl it into this tantalising vortex. The larger the rock and the closer one got to the edge during the act, the greater the kudos. Being terrified of this shaft as well as the hundreds of other lesser, but equally dangerous ones scattered round the bush I never went too close. I would always allow enough space to tumble head over heels several times before I'd reach the edge. It was a spine-chilling thrill to hear the measured reverberating booming of a large rock bouncing off the sandstone sides of the shaft: sometimes in chorus, sometimes in eerie silence, the long seconds would be counted until the final resounding splash – or in dry mines a dull thud – was heard. Then using a doubtful formula from heaven knows where, someone would authoritatively pronounce the depth of the shaft. Gosh, according to those calculations, some of those holes were deep.

I liked Mr Kellam, the old man who gave us the milk but, because of his long lean build, I was confused by the name "Porky", by which he was mostly called, though with us, only in his absence. The house and its dairy equipped with a separator were the only buildings still standing at Bluchers. At first I thought Mr Kellam lived there, for the house looked as if it was inhabited, but I later learned that he rode his bike twice daily from his home in Maryborough, to milk a few cows and separate the milk.

There were a number of fruit trees around the house, and down in one corner of the paddock, a huge old pear tree. We were granted permission to compete with the various species of parrots and human raiders for its woody fruit, which we considered "beaut".

That privilege continued for many years after the supply of skim milk ceased to provide the custard for the stewed pears.

Venerable "Porky" had an amazing knowledge of the history of the surrounding bush. He passed on to us the sites of long-gone schools, hotels, and other things that were "documented" only in the minds of such witnesses and later only known to those like us, who as youngsters were fortunate enough to have heard their tales.

* * *

Although we were managing reasonably well with the euky-sticks and stump-wood, Dad decided we needed something a bit more substantial. During the cooler months each year, the Forestry Commission always marked areas of the bush into small sections in which they blazed certain trees with a tomahawk, that they considered would be suitable for posts or sleepers. These areas, known as "household blocks", for a small fee, were made available for people to cut the unmarked trees for their firewood. Dad bought one of these blocks. He then lashed out and bought a new hickory axe handle, which he then proceeded to laboriously scrape with broken glass, until it snugly fitted the head of our old "*Plum*" axe. He then spent a couple of days with a file, making the axe sharp enough to do the work.

The forest bailiff was very considerate, and granted Dad a block not too far from our camp. Cutting the block out was quite an event for us all. Dad did most of the felling, as well as cutting the trees up into five-foot lengths. It was not that my older brothers weren't anxious to share the task, but because Dad was over-cautious about accidents with razor-sharp axes. He was haunted by the injuries he had seen inflicted by such axes in the hands of inexperienced people. But there were plenty of logs to be carried and stacked into heaps for the bailiff to measure and to assess the tariff. Jack and I eagerly helped, carrying the small logs to the heaps and dragging the unwanted bushes into heaps for their mandatory burning.

The cutting of the 24-ton block was done with such proficiency that the bailiff congratulated Dad on the fine job. He was especially impressed by how low the stumps were cut. As a reward, the bailiff invited Dad to cut down as many of the high stumps scattered through the bush as he liked, free of charge.

Thankfully Doll was available to make her last contribution to our family's welfare, by hauling the wood home.

11

Pleasures, Problems and the Promised Land

We were not overwhelmed by visitors during our stay at that first camp, but Reg Hovey and Sid Murray dropped in quite often. They came mainly for the companionship of my three eldest brothers. Louis and Sid were keen on ballroom dancing – or as they always emphasised, *modern* ballroom dancing. Often on a pleasant afternoon they would "glide" over a swept patch of hard bare ground, without partners, whirling to an endless oration of "quick" and "slow", in an assortment of combinations, which I presumed was a substitute for music.

It wasn't long before Keith also became "infected" with this dancing obsession, and although it would be a year or two before he graced a dance-hall floor – due to the lack of suitable clothes – countless hours were spent learning and practising various steps. In later years, all three were locally acclaimed for their dancing prowess: perhaps those hard, rough, clay-loam clearings acted like the double-weight armour Roman soldiers are said to have used in training, to give them a bit of an advantage when it came to the real thing using normal gear.

There was always an air of reverence about the conversation when Louis and Sid spoke of the superb candle-greased floors they had encountered in various halls. The reverence was worthy of the Almighty himself, when they spoke of "Leggets" – which they frequently reminded us was a grand dance palace in Melbourne. Often during these visits, dancing would give way to music and singing: Louis, Sid, and Lloyd were all competent with the mouth organ. A reasonably good mouth organ could be bought for a few shillings, and despite the fact that they all seemed to be German imports, most had dinky-di Australian brand names, such as "Kookaburra", and "Boomerang". There can be few sounds more soulful than the quivering notes of a mouth organ playing a sentimental melody by a campfire at night in the Australian bush – especially in the midst of uncomplaining poverty.

Even though Dad used to say I went to bed with the chooks, I knew the enchantment of those evenings by the fire. In a mental twilight from my bed, I was conscious of that music and the chatter that often extended deep into the night, until the dying embers closed the session.

* * *

Mr Chapman, usually with at least one of his – to me – grown-up sons would often drop in to see how we were faring, and from time to time Dad, with various combinations of his sons, would wander across the bush to inspect the progress on the Chapman building. The walls were mud, but unlike most of the mud-houses around our town, which were made of pre-moulded bricks, they were using a scant supply of planks, to form long moulds in situ, which were then packed with mud. After the mud had dried sufficiently, the boards were moved further along the wall. This process was repeated again and again. Waiting for the mud to dry made progress tediously slow, and as the walls rose a few inches higher with each course the work became progressively harder.

In spite of his own problems, Mr Chapman had a genuine concern for our wellbeing. In any conversation with Dad, the options for quickly "getting a roof over our heads" seemed to come up. With winter approaching, Dad was also concerned about our plight, but there was no acceptable solution. Mr Chapman also stressed the importance of Dad getting a piece of ground of his own. Dad wholeheartedly agreed, but in our circumstances that seemed to be a hopeless dream.

There were often great discussions about house plans: hours were spent drawing endless concepts on any suitable patch of bare ground. The sketches were usually to a slightly larger scale than one would expect on a formal blueprint, but always small enough to be drawn without the necessity to move from a squatting position. Dad's plans were always richly innovative: some of his designs could have turned the architectural world upside down, had finance been of no consequence. His obsession with the importance of fresh air and sunshine was always the inspiration behind those unorthodox visions. Mr Chapman would listen and make constructive comments, but was always respectful of Dad's thoughts. However, he was not one to flit off in flights of fancy: his plans for us were always very basic, but sadly even they were beyond our grasp. So, as autumn drifted into winter, there were no preparations for whatever it would bring.

Soon we were constantly turning, as we sat or stood around our campfire in the evenings: at times beneath the brilliant sky of a still frosty night, the spine-chilling husky bark of an errant fox would bring an excited response from the scattered neighbourhood dogs, and when the moon was bright, the bush curlews paid homage to the glory of the night, with their plaintive high key drawn out notes and cackling shrieks. On other nights, all nature's sounds were of the wind: it drove the racing clouds, and played a symphony of timelessness, as it stirred the trees around our camp. Like a living thing, it whispered in the trees above; then suddenly the whisper was a roar, as muted "whip-cracks" from the wildly flapping tents beat in abandon to the whims of the whirling gusts. Then, to nature's baton, a gentle interlude, as the wind departed to stir the crowns of other trees with ever changing roars and murmurs, that rose and fell in accordance with the direction and distance of its vagaries. Such nights possess a strange beauty that seems to bring one close to the essence of the universe.

It wasn't until July, when we received almost four and a half inches of rain, that I knew the discomfort of camping in really wet weather. It was cold and miserable, and the only place that offered any comfort, was bed. Even then, it wasn't all roses, for we soon discovered that the tents were not completely leak proof in heavy rain. Any accidental or misguided touch of the calico roof was enough to start an incessant drip. Sometimes the seriousness of such drips could be reduced by running the fingertip from the offending spot down the sloping roof to the walls, thus creating a path, which the water would follow rather than drip. However such action was never taken lightly, for at times it could exacerbate the situation.

It was also disastrous – as poor Auntie Mag found out after that first heavy rain – to allow any object to touch the tent roof.

Auntie Mag was a great hoarder: she had saved in mint condition, probably every non-perishable Christmas and birthday gift and card she had ever received. Many of those "treasures" were safely stored in her seafarer's chest, which though slightly smaller, was similar to the family tin box. The overflow was stored in stout cardboard boxes with neatly fitting slip-on lids. In the restricted confines of the tent, these cardboard boxes had been neatly stacked on top of the trunk, and unfortunately the top ones were pressed against the tent roof, near the wall. Although the rain had continued throughout the night, it was not until the light of day that the disaster was discovered.

Within my memory, Auntie Mag had accepted all our previous misfortunes with no indication of the anguish she must have felt, so I was not prepared for her reaction to this latest situation.

Perhaps the abysmal weather outside, and the sheer misery within the dank tent, where the rain had seeped beneath the walls and turned the dust of the earth floor to mud, accentuated her sense of loss, and induced a feeling of hopelessness in her courageous soul. As she sorted through her sodden keepsakes, for the first time I saw her cry. As I write, I relive my feelings of that moment: the staff on which I so heavily leant, was crumbling. The despair I felt was not for myself, or even for the damaged goods, it was because there was no way I could ease dear Auntie Mag's distress. Reminiscing years later, it seemed incongruous that Auntie Mag had broken down over this particular mishap, after calmly enduring so many more serious trials of life. Eventually the answer was to come: this was solely her loss; there was no one else who needed her comfort and support.

The cold, drizzly rain continued throughout the day, but more penetrating than the rain, was the gloomy atmosphere that imbued our beings. However, in the feeble sunshine of the following morning, things seemed much brighter: surprisingly, it was soon discovered that most of Auntie Mag's damaged souvenirs could be salvaged, while those in the trunk were still as good as new. What's more, because of the hard ground, and the air gap under the walls, the tent floors were already beginning to dry, so it wasn't long before we began to enjoy our lives again.

It was during that wet spell that I became aware of how important bags were. A three-bushel jute wheatbag would be thrown around the shoulders, and another bag with one half tucked into the other half lengthways, formed an extended pixie-type head covering. The finely woven 70-pound hessian sugarbags were preferred for these hats, but because they were a much sought-after item, the rougher, larger wheat bags often had to suffice. One of the reasons sugarbags were scarce, was because they were also in demand for the manufacture of gunny bags, which were the universal haversacks of impoverished Australian males of that time. The gunny bags were very easy to make. The top half of the sugar bag was simply turned down over the bottom half and a rope of suitable length for the person concerned was tied to the two top corners. A walnut sized stone was inserted between the fold of the bag above the knot, to prevent the rope from slipping off. Few men or boy pedestrian shoppers – and even those prosperous enough to have a bike – were without one. Bush workers – and manual workers in general – almost inevitably used them to carry the day's meagre rations, either over their shoulders or on the bar of their bike.

The onset of winter quickly brought to our notice, the inadequacy of our thinning blankets, for our raw lifestyle. It was necessary to urgently supplement them with coats, newspaper, and jute wheabags. At first the wheatbags were used as single units, but these were soon upgraded into much more practical waggas. These were produced by simply sewing bags together with twine and a bag needle, until the "blanket" reached the required size. More affluent families disguised that humble fabric with a colourful cover of some inexpensive material, which allowed the article to masquerade as a more socially acceptable quilt.

Forty years or so later, I was shown a wagga that had become a family heirloom. This up-market example had been covered with outdated samples of suit material that had been donated by a travelling salesman. The squares of various colours and patterns had been stitched together patchwork style, over the bags.

Waggas were oppressively heavy: they would virtually pin a small child to the mattress, and create the environment for nightmares, or in times of restlessness, consume the energy that a night's sleep should restore. For those reasons, a lighter version was often made. This was achieved by cutting the bags open, and using a single layer of the fabric. However halving the weight reduced their efficiency by the same degree.

Our main source of bed-warmth and comfort on those wintry

nights proved to be the unmortared bricks that enclosed our stove: they were marvellous bed-warmers. Selecting bricks of the optimum temperature, and wrapping them in paper or suitable cloth, soon became a nightly ritual. Jack and I were considered too young, to be trusted with this potentially hazardous task, so Dad – with the diligence of a male mallee fowl determining the temperature of its nest – prepared our bricks. The older members of the family prepared their own, often with varying degrees of mishaps, when overheated bricks scorched their wrappings and the bedding. On rare occasions, they even burnt the feet that sought their warmth. Overall though, the hot bricks were a resounding success.

We soon learned the wisdom of keeping the blankets up over our ears as we slept; even so, before the winter was over, the upper rims of my ears were the texture of cauliflower, from sore and itchy chilblains. Louis and Lloyd didn't just cover their ears: they slept with their whole head literally tucked in under the bedclothes. This action really worried Dad, he feared they would suffocate. He repeatedly lectured them on the folly of this deplorable habit: he even went to the trouble of making the rounds – often several times a night, to physically extract their somewhat stifled heads from that potentially suicidal situation.

For me, thunderstorms were the most frightening events of our camp life. I didn't mind the thunder, for it had been explained to me that once you heard it, the danger from that particular strike was over. But not far from our camp, the remains of a large grey box tree that had been shattered by lightning, dramatically illustrated just what lightning could do.

Dad often warned us never to take shelter under a tree during a storm but because our tents were surrounded by ironbarks, necessity forced him to accept the situation. It must have really worried him. When severe storms were approaching, we kids would be terrified, so Dad would tell us to get into our beds and we would be safe. Having no reason to doubt Dad, we would promptly take to our beds, where with his trusted assurance, we would feel secure. Looking back, that advice seems strange, Dad, being well versed in the ways of bush survival, would have been well aware that being in bed did not reduce our vulnerability one iota. I can only conclude that being unable to do anything about it, he realised it would be best for us to at least face the danger without fear.

Over the years, I have seen many trees struck by lightning in the vicinity of our two old camps, and realise just how significant the danger was.

* * *

One pleasant afternoon, Mr Chapman arrived at our place somewhat excited: I gathered from his conversation with Dad, that he had heard about a three acre Crown land block, more or less just over the hill, that adjoined the western boundary of the "park", that could be available for lease from the Lands Department. He explained that part of the block was once a market garden, but the venture had been a failure, and the lease had long since lapsed. He thought the lease fee would probably be three pounds a year, but we could worry about that when the time came, the main thing was not to waste any time before looking into the matter. It all seemed too good to be true: an immediate cursory inspection was warranted.

It was one of my not infrequent days away from school, so Keith and I were available to join the expedition. In high hopes we headed up the hill through the "park", towards the afternoon sun. Although the journey was only a few hundred yards, there were a few stops as features of the landscape were noted and discussed, especially from the vantage point on the top of the hill, where we were surrounded by four contrasting landscapes.

I remember getting a little impatient with these seemingly needless delays. I now wonder if it was perhaps an unconscious postponement of viewing the "Promised Land", in case of disappointment.

Eventually we reached the "park's" western boundary fence, and climbed through into the enticing real estate. Although we had been in our camp for some months by this time, and this area was so close, it was completely new to me, and the rest of the party seemed to be in a similar position.

No sooner had we left the "park", than we confronted two rectangular slate quarries, running in a north-south alignment. The larger one was many times the size of the ones near our home camp. It varied in depth from near ground level at its southern end, to a sheer wall of some 20 feet at its northern end where a narrow steep-sided neck-like channel connected it to the much smaller and uniformly shallower excavation. The possibilities of the larger gaping hole were immediately evident to the fertile minds in our group: it could be made into a fine dam.

After an exchange of suggestions concerning the civil engineering implications of such a project, we moved on to assess the block's other features, and more importantly, find the survey marks that designated the area: that was when we struck our first disappointment. It didn't take long to find the first survey mark: it consisted of a square sawn wooden peg, with trenches a few inches wide and deep, and a yard or so long, radiating out to indicate the direction of each boundary. Calculated searching soon located the corners of the block, and that was when it was realised one boundary cut the quarry in two. So much for our grand dam.

"But just a moment," someone said, the survey marks indicated there was another apparently vacant block about the same size, adjoining the first block – perhaps we could lease them both? If we could, it was agreed, it would be an even more desirable property. The whole quarry would be included, and the soil in the shallow gully that adjoined the south end of the quarry was much better than that on the grassy acre clearing half way down the blocks where the old market garden had been. As we inspected the site of the old garden, there was general bewilderment when someone mentioned how strange it was that there was no dam nearby. After a few minutes of serious discussion, incredible as it seemed, it was agreed that the water must have been carted to the spot. No wonder the project failed.

It was instantly decided that our local member would be approached as soon as possible. We wended our way back home in an atmosphere of high euphoria.

As soon as it could be arranged, a more comprehensive family party was assembled, and a detailed inspection of the blocks met with unanimous approval. Dad was very enthusiastic, indicating possible sites for our house and tennis court. He also pointed out several strategically placed trees, which would provide ideal shade for cars or tethered horses. I visualised them being used on a pleasant Sunday afternoon, when friends and neighbours dropped in to leisurely sip tea, as they waited their turn for a friendly game of tennis. Had I, at that time, heard of how American plantation owners would sip mint julep on their cool verandas, as their slaves toiled in the cotton fields, my mental picture would have been greatly enhanced. Yes, the two blocks certainly held the promise of stately country living. For Dad – a battler who was intensely mindful of the evils of the class system – at times allowed himself the indulgence of such aristocratic day dreams.

For the next few days/weeks/months, I was not privy to the details of the negotiation concerning the land, but I was well aware that movements were afoot, and that George Frost was favourably involved. I did discover though, that there were technical reasons why Dad could not lease both blocks, but there was no impediment to Louis leasing the second one, so slowly but surely, things proceeded along those lines.

12

Steady As We Go

Meanwhile, it was "steady as we go" around our camp: on moving to the bush, Dad had continued his usual practice of rising first each morning to light the fire in the stove and take every member of the household a "wake-up" cup of tea. What's more, he continued to do so virtually every morning for years to come. Dad seemed to get a lot of pleasure out of spoiling us in this way, for most mornings we would hear him singing scraps of favourite songs he had learned over the years, and they added up to quite a repertoire.

Other songs were those that he had learned from his father. There was one about Lord Horatio Nelson's "gallant" death at the battle of Trafalgar, and others that glorified the highlights of England's nineteenth century wars. When Dad sang those he would scoff at the foolish heroic sentiment they conveyed, especially one song about that idiotic Charge of the Light Brigade during the Crimean War.

As one would expect, many of his father's songs he sang to us were of a nautical nature. I suspect Dad's version of *Rule Britannia*, may have been a parody on the old song that was meant to stir the heart of every Englishman; if it wasn't, it was patriotism going over the top:

It was on the deep Atlantic,
In the equinoctial gales,
That a young fellow fell overboard,
Amidst the sharks and whales.

He went right down so quickly,
So headlong first fell he,
He went out of sight like a streak of light,
To the bottom of the deep blue sea.

Singing Rule Britannia,
Britannia rule the waves,
Britons never never ever
Shall be slaves.

Louis would always substitute the last two lines of that final verse with:

"No more Chinamen allowed
In New South Wales".

Another of the nautical songs we youngsters particularly liked was *The Pirate's Song*. Even though I heard it so often, only scraps of the song remain in my mind:

I'm afloat, I'm afloat,
On the fierce rolling tide,
The sea is my home,
And the barque is my pride.

I heed not the monarch,
And I fear not the law,
While I've a compass to steer by,
And a dagger to draw.

And never a slave
Or a coward shall I kneel,
While my gun carries shot,
And my belt holds a steel.

Up up with the flag,
Let the sheets kiss the wind,
And I'll warrant we'll soon
Leave the seagulls behind.

With thunder above us,
And darkness below,
Right onward, right onward,
So merrily we'll go.

But this rebellious sentiment with which we were imbued, wasn't restricted to pirates or old England, we were frequently given a recital of *The Wild Colonial Boy*. One of our particular favourites was *The Stockman's Last Ride*. Dad sang it to a different tune and words to any version I have heard before or since, I think his version had more appeal and the words seemed more Australian and less corny.

It was also from Dad that I first acquired a lifelong appreciation (except for his occasional abhorrent aberrations of racial intolerance) of the works of Henry Lawson. He graphically exposed the social injustices and the heartbreaking lot of so many Australians. Dad would recite such as *Faces In The Street* and his favourite *The Shanty On The Rise*. The words moved me greatly, and helped awaken me to the finer aspects of Australian culture – mateship, generosity and the obligation to rebel against the economic tyrants of our land. Such traditional convictions still prevailed within the common people of our Australian community during my younger years. Sadly, such qualities have now been largely superseded by the overbearing American culture of triviality, selfishness and greed.

* * *

A bit of excitement – diminishing with the seniority of the members – ran through our family, at the birth of a kid to the old white goat. He was dark brown, with big ears and a lovable demeanour. As with Donk, unbeknown to Jack and I, he was neutered, and as a result, he also grew into a big docile sturdy beast. There was always doubt about whether his somewhat dopey demeanour was natural or artificially induced, I think the evidence indicates it was the latter. Within a few days of his birth, this bright kid was a firm family favourite, spending much of his time mingling with the humans. It was this association, together with his astuteness in attaining self-comfort, which almost led to his death and greatly changed his behaviour.

It was common practice in cold weather, for various members of the family to sit in front of the stove. Often when either Dad or Auntie Mag was doing so, I would climb onto their knee. Even now, I feel again the ecstasy of those occasions: I felt so secure in the aura of their love, especially when Dad held the palms of his hands at the open firebox, then transferred the warmth to my icy hands, knees, and ears. It was heavenly. Often the person at the stove would also warm their feet in the open oven, and sometimes when they finished warming themselves, they would forget to shut the oven's double doors.

After one such session, Auntie Mag on noticing the doors open closed them, then continued on with her work, which included keeping the stove stoked. Some time later, Keith appeared on the scene, and heard pathetic bleats coming from the stove. He quickly opened the oven to reveal the slightly singed and bewildered looking kid. It was indeed lucky that Keith arrived, for Auntie Mag with her depleted hearing, would never have heard the muffled bleats, and it would have been far too late when she detected the smell of scorching hair.

He didn't appear to have suffered any serious physical damage, but from that time on, he was accustomed to emitting a strange noise. Keith, who was always on the lookout for unusual names for family pets, quickly saw the potential of that sound, as a name for our new pet: we all agreed his name should be Burbler.

This kid proved to be the harbinger of the many problems the goats were to cause in the future. Soon after his adventure in the oven, he was tripping along one of the horizontal poles that supported Chapman's tent, when he slipped and went through its ageing fabric. It was a major calamity for us, for no matter how hard we tried, it was impossible to make satisfactory repairs with wheatbags – the only material available.

Burbler's mother proved to be a prolific milk producer, so our supply of milk was greatly increased and often exceeded our normal household requirements. Because Dad considered Keith had been left with delicate lungs after his childhood bouts of pneumonia, this spare milk was given to him to keep in his tent, to drink at will. At first either Auntie Mag or Dad milked the goats, but Jack was keen to learn, though many months would pass before he mastered the art, and by that time I was a willing apprentice. Looking back it seems strange that Lloyd, who seemed to be the "rouseabout" of my siblings, never took on this task. He shared the job of shopping for groceries with Dad and seemed to always be the message boy, but milk the goats – never. Keith didn't milk them either, but no one would have suggested that he even try, it would have been out of character for him.

* * *

During our first year in the bush, meat and vegetables were scarce. We saw only the lowest cuts of meat, and a portion of our meat supply was still rabbit and hare but even they were never plentiful in the areas close to home because so many others were in poverty too. The pressure on their populations close to the town was drastic. Although rabbits were in plague proportions further afield, lack of transport put them beyond the reach of most poverty-stricken people in town. Vegetables however, were the biggest problem: the only kinds I associate with that camp (except at Christmas) were dried peas and haricot beans which had to be soaked in water overnight before cooking, and potatoes and onions. There never seemed to be any shortage of onions: they were prepared in every conceivable way, and a pan full of nicely browned fried onions, with fresh scones, was considered by us all, to be a splendid evening meal. Even when onion was not part of our midday dinner, raw onion – mostly the cheapest Brown Spanish – to which most of us were virtually addicted, was always available as a garnish.

Almost daily, as the main item of one meal – usually tea – Auntie Mag produced some type of scones. They were usually eaten with honey. With fried scones, the dough was simply rolled out, then with a series of straight knife strokes cut into palm-sized sections of assorted shapes. They were then cooked in a greased pan. At times when cold meat was available, we would have fried pasties. For these the scone dough was rolled thinner, then cut into bread-and-butter-plate size circles, then folded in half over a filling of minced meat and onions. They were really good – especially with tomato sauce. Auntie Mag also made what she called pan scones. A pan scone was about two inches thick when cooked, and filled our big frying pan with the arched handle with a swivel ring at the top. The pan scone was not fried, instead it was cooked in a floured pan, and ended up with a hard tough crust, but the inside was light and fluffy. It was used as a substitute for bread, and possessed reasonable keeping qualities.

Scone dough was also the basis for another of our regulars – roly-poly. Dad often made these as well as Auntie Mag, but no matter who made them, they were always produced in pairs. The dough for these was rolled out; spread with jam – mostly plum – then rolled up and put into an unbleached calico cloth and boiled. The finished products were about 10 inches long and roughly four and a half inches in diameter. Two of them just fitted nicely side by side in our large oval cast-iron boiler. The ends of the cooked rolls were moulded to the intricate creases where the cloth was tied, and because roly-polies were dusted with flour before they were rolled in the cloth, they were covered with a firm jelly-like skin. Although the ends were tasteless, they had a pleasing appearance, which made them desirable to children, until they discovered they were somewhat bereft of jam. When cooked, these rolls were cut into slices about an inch thick, and eaten with cold milk.

When eggs and milk were plentiful, Auntie Mag would make what she called French pancakes. These pan-sized delicacies were usually sprinkled with sugar and a squeeze of lemon juice, before being tightly rolled up and eaten with much enjoyment. These simple foods were very important in keeping hunger at bay.

* * *

As winter drew to a close, the bush around us was a yellow blaze of breathtaking beauty, and the air was filled with the perfume from the fluffy blossom of the golden wattle.

Then spring was with us: among the nearby sandstone outcrops, wild orchids bewitched us with their subtle beauty. It didn't matter to us that we lumped two genera of orchids (Glossodia and Caladenia) together, and called them big blue, small blue, pink and white cockatoos, or that our "late-leopards" were in fact tiger orchids. Cowslips, green-hoods and other unnamed orchids mingled with chocolate lilies, intriguing trigger plants, and a host of other hardy flowers. Modest shrubs that had been so easy to overlook, now demanded our attention as they flaunted a rich display of flowers in many colours and intricate shapes. While flat on the ground, the pretty sundews spread their dainty sticky reddish rosette, which attracted and entrapped the unsuspecting insects on which the plants feasted, then – as if to hide their grisly deed – they "shamefully" covered themselves with a beautiful single flower of pristine white.

Towards the end of October two coming events began to occupy our thoughts and conversations. The first one was bonfire day. I could remember the one we had the year before in our old paddock by the school, and that I was more scared than thrilled by the occasion. However, this year I was anticipating the event with enthusiasm. I eagerly helped my older siblings to drag suckers that they had knocked from stumps a reasonable distance from our camp, up to the top of the big hill in the park. We didn't stack them in a heap though, but left them scattered over a wide area, for bonfire builders had to be ever vigilant to protect their work against marauding raiders – other kids who were always anxious to celebrate bonfire day early.

About the same time as we began to prepare for bonfire day, another approaching event became a topic of conversation – I suddenly became aware of horse racing. It was a subject I could not remember being discussed before, but now this race, called the Melbourne Cup, seemed to be of great importance. I had heard of Melbourne, but it seemed so remote it was not part of my reality.

The talk of racing set Dad reminiscing about his adventures as a paper-boy in Collingwood, which had brought him close to the activities of John Wren and his tote.

On the eve of the first Tuesday in November, Louis arrived home with a list of strange names, which I was told, were those of the horses in the big race. In a festive atmosphere, the names were cut out and placed in a hat, then in turn from youngest to eldest, we drew them out, until the hat was empty. That was my first experience with a sweep, and although Auntie Mag said, "It's a funny old sweep without prize-money," we all joined in the spirit of the thing, and I found it most exciting. Throughout that evening, and all next day, the names of the horses I had picked, mingled with the expectations of our bonfire that night. It was late on Tuesday afternoon when Louis came home with the name of the winning horse. Even though it wouldn't have made the slightest difference, I felt badly let down by those names in my pocket.

There wasn't much time to brood, it was the 5th of November, and we were busy with our bonfire. Straight after school on bonfire day, it was all hands to the task of building the actual bonfire, from the large amount of bushes that we had scattered over the top of the hill. First a selected long sapling-spar was planted in the ground to stabilise the bushes that would be stacked to a height of around 15 feet. Many of the local bonfires were built around living trees, but Dad strictly forbade that practice.

Although the older boys diligently did the actual building of the stack, it was only a minor job compared with actually collecting the bushes, so the job didn't take long. However once it was built, it was essential for someone to stand guard until lighting time after dark. Sadly, even as we stood guard, we watched spasmodically, the pre-darkness beacons, that indicated spoilsports had destroyed the hard work and expectations of other more trusting youngsters. Sometimes even guarded "bonnies" would be torched, when a less vigilant guard was outsmarted.

Soon after dark we lit the fire, which coincided with the dozens of other blazes all around the town, as well as others to be seen miles away. I don't think we exaggerated when we agreed that our fire was not disgraced in comparison with the best of the others, for when the leaves were compacted by stamping, as was the case with ours, the fires maintained a good blaze for much longer.

The biggest were always placed on prominent points, but the hill on which ours stood, was the highest point within the borough boundary. That fact, gave us a fine view of the celebrations elsewhere. Although we didn't have many fireworks – just a few small cheap crackers and a few sparklers – whizzing and throwing sticks with burning or glowing ends, helped to make the event a success.

Dad reluctantly allowed us to have our bonfires, although he did not approve of the occasion the event celebrated and encouraged us to call it bonfire day, rather than Guy Fawkes Day. He greatly disapproved of the practice of placing an effigy (commonly called a Guy) on top of the pile, and lectured us on the symbolic barbarity of such an act.

With the warmer days, some of the evenings were quite pleasant, and there was a general reluctance to go to bed as early as we had in the cold weather. Most nights there was no need for a campfire, so we lost our rallying point, and with only a sparse supply of kerosene for our dull hurricane-lantern, the range of evening recreations was limited. However, the ingenuity of Lloyd and Auntie Mag, enabled them to extend into the night their favourite pastime of reading which because of our problem with lighting, had been strictly a daytime activity. In fact during cold or wet weather, most of their reading was done not only in daylight, but fully clothed, in the relative comfort of their respective beds. Now the incentive of warm nights had inspired them into making a luminosity breakthrough. They discovered that by gathering a good supply of mostly sticks before dark, they could sit in front of the stove, with the wide double doors of the firebox open, and by frequently recharging the fire sufficient flickering low-quality light enabled them to read the loaned or donated material well into the night. Dad wasn't very happy about this activity, he said it would ruin their eyesight, but in the absence of scientific proof, they decided to put Dad's theory to the test.

It was uncanny how competent we had all become at finding our way around the camp, even on the darkest nights. We had all unconsciously plotted the position of each tent peg and guy rope, as well as trees, stumps, rock outcrops, the park fence and other hazards of the night. Dad really got angry with us for "setting traps", which was his term for leaving things in unexpected places where people could trip over them. The general compliance with this obsession was a major factor in enabling us all to negotiate our domain with such confidence on those dark nights. We always tried to complete the essential activities, such as having tea before dark. The stove was usually burning from before breakfast, until the last member of the family went to bed, so the cheap flickering light from its open firebox doors was considered adequate illumination for most of the camp's nightly tasks. Since that first night in the bush, when our lone lantern was in such demand, its importance to our nocturnal activities had greatly diminished. It was no longer habitually lit at the onset of darkness, but was reserved for occasions when extra light was needed away from the stove.

During our brief time in the bush, I had already seen the rhythm of nature change with the seasons. With winter came the flocks of green parrots to feast on the nectar from the flowers of the red ironbarks, and the blaze of wattle gave way to the flowers of spring, and the busyness of nesting birds, but summer came on the wings of mosquitoes and flies. I soon learned how the intimidating buzz and painful bites of mosquitoes could make a pleasant evening almost unbearable, and the torment they could cause during restless sleep. Luckily though, a cheap partial solution to the mozzie problem was at hand. On any warm calm evening, several small fires of smouldering dried cow dung, would be strategically placed around the camp. The mozzies didn't like the smoke these fires produced, but I loved the soothing aroma.

One of my earliest religious lessons –

All things bright and beautiful,
All creatures great and small,
All things wise and wonderful,
The Lord God made them all –

made me wonder about mozzies: why did He do it? Though I was grateful, that He had fitted them with a warning "siren", and made them so fragile that a puff of wind would almost put them out of action.

Numerous though the mozzies were, compared with bush-flies, they would have to be regarded as an endangered species.

It is hard to imagine just how thick the flies were. At times they would have to circle for ages before they could find landing space on our backs. Our backs were so crowded, most of the flies didn't risk a jaunt to lick our eyes or crawl up our noses. They were just content to sit. They were also very fond of our humble food, so as we didn't have any fly spray, at meal time there was more waving over the table than you'd see in the same space at a 1950s royal visit.

At times, numerous flies would meet their end in scalding cups of tea. Often it was embracing couples that made the plunge – not in suicidal despair like Romeo and Juliet, but in the careless pangs of unbridled passion. For a while there were so many cups of tea being tossed out, it caused a serious increase in our consumption of potable water. However, it was not that aspect that changed our attitude to this matter, it was the inconvenience of having to repeatedly pour fresh cups of tea. The bolder members of the family soon began to spoon, spill, or simply flick single suicides out of their cups, and gradually it became common practice – except when we had visitors. "Passion cups" though, were a different matter, drinking those seemed just a bit beyond the pale.

At night, the dormant flies clustered in untold thousands along the ridgepoles inside the tents, and under the shelter that covered the table, their glistening wings and black bodies blending into a single unbroken form. For a few nights we watched the ever enlarging swarms, and when the sun warmed the tents in the morning, flies would fill the air like a swarm of bees, before following us outside.

Early one morning, we awoke to see Dad standing by our bed, holding a large loosely rolled sheet of newspaper. He explained that he was going to burn the flies, and told us to put our heads under the blankets. We obeyed, and within seconds our bed was a-buzz with flies. It was even worse when we uncovered our heads, hordes of flies were over the bed or cascading onto the floor, and the flies that were on the pillows, gravitated into the bed with us. To avoid setting the tent on fire, it was necessary to briskly move the blazing paper under the flies. As a result, their bodies weren't damaged at all. The procedure did little more than remove the tips of their wings, but it made flight impossible. It isn't pleasant sharing a bed with such handicapped flies, and it was virtually impossible to brush them all out. However their loud persistent buzzing made it easy to get up. It wasn't long before the ants and insectivorous birds were busy collecting the casualties and by midday they had all been removed.

Despite that morning massacre, that night the ridgepoles were again textured with myriad flies. Admittedly, the quantity was slightly reduced, but their numbers were still astounding, never the less, it did slightly reduce the fly problem, so that ritual continued throughout the summer – and through the warmer months of all the following years that we spent in our tent-camps. Each morning, the flies were subjected to a fiery attack, and each night, reinforcements filled their places. I still wonder though, if it was skill or just good luck, that saved Dad from burning down one of our tents, for in the heat of summer, they were tinder dry.

13

My First Bush Christmas

Soon after our exciting day with the Melbourne Cup, and bonfire day, thoughts of Christmas began to occupy our minds.

Although my family tried to live by Christian principles, we tended to play it low key. Auntie Mag was an unquestioning Christian, who steadfastly upheld the best teachings of her Presbyterian faith, but she had stopped going to church on leaving Evansford. We all had been christened Presbyterian, and my older brothers and sisters had regularly attended Sunday school. The girls and Jack had continued right up until the time we moved to the bush. Most of my knowledge of Christianity was what I had learned from Auntie Mag, and a lot of that was about Christmas, which we all loved even though there weren't many gifts. Auntie Mag started to worry about getting a small gift to send to a friend with whom she had exchanged Christmas gifts since childhood; and getting the Christmas puddings made. She was also concerned about how the stove would perform in its exposed position, when she cooked the Christmas cake. The biggest problem though, would be finding the extra cash to buy the dried fruit and almonds for those items.

Fortunately that hurdle was somehow overcome, and with plenty of time to spare, a big Christmas cake was wrapped in paper and stored away in a large airtight tin, and two fine plum puddings – still in their unbleached calico cloths – hung safely from the ridgepole of "Chapman's tent". Come flood, fire or famine, Auntie Mag would ensure that those luxuries wouldn't even be sampled until Christmas day, and one of the puddings would survive past

Christmas, and be eaten at our midday-dinner on New Year's Day. While we were young, Auntie Mag always left making the Christmas puddings until the weekend, for she respected the tradition handed down through past generations, that everyone should have a chance to stir the mixture and make a wish. My wish this year was a simple one – that we'd all live forever.

Even school was imbued with the Christmas spirit. We began to relearn the carols I had loved so much the previous year. *Silent Night* and *The First Noel* seemed even more beautiful, as my imagination created wonderful scenes of those holy places long ago. I liked *Good King Wenceslas*, and *A Partridge in a Pear Tree*, but they failed to stir my sleeping spirituality.

Another thing that was making school more interesting, was the large garden compost heap on the bush side of the school, it was covered with long lush grass. Being in the "Bubs", at the end of the day I was released from class about a quarter of an hour before Jack. I used this time to pluck an armful of grass, which I would proudly carry home for the goats, which gratefully accepted it as a supplement to their normal diet of the local flora. It gave me a warm feeling of self-satisfaction; I felt I was doing something worthwhile to assist the home economy, for I was sure such good grass would increase the milk supply.

After that first momentous day at school, I quickly decided school wasn't all it was cracked up to be and my dislike of it grew daily. It was then I became aware of the fact that attending school was not compulsory until the age of six. Dad thought six was the right age to start school and only agreed to me starting at four and a half, because I was eager to do so. I took full advantage of this situation and made little more than "guest appearances" at school until I was that age.

What's more, even on those days when I was at school, I would frequently lapse into long spells of daydreaming about the things I would do when I got home. In view of those facts, I need hardly say that my scholastic performance was not brilliant, resulting in me spending eighteen months in the "Bubs". Then – a head taller than anyone else in my class – I was promoted to grade one, at the beginning of 1936. Jack, who was a dedicated student, had earned his promotion to grade four.

As we eagerly headed for home after school on break up day, to a whole month of freedom, Jack and I were in high spirits. The feeling of elation transcended thought alone, everything seemed grand and wonderful, and much of that was due to the mystic expectations of Christmas.

It wasn't the thought of being showered with gifts, for in my world, even Santa Claus had been defrocked. The previous year, when we were still in our old home, with tingling excitement, I had hung one of Dad's big socks at the foot of my bed on Christmas Eve. Jack had also hung a sock beside mine – I don't know if he was still a believer, but if he wasn't, he did nothing to diminish my faith. Keith and Lloyd had scoffed at our socks, they said they wouldn't hold enough, and showed us the chaff-bags dangling from the high ends of their iron beds. The rest of the family rose to the spirit of the occasion, and solemnly warned them that their greed would raise the ire of the overweight saint, and he would leave them nothing. Encouraged by the banter, I giggled at their folly and anticipating some appropriate reaction from Santa to their greed gave me as much joy as the thought of what might fill my sock.

I can still feel the thrill of waking on Christmas morning to find my sock filled with boiled lollies and mixed nuts. But the clearest memory of that Christmas morning, is my childish hilarity at the feigned performance by Keith and Lloyd, of being "censured and shamefaced", as each forlornly displayed a tatty cabbage leaf that Santa Claus had left in their bags, to mark his disapproval of their greed. Later that morning as the neighbourhood kids compared what the old man in red had left, it was obvious that social standing had a big influence on Santa's generosity – he worked to a sort of adverse means test. It was probably partly due to that aspect, that my family didn't put much value on maintaining the myth, for now a year later, to me, the story of Santa Claus was just another fable.

We were all up early and in good spirits Christmas morning. After breakfast there was an excursion into the nearby bush under the leadership of Keith, to select and carry home suitable suckers, which were placed around the stove, kitchen/eating area, and at the openings of the tents. I suppose that was a bit absurd, seeing we were literally living among the gum trees, but it did add to the magic.

I discovered that Christmas morning wasn't a time for relaxation. Under difficult conditions, made utterly intolerable by the swarms of bush-flies, Auntie Mag managed to get a large rooster stuffed with a mouth-watering mixture of breadcrumbs, onion and herbs, which even in its uncooked state tasted as good as it smelt, into the oven. By our standards, there was a generous supply of fresh vegetables. Some of the vegetables, I suspect, thanks to the unselfish generosity and caring community of those days of general hardship, would have been from the gardens of thoughtful acquaintances. Our budget would never have permitted such an indulgence. As Jack and I podded the fresh green peas, there was discussion about the light coloured potatoes with thin slightly-flaky skins: I gathered it was something of an achievement to have new spuds for Christmas.

With the rooster in the oven, the vegetables prepared, and one of the plum puddings bubbling away in the boiler, the time had arrived for a cup of tea and a slice of that long awaited cake. The taste and texture of our Christmas cake exceeded all expectations, and each of us conveyed that assessment to its maker by word or gesture, but we didn't make a feast of it. For months after, special occasions would be celebrated with a small portion of that large cake.

By the time we finished morning tea, the glaring sun was threatening to cause us some discomfort during our feast. Although our camp was among ironbark trees, they were mostly young, and only threw a patchy shade. However, some 60 yards away, on the town side of the camp, was a large spreading grey box, growing in close company with a couple of huge old ironbarks. Together the trio presented a sizeable patch of good shade. With the prospect of a classic hot Australian Christmas Day, someone suggested that the table and makeshift seats be carried over to the beckoning shade.

It would take considerable effort to carry the heavy table to the shade, and serving the dinner so far from the stove would exacerbate the problems we already faced, but in the interest of enhancing the Christmas spirit, the idea was wholeheartedly accepted. Auntie Mag had retrieved from its secure storage another vestige of our former prosperity – a top-quality damask tablecloth. As she carefully spread this immaculate cloth over the table, it gave a bizarre hint of class to the rustic setting of our Christmas feast. So began a ritual that made that cloth an integral part of all such notable celebrations during our years of poverty in the bush.

The appetising aroma of seasoned roasted poultry engulfed the table, summoning hordes of bush-flies to our feast. There was gravy for the poultry, freshly made mint sauce, new potatoes, peas, and other vegies, either boiled, or – like the whole onions – roasted.

Then we scoffed the pudding with sweetened goats' milk white sauce. Auntie Mag modestly acknowledged our appreciation of our meal, but stated the white sauce really needed brandy. To conclude the feast, the teapot and iron kettle were carried over, and we sat around repeatedly drinking cups of tea, until the contents of both were exhausted.

When I mention having a cup-of-tea, the statement is far from being literally correct, for at that time our drinking vessels were an assorted collection. Apart from three or four intact cups with matching saucers, which we reserved for visitors, very few were genuine cups. There were a few in daily use but they were either without handles or chipped, but never cracked. Neither Dad nor Auntie Mag could tolerate what they perceived as germ-breeding abominations, so in spite of the shortage, they would be discarded without hesitation. Even so, these imperfect cups, and a chipped enamel mug, fell short of the demand, and often the older members of our family resorted to empty Nestles condensed-milk tins. Many of our acquaintances also used these tins for cups; a few even upgraded them to "proper mugs" by soldering tin handles on them. We didn't have the means to do that, so we had to depend on a piece of paper or rag, to insulate hands from the hot contents.

For some time after dinner, we were so full and listless we just lolled around. After a while, most of the party assisted in carrying the dishes back to base, and after the kettle was re-boiled, the big job of washing up was performed in the large dish reserved for that purpose.

It was decided to leave the table where it was, until after tea, so when the washing up was finished, everyone again gathered under the trees, where the shade offered the best prospect of relief from the sweltering heat. High in the treetops all around, the diffused dreary hum of unknown insects set a background for the trills of the black cicadas, that shared those leafy realms, and made we post-feast humans content to simply laze around. So apart from a mid-afternoon cup of tea, there was little activity.

Auntie Mag had also, as she said, ". . . gone to the bother of making a few special things for tea". One of the items I particularly remember was Lemon Snow. As they would say these days, its production was very labour intensive, just the job of beating the egg whites with a spring whisk was a marathon task, and trying to keep it cool by covering it with damp cloths was practically hopeless. Yet in spite of that, the final product had me looking forward to Christmas tea. The Lemon Snow was to be served with stirred egg custard, which we knew quite well and loved, so the anticipation of having that with something with the exciting name of Lemon Snow ensured the combination was a special treat.

After tea, when the sun had disappeared behind the big hill and the pleasant aroma of smouldering cow dung was keeping the mozzies down to tolerable numbers, it was time for reminiscing about Christmas days in other years. Mostly they were stories from the happy days before we struck hard times. At one stage though, Dad drifted back to his years as a youth in a small Gippsland settlement.

He recalled the Christmas afternoon, when the teenage son of the large family, who treated him like one of their own, was drowned during an after dinner swim with some of his mates. It wasn't hard to visualise the neighbours gathering to give their help and support, and how, late that Christmas afternoon the sound of hammering from the smithy broke the forlorn atmosphere, as someone fashioned a grappling iron in order to retrieve the body. To Dad, those memories were vivid, but to me the story was as remote as the manger in Bethlehem, but the pathos it invoked enriched the nostalgic atmosphere of the day.

The reminiscing continued well into the night – long after Jack and I had wandered off to bed without the aid of a light.

It was that wonderful day that deeply imbued my spirit with the magic of an Australian bush Christmas. That indefinable something, that – at least in those days – seemed to bring out the best in human nature in both believers and non-believers, had created in me a beautiful, hypnotic emotion, which is still evoked by the mere thought of Christmas.

14

Improving Our Lot

Although nothing unusual happened, the week between Christmas and New Year's Day did seem special. All the older generation seemed to agree that the year had gone fast, which I gathered was a good thing, for most also expressed the hope that 1936 would be a better year. It was in that week, I first became aware of the many traditions and activities associated with New Year's Day. I heard about New Year resolutions, and the New Year's Day Highland Gathering, which had been held in Maryborough since its foundation during the gold rush. But the full significance of the occasion came when Dad awoke us just before midnight on New Year's Eve. We heard the eerie blended sounds of the town clock striking, the knitting mill's whistle, hooting trains, distant bagpipe music, and muffled singing of *Auld Lang Syne*, wafting up from the town's heart, through the midnight calm. As we had no working timepiece, Dad's timing was quite a feat.

How could I fail to feel there was something wonderful about it being 1936?

All next day the sound of bagpipes, side show music and spruikers, with the pounding of the drum from Jimmy Sharman's boxing tent, drifted up from Princes Park, which is the venue of our town's prestigious annual event. The seventh day of the new year was my sixth birthday. My family made me feel that it was a very special day, but when Auntie Annie and Sis arrived with a fine iced birthday cake, complete with six curly candles, my day became the stuff of fairy tales. I was not to know then that Auntie Annie and Sis would faithfully perform this ritual right up to my twelfth birthday. Looking back I wonder if they plodded that rough dusty bush track in scorching heat, just to give me a birthday treat or a tacit homage to their departed sister and friend, my mother. I like to think it was a bit of both.

Sometime during the holidays we had another visit from Auntie Tot, with as was usually the case, her quiet good-natured sister Auntie Deb and husband Uncle Jim. On their unexpected arrival, my heartbeats lifted at the prospect of seeing our much-loved sister Yvonne again, but our hopes were soon dashed by feeble excuses for not bringing her with them. Auntie Annie was also with them, and this time they did accept the offer of a cup of tea – probably for the purpose of tasting Auntie Mag's Christmas cake. Tasting each other's Christmas cakes was a popular ritual in Mum's family. Tot and Deb had each brought Auntie Mag a slice of their own cakes. Even though the slices were quite small, when Auntie Mag decided to taste them over the next few days, she did exactly the same as she had done with the slice Auntie Annie had delivered on my birthday: she cut each into three, so Jack and I could share the treat. Although those morsels were nice, loyally we expressed our honest assessment – they were not a patch on Auntie Mag's cake.

Again Auntie Tot pressured "Maggie" to return to Evansford; again my heart was chilled by the fear that she would capitulate. Poor, emotional Auntie Deb simply could not cope with our seemingly hopeless situation, and was moved to tears by our plight, but like her husband Uncle Jim and faithful Auntie Annie, she respected Auntie Mag's right to steer her own course.

Although my family was in no way royalists, we could not completely overlook the considerable community mourning over the death of King George V, in January of 1936. Even Dad seemed sorry, and expressed that "He wasn't a bad fellow". At the same time, because of his occasional excursions to mingle with the lower strata of English society – such as the London East Enders and the Welsh coal miners – Dad had great expectations about Edward, the Prince of Wales, and him becoming king. Dad's admiration of Edward even increased over the next few months, as his liaison with the American divorcee, Mrs Simpson, outraged much of the British Empire. Dad said he showed strength in standing up to the British establishment.

Early in the New Year, to great jubilation, news came through that the applications by Dad and Louis, for the occupation leases of the much-desired six acres over the hill, had been granted. The annual combined fee would be the considerable sum of six pounds, and although they would be minimal, there would also be Council rates. However, this problem was somewhat dulled by the euphoria of the moment.

Unlike our original move to the bush on the 14th of March 1935, the actual date of our move from the squatter's camp to our new leased selection is not remembered. However, there is general agreement it was in February 1936, and it is certain that instead of being a one-day affair, the move extended over several weeks.

It was decided that the new campsite would be a sparsely treed flat area adjoining the western precipice of the quarry. Although Keith would not be 16 until May, he was the first to fold up his tent and move to our new lease, where he was the sole occupant at night.

During that time some preparatory work was carried out. Ever helpful Mr Chapman had given us an excellent galvanised-iron lined mud-brick mould, so Keith got busy and made some high quality mud-bricks from the subsoil nearby. After prolonged discussions concerning the most appropriate site, he set to work building a dunny on the highest hillock of the consolidated overburden from the old quarry, which the building would overlook. He even managed to get enough kerosene tins to cut open for its roof. The seat was an old modified washstand, and an opened kerosene tin with a wire handle served as a pan. A proper door though, was too much of a hurdle, so we had to be content with a curtain of opened wheatbags sewn together. In the years to come, we kids would mostly hitch the bags up, so we could gaze out over the quarry and watch the parade of nature, as we sat and pondered. When this promise of better things to come was completed, with mock formality, I was given the honour of "christening" it.

In those weeks, a three-sided building, which opened to the east, was also built. It faced the northern end of the main quarry. Although this "family room" was built mainly from the materials that had formed the community shelter of our first camp, it was a much more substantial building, measuring about 15 by 20 feet. Once again the sides of the old piano case joined a variety of materials to form the walls. The roof, which sloped away from the open front, incorporated our two 10-foot sheets of black corrugated iron among an assortment of other old sheet-flat-iron, yet in spite of its improvised design, it proved to be remarkably leak proof, and served us well. Finally the stove was moved over and dry-bricked into the centre of the open side of the building, and the opening to the left of the stove was filled in. No attempt was made to place a door or even a curtain at the right of the stove, because as the shack had no windows, the opening was needed for light and ventilation. With the stove in place, there wasn't much sense in maintaining a presence at the old camp, so the move was quickly concluded.

Two tents facing southeast were placed in a line more or less behind the kitchen. Lloyd's tent faced the same direction, but was about 10 yards in front of the other three, and was some 50 yards from Keith's tent, which was at the far end of the little quarry at the extreme northern end of the camp. While the rest of the family were content with the naturally hard but dusty earth floors in their tents, Lloyd set to work gathering an assortment of red bricks, and proceeded to fastidiously pave his tent. At first, because bricks were hard to find, it was just a path beside his bed, but as suitable whole or part bricks were scrounged, it was extended to the whole floor. The finished job was excellent, as was Lloyd's housekeeping. This made his tent the pride of our camp.

After a few days, when the bustle and trauma of shifting to the new camp waned and normality returned, one pleasant evening, Dad, Lloyd, Jack and I decided to visit our allies in hardship, the Chapmans. Our family still felt a strong sense of appreciation for the fellowship and the practical assistance Mr Chapman had given us. We spent a very pleasant few hours at their home, in an atmosphere of renewed hope – especially for us, as things seemed to be looking up.

The Chapman household was now about twice the distance it had been from our old camp, and as an accepted route through the bush had not yet been established, there was quite a bit of uncertainty and dispute between Lloyd and Dad. As we plodded our way home in the pitch darkness, I became desperately tired, and eagerly accepted Dad's offer of a piggyback. When we were within a hundred or so yards of home, a serious dispute began between Dad and Lloyd, about the pathway through a dangerous strip of old reef-mines that bordered our town-side boundary. We were all well aware that among the several shallow diggings were two lethal shafts that were around 80 feet deep. The disagreement became so profound, that our paths parted. As Lloyd began to move to our left, there was an exchange of cautionary shouts between both Dad and Lloyd, as they warned of each other's impending doom.

Dad's desperate concern for Lloyd's safety must have diminished his normally practical judgment, for he changed course and headed towards Lloyd, some 20 yards away. Almost instantly, the broad back to which I clung was violently flung forward and down. An instant later, we hit the bottom of the broad excavation into which Dad had stumbled. In the darkness, there was overwhelming relief that we were both conscious. But in the blind confusion, there could be no quick assessment of our injuries and as we groped our way out of the 4 feet deep hole in the darkness, there was still the danger of the deep mine shafts. At no time did it cross my mind that I was seriously hurt, but Dad was frantically concerned for me, yet he was completely indifferent about his own injuries. It was no surprise that later inspection confirmed that I had suffered only a few minor cuts and bruises. Dad however, besides suffering a much more severe form of my abrasions, had also received substantial back injuries which in the absence of affordable medical attention, caused him severe pain for many weeks. He was never again able to do any heavy work, without risking a prolonged return of the severe symptoms.

A family inquiry, held next morning at the site of the misadventure, proved beyond all doubt, that had they each continued on their selected way, both paths would have led them safely through the "minefield".

Dad never lost sight of the grave potential of his folly: the hole he fell into could very well have been the deep shaft just a few perilous feet away.

As soon as we settled in, Keith became very active with earthworks. Looking back, I think he had a leaning that in other circumstances could have led him to be a civil engineer. With only a pick, shovel, crowbar and a twin-shafted billycart he had made from a fruit case, and a pair of old pram wheels, he proceeded to make the old quarry into a dam, to store the water from the soon expected rain for our domestic use. This necessitated building a small bank across its shallow southern end. It was then necessary to dig a narrow cutting through the lowest part of the pile of overburden on the quarry's eastern side. From that cutting, he dug a contour drain to a higher part of the gully, to catch the water run-off that previously passed the quarry. The scheme was very successful: after good rains in June and July, the quarry overflowed. What's more, good rains continued for the rest of the year, so we had plenty of water for our goats and chooks, and for the treasured pot plants Auntie Mag had struggled to keep alive, since we moved to the bush. The much talked about vegetable garden now seemed a viable proposition.

If necessary – although it was badly discoloured with clay at first – the water could be used for washing the dishes, clothes and ourselves, but luckily, a small quantity of much better water was available from an old excavation that had been dug in the hard slate. Only a few feet deep, its sides and bottom were virtually solid sandstone, which gave it remarkable water retaining qualities: it seemed never to go dry. Our nearest neighbour, Mr Chester, told Dad it was thought to be a spring, and had been used as a water source by the hotel that once stood a few yards away. But even though we soon found out it was not a spring, we continued to call it "The Spring". Although its water was ideal for washing ourselves, our clothes and dishes, the water was a light weak tea colour and slightly tasted of gum leaves, so it was not the best for drinking.

Luckily, good fortune smiled on us. One of our neighbours, the Hills – who lived just over the hill on our town side, behind the showground – graciously offered us potable water from the taps of their reticulated town supply. Being only a few hundred yards away, it could be quickly fetched in the billycart that Keith used for his earthworks. The older male members of our family usually brought two kerosene tins full at a time, but Jack and I in combination, could only manage one tin full. These trips to Hills for water during the magpie-nesting season became quite hazardous for me. Jack – and later Valma and June – along with my older brothers, could make these trips in peace. I, on the other hand, would be viciously dive-bombed. Because I was a bit of a daydreamer, I would not hear the birds coming, so on several occasions they gave me a painful wound by actually piercing my scalp. My family never tormented the nesting magpies, so why they picked on me seemed strange until someone realised I vaguely resembled Artie Cook and that one of his favourite recreations was tormenting the magpies at their nest.

The aforementioned showground covered an area of about five

acres and contained a fine oval and several sizeable buildings, yet, to me, these amenities seemed to be only used once a year on show day, which was always held on Caulfield Cup Day in mid October. The showground was completely surrounded by a very high corrugated-iron fence. The fence appeared to be human proof, but I soon learned that at this time when even the minimal entrance fee to the show was considered exorbitant to many poverty stricken residents, it proved to be no match for the ingenuity of the local young larrikins. The night before the show, these youths would surreptitiously loosen the nails on one side of selected sheets of iron around the ground, so that next morning they could be opened and closed like a door, to allow free admittance. But there was still another hazard to be overcome, the show officials engaged a horseman equipped with a stock whip, to ride the internal boundary. The effectiveness of this was more psychological than practical, for the horseman could not be in all places at once. It was several years before we could afford to go to the show and unlike lots of the local kids, we were too law-abiding to use the unmanned "gates".

Somehow in those first few busy months, Keith and Lloyd found time to construct a fine goat yard and shelter, using upright sticks in contact with each other. It was built on the far side of the quarry opposite our kitchen, and measured about 45 by 16 feet. Three sides were bound with light scrap wire from the rubbish tip, to number-eight fencing wires that had been tightly strained between posts. The park fence was utilised for the long fourth side. The opposite long side ran parallel – and was perilously close – to the deepest face of the quarry. For the comfort of the goats, and those who milked them in wet weather, a gable roof about 12 feet long, thatched with gum tree branchlets, was placed over the centre portion of the yard. The finished structure looked delightful, and was henceforth known as the "Goat House".

No sooner had Keith finished the first stage of his water project, than he began a much more ambitious scheme of constructing a bank from the low south end of the quarry, across to the other side of the gully which would roughly double the capacity of our quarry-dam. With the tools at his disposal, this was a mammoth challenge. After discussing the method of construction with Dad and some other practical old-timers, he began the task with great diligence.

For many months, he toiled with pick and shovel, to dig away the hard earth from the up-gully side of the bank he was constructing. Even a proper wheelbarrow that could be emptied with ease would have been a big improvement on the hard-to-wheel, and empty handcart. It wasn't just a matter of shifting the earth to the bank site. Along its whole length, the structure incorporated an 18-inch wide crowbar-rammed core of yellow clay, which he also dug from a virgin deposit, in what would eventually be part of the dam.

Around this time Keith began a lifelong interest in beekeeping. It began when our kind-hearted benefactor, Mr Chapman, who had a few beehives, gave Keith a hive and the rudimentary instructions on beekeeping. Although he didn't say so, it was clear that it was his hope it would enhance our dietary needs. Keith excelled at the art, and in a short time he had built his apiary up to several hives. Evidently, a local apiarist, Mr Phillips, heard about Keith's natural affinity with bees at a time when he was looking for someone to assist him in the business. He hired Keith, on an occasional basis, to help when he was extracting or shifting his hives to a new site to follow the honeyflow of the eucalypts. Although the wages were pretty poor, Mr Phillips agreed to shift Keith's hives around with his: this would greatly increase their honey production. He also helped Keith extend his own apiary.

Dad was also friendly with Mr Phillips, and occasionally, I accompanied him on visits to their home. They talked in the prim little sitting room where the shine of the polished floorboards reflected the energy of his devoted wife. Mr Phillips – who appeared ancient to me – would lean back in his comfortable armchair, smoking his pipe with the dignity of a sage. That's why it seemed so incongruous that, every now and then, he would clear the gooey pipe induced phlegm from his throat, and direct the results to a selected portion of the shiny floor several feet away. Instantly, without a word, his attentive wife – somewhat reminiscent of an eager dog fetching a ball – would whip to the spot, and remove the revolting bronchial splash with a cloth she kept at hand. In spite of this bad habit, I liked Mr Phillips, and thought Mrs Phillips was a lovely old lady. She always offered me some treat, such as a homemade biscuit or piece of cake, and luckily for my delicate sensibilities, she always consented without offence, when I politely asked, "Can I keep it for later?"

On one occasion Mr and Mrs Phillips contacted the school offering a donation of some books. There appeared to be a tradition among the teachers at our school to reward pupils for any thing they considered to be commendable. This day, I was the recipient of such an honour and as a reward another boy and I were sent forth to collect the gift. I was delighted at being selected for this mission and felt extremely smug that, unlike my companion, the school's benefactors were not only known to me, but gave me an effusively friendly greeting.

In the younger grades, such rewards usually consisted of being allowed to select a lolly from an assortment they mostly kept in a wide mouthed jar. Surprisingly despite being such a poor scholar, I often qualified to be rewarded with a lolly. Mostly the reward was for particularly good behaviour and manners in class. Although they were not my favourites, I invariably selected a toffee or nougat that was wrapped in paper with the ends twisted. They were always given with strict instructions that they were not to be eaten in class. That condition never bothered me at all: for although they were less than an inch long, I would always take them home and – resisting all protests – equally divide them into the number of my kin at home.

15

Routing the Child Stealers

Leasing the blocks had a beneficial psychological effect on my family. Even I sensed we had taken the first step up the long ladder that would lead us from the pit of hopeless poverty to financial and social redemption. There was even a change in our diet, when Dad realised that mincemeat could be obtained from the butcher for only four pence a pound. Fried patties of either straight mincemeat, or mixed with chopped onions and thyme, were readily accepted as a delicacy by us all – especially when we had tomato sauce. I cannot remember ever hearing a complaint about the frequency with which they appeared on our dinner plates. Dad also began to regularly make a heavy concoction, that he called "concrete stew". The recipe consisted of several pounds of egg-size mincemeat balls, onions, potatoes, and any other vegetable that was available, or at times, when vegetables were very scarce, weeds such as trefoil and marshmallow. It was certainly filling, but I didn't like it much. Although our food was austerely basic, it was always well prepared and skilfully cooked. What's more, apart from the normal pre-meal pangs, I cannot remember ever being hungry.

Occasional handouts supplemented our scant supply of "susso" clothes. However, only a few of these "cast-off clothes" – as Auntie Mag called them – were even moderately good and mostly we received them in an unwashed state, stuffed in wheat or sugarbags. Having to receive such clothes was a far greater indignity for Auntie Mag, than living in tents in the bush. After discovering that some of the first bundles of clothes we received were bug infested, they were always opened well away from camp, where the very few wearable and other useful garments would be sorted out. Any garment that could stand the treatment was boiled in our old large brass preserving pan or a kerosene-tin bucket, while those that could not be boiled, were soaked in soap and water for a few days, and then thoroughly washed. These included even the oldest overcoats – I especially remember one with a tatty fox skin with a ghastly mummified face still attached, draped around the collar – for they were valuable additions to our beds on cold nights. Selected dresses and other garments of suitable material that were past wearing were also washed and trimmed down to serve as towels. By this time the only real towels we possessed were a couple of threadbare relics reserved for visitors to dry their hands on. Auntie Mag would also retrieve bits from some of the unusable garments that she thought "could come in handy", as patches for our everyday outfits. The remaining rubbish would be burnt on the spot. But even with those precautions, on occasions – due to kindly donated clothes – a bed would have to be debugged with kerosene.

Despite all the imperfections of our household, we were all well fed, reasonably clothed, healthy and members of a caring united happy family, and only fools would see us otherwise. What's more, we even had a proper dunny now. Another thing in our favour was that Dad didn't smoke and was in all reality, a teetotaller. I had never seen grog of any kind in our home, and Dad never went to the pub. Even at the age of six, I realised the difference the habits of the father made to families in poverty, and knew how lucky we were in that regard.

For those reasons, the events of one Saturday came as a bit of a shock. Just after we had finished our midday dinner, two government officials, impressively dressed in business suits, arrived at our place on foot, with a briefcase containing the usual paraphernalia of public servants of that time. It was obvious that they had failed to find the track through the bush and had parked their car some 300 yards away at the far end of our block.

Dad had steel-hard whiskers, so because his cutthroat razor – despite being frequently touched up on the razor strop – was getting rather blunt, there was often a considerable time between shaves. But he always shaved and donned his well-worn best clothes when he went to town. On this particular day, he hadn't been down the street for some time, so the black steel-like bristles that "adorned" his face and his solid six foot build belied his normally placid nature, and conjured up thoughts of wild men from the backblocks.

He politely greeted the strangers, and waited for them to state their business. He probably thought they were from some religious group, in search of converts. Although not very religious himself, Dad always treated such people with courtesy. He would always patiently listen to their views, and then join them in friendly discussion. Our visitors soon made it clear that they were from the Child Welfare Department, and were there to investigate a report from a concerned informant, that Jack's and my welfare was in dire jeopardy. Papers were produced, and they officiously began to ask impertinent questions about our financial position and personal questions about all the individuals of our family. They even demanded details of our goats and chooks, and the extent of our food supplies. Dad was ever so patient and truthfully answered their questions with the dignity that so naturally came to him. Dad seemed to be confident that he had allayed the concerns of his inquisitors, during the hour or more that they talked near the edge of the quarry in front of our kitchen. Then with the situation finally talked out, Dad politely walked away, while the intruders conferred.

After a few minutes, they rejoined Dad, who was standing in front of the tent next to the one Jack and I shared with Auntie Mag. Suddenly it became a case of a match in a box of firecrackers. They informed Dad, "After assessing your situation, we will be recommending that the two young boys be institutionalised until your circumstances improve". Instantly, a swell of angry passion engulfed Dad's whole being, as his clenched fist struck the centre post at the door of the tent so violently, that the whole structure quaked. The two officials were visibly startled and somewhat disoriented by Dad's drastic change of mood. They began to back away towards their distant car, struck dumb by Dad's blistering tirade, as he ordered them off the property. When Dad picked up the axe that chanced to be close at hand, although he made no threats, they really scarpered.

We were all somewhat traumatised by the unprovoked attack on our family structure. Over the next few days, we anxiously awaited an official reaction to Dad's ferocious outburst. Surely such an action would be further damning evidence that he was an unfit guardian. Thankfully as the days turned to weeks, then months, there was no reaction: the threat of an institution never again troubled our young minds.

One Saturday morning shortly after that absurd threat to our family unity, Dad, freshly shaved and as neatly dressed as circumstances would allow, unexpectedly invited me to accompany him on the long walk to the main street. I accepted the invitation, so shortly after we set off together. I vaguely presumed it was a consolation prize, because – as was mostly the case – Keith would not allow me to accompany him and Jack on a rabbiting excursion through the bush to Mosquito, the site of a once bustling gold town of that name.

On reaching High Street, instead of heading for Fishers, the impressive hardware and grocery store or the butcher's shop, which were usually the only ports of call, we made straight for the shop of C. J. Wilks, Watchmakers, Jewellers and Opticians. I was completely mystified by this unexpected action, and then suddenly my ears pricked – Dad mentioned clocks. Soon the most glorious alarm clock I had ever seen was on the counter – it was the "Big Ben Repeating Alarm Clock". For me, the salesman's pitch about its illuminated figures and hands that could be seen in the dark, and his demonstration of its repeating alarm, instantly dispelled my longings for that 15 shilling pocket watch I had seen illustrated in the *Weekly Times*, before we left the house near the school. And what's more, we could have the Big Ben for 12 shillings and sixpence. Even so, I haven't the slightest idea how our budget was stretched enough to cover that huge expense.

There was much excitement when we arrived home with the clock I couldn't help feeling I was the only one who didn't know the reason for our trip to town. There had been talk of late of how we really needed a clock. I had become the subject of subtle persuasion to change my desire for a watch, to a more practical alarm clock. Although the novelty soon wore off, it's a wonder we didn't wear out the repeating alarm on the first day. I was very proud that the Big Ben clock would henceforth be known as mine. Of course, I knew it was in name only, but I felt good about the honour.

16

Our New Neighbourhood

From our camp, one could look down the slope across the cleared acre site of the old market garden to where a clump of old yellow box trees lined the bush track that crossed our blocks, just short of our unfenced western boundary at the scrubby official road. This road would later be named Poole Street, in honour of a worthy councillor of those days, Sammy Poole.

On the other side of Poole Street, a fence of five plain wires topped with a barb designated the boundary of Joe Marshall's property. Joe – commonly called "old Joe" – was the "patriarch" of various members of the Marshall "clan" who lived in several dwellings, scattered on that side of the street. It wasn't long before we got to know most of the Marshalls by sight and some of them quite well, with varying degrees of cordiality.

Lifting the eyes to the rising slope of Blackman's Lead, about a mile further on, a yellowish-red clay patch that had been stripped of its gravelly gold bearing surface showed clearly through the trees, as did the raised embankment of the railway line that ascended the steep rise towards Ballarat.

When the nights were frosty, from our beds, we would listen intrigued as the heavily laden goods-trains laboriously attempted to climb the steep slope from our railway station. Old identities would tell us how Mark Twain, on a visit in the 1890s, referred to Maryborough as "A railway station with a town attached and a couch for every inhabitant". After a few slow earnest puffs from the steam engine – or engines in the case of a double-header – there would be a burst of frantic fast puffs as the wheels slipped on the icy rails. Then we would hear the train retreat, as its crew released a sprinkle of the contents of the locomotive's sandbox onto the rails to enhance the grip, before they tried again. Often this procedure had to be repeated time after time, before it got up the hill. In extreme cases, the pilot engine from our extensive railway marshalling yards, which was the junction of four incoming lines, had to be sent to assist by pushing the floundering train from behind. Eventually, a flurry of regular free flowing puffs that would quickly fade into the distance told us the train was over the hill and on its way.

Some 20 miles further on, above Blackman's Lead, in ever-changing hues of grey and blue, the Pyrenees Ranges marked our western horizon.

We still had exactly the same neighbours, but while some were now further away, some of them were much closer. Now some of their homes were in sight, two being quite close.

Mr Chester was our closest neighbour. His house was situated among old ironbark and applejack trees, on a Miners Right Claim, close to the bottom of our town-side boundary, about 200 yards from our new camp. He was a big quietly spoken man of Cornish parentage, with a friendly gentle nature and an air of dignity that seemed in keeping with the dark three-piece suits he invariably wore. Sometimes however in hot weather, when unaware of our approach, we could find him "stripped" to his buttoned-up waistcoat.

He soon became a friend to us all. As soon as he got to know Dad, their debates and discussions on the frightening world affairs of the 1930s prompted him to offer Dad his copy of *The Age*, after he finished reading it. From then on, the day-old *Age* was collected each morning. For me, this ushered in an age of enlightenment. In appreciation of him passing on his newspaper to us, Mr Chester was offered a daily supply of goats' milk, which was about the only worthwhile thing we had to spare. The offer was gratefully accepted and thereafter it was delivered each morning when we collected the paper, or by a special visit when there was none to collect.

Not within my memory, had a daily paper previously been available to our household. We had even stopped getting the *Weekly Times*, months before we left the house by the school. Now our conversations became much more informed, on both Australian and world affairs, and sadly, to my ever-eager ears, even more frightening. At a time when I was yet to see a wireless, the newspaper certainly extended my horizons. I met my first comic-strip characters, and so began years of eagerly awaiting the next instalment of the adventures of Curly Wee and Gussy Goose. Keith, who was somewhat obsessed with world events, would deliver the goats' milk most weekdays, and collect and scrutinise the paper. But on Saturday or holidays, we kids usually beat him to the gun.

Jack and I often visited Mr Chester with Dad and were always readily invited into his clean and tidy dwelling, and extended the fullness of his hospitality. When Valma and June came home, we kids often paid him a visit by ourselves, either to collect the paper, or just on social calls to inform him of our latest trivial adventure, to which he would always respond appropriately. We loved having Mr Chester share his great knowledge of the history of our immediate area – where he had spent much of his life – and of Maryborough in general. What wonderful hours we spent in that tidy, narrow brick-paved space between his house and the neat little gate that was framed by verdant bridal creeper. It was obvious he enjoyed our companionship as much as we enjoyed his, for it wasn't long before he began to treat us with a modest bag of lollies, after each of his fortnightly visits to town on pension day. Considering Mr Chester's firm friendship with my family lasted until his death in the early 1940s, it was strange that not even once did he visit our home – perhaps he thought our poverty might cause mutual embarrassment.

Just a few yards to the town side of Mr Chester's neat mud-brick and brick house, was a very similar establishment. This was the home of an old lady named Miss Jones, who seemed to be something of a recluse. She was Mr Chester's Auntie, and like our Auntie Mag, was very deaf. We probably would have overlooked her presence, except for occasionally seeing her attending the few hardy plants of her struggling flower garden, and her daily visits to fetch water from a neat little square water hole. The water hole was identical to the one where we had watered the goats that evening on our way to the bush. Mr Chester told us the dam had been made for the old lady's exclusive use. The fact that the dam was now inside the boundary of our selection, and only about a hundred yards from our encampment, didn't bother my family at all. We respected her exclusive rights to the water, and of course named it

"The Old Lady's Dam". Almost daily, she would also make treks across our unfenced blocks into the bush beyond, to collect big bundles of sticks, which were evidently the main fuel for her fires. Although at no time was there ever hostility between her and my family, neither she, nor we ever made any attempt to establish an acquaintanceship.

Our regular path to school was over the big hill that shielded our place from the town, then down between two dwellings that were each occupied by an elderly bachelor. The rambling old mud brick house on the left, which faced the unformed Carrick Street, belonged to Mr Charlie Harrup, who I gathered was deaf and something of a hermit. We youngsters never spoke a single word to him, but often as we passed we heard a low moaning dirge, which we were told was him singing.

The neat, unfenced two-roomed weatherboard hut on the right side of the track was on Crown Land. Like many bush dwellings of that time, it was there by the provisions of the residential clauses of the Mines Act. This was the home of Mr Bill Ellis, who suffered severe chronic asthma, which necessitated him making two trips daily to the local hospital for what he said were morphine injections. Unlike Charlie Harrup, Bill was quite the opposite of a hermit, being universally known throughout the town, and on friendly terms with all he knew.

After passing between those two houses facing Carrick Street, we would turn left at the bottom corner of Charlie's block, into the top end of Hubble Street. At that time much of Hubble Street was only an unformed track with a few houses on one side and only bush and the Prisoners' Dam on the opposite side. The land between Hubble Street and Carrick Street had long since been surveyed into street-to-street half-acre blocks.

There were six houses facing Hubble Street. The first one was occupied by the Williams family and was set well back on the block. Four of the houses were on the better part of the street down near the Prisoners' Dam. The first of these houses belonged to the Cooks.

17

Ventures Into Reef Mining

Although Dad was still suffering with his back injuries, he and my two oldest brothers were still spending considerable time prospecting on the old, alluvial goldfields of our forest. Thanks again to the ever-generous Mr Chapman, our gold-processing equipment was dramatically upgraded when he gave my family a beautifully constructed gold cradle. Gold cradles would be short priced in any competition for history's worst designed mechanical appliance. The pay-dirt is placed at the top while the rockers are at the very bottom, so with each rock, the heavy unbalanced weight of the dirt at the top causes physical strain on both sides of the point of balance. But owning a cradle carried considerable kudos, and really speeded up the gold washing process. Our prospectors set up their new acquisition in the mostly dry creek in Shicers Gully, at Bluchers. It was necessary to dig two or three feet through the loose gravel to obtain the few inches of gravel and silt on the solid creek bed, which contained the gold. Usually, the amount of water needed for washing the dirt would seep into the hole. The water was mostly scooped from the hole with a seven-pound jam tin attached to the end of a long sapling handle. Again, there was always enough gold to tempt them to gamble greater effort, but for them, there was never a jackpot.

After some time – owing to Dad's continuing back problems – Louis and Keith, more or less, branched out on their own. Keith was trying his luck on what was known as "the yellow clay patch", just behind the Carisbrook Reservoir. To assist in the difficult process of washing clay, Keith had obtained an large old metal tub, in which he soaked the gold-bearing clay overnight, before panning it the next day. The gold at the yellow clay patch was described by the old hands as "shotty", and consisted of specimens varying from wheat grain size, up to a couple of pennyweights. There was virtually no fine gold. Unfortunately, although the results of Keith's efforts looked wonderful in a small bottle of water, the quantity seldom justified the drudgery required to obtain it.

Around this time, I became aware that the words indicator and indicator-gold were popping up in any conversation about mining. When I enquired, it was explained that while a countless number of quartz seams were to be found in the slaty bedrock of this area, only a very few were likely to lead to gold: for this reason they were keenly sought after. Their location was often betrayed by the presence of coarse surface gold. Occasionally we would hear of someone finding an indicator, but their hopes of it leading to substantial gold mostly proved to be just dreams.

Probably because of all that talk, Louis became disillusioned with scavenging the worked out alluvial fields, and set his aim at higher things, to be more explicit – reef mining. To further this ambition, somewhat unexpectedly, Louis came to some sort of arrangement to be the offsider and protégé of Joe Fossey, an elderly miner who was working a reef mine, which at that time was over 80 feet deep at Bluchers. For quite a few months Louis was almost ecstatic, for the association was one of harmony and mutual respect.

In view of that situation, it was quite a surprise when Louis announced that he and a mate of similar age, Joey Price, had formed a partnership, and had received a mining grant to establish a reef mine on a claim they had staked, about half a mile south of our camp. Apparently our new camp was situated on the Portuguese Reef, which from our place, ran along the low range of hills that extended for miles through the bush to the south, but appeared to end just a few hundred yards to our north. An important condition of the grant was that to receive the meagre financial incentive to seek gold, the depth of the shaft had to increase by at least one foot each week. During the first few weeks, that was not a problem, and within a short time the mine was an impressive sight. As was the custom with such mines of that time, the miners had constructed a log frame around the top of the embryonic shaft and on this they had mounted a fine new windlass.

Another purpose for the log surround was to prevent any loose mullock or other things from accidentally falling down the shaft. The mining inspector was very impressed by the structure and the diligence of the relatively inexperienced young miners.

From just below the surface, this portion of the Portuguese Reef proved to be extremely hard, so after just a few feet the wage of a hefty pick stroke was little more than a puff of dust. In view of the hardness, they were forced to abandon the pick and resort to hammer and gads. But even with hammer and gads, partly because of their minimal experience, progress virtually ceased and a visit from the mining inspector was imminent. Happily, their ingenuity considerably surpassed their mining skills, so with a fraction of the effort required to extend the shaft the required distance, they raised the windlass another log higher. The inspector appeared not to notice the ruse, logged them an additional foot, and recommended the use of explosives. Soon they were in possession of a generous quantity of highly subsidised gelignite, detonators and fuse. Although Louis had worked for a short time with his skilled mentor, he still didn't know much about using these highly dangerous materials.

I feel sure they would have received a few handling instructions from the friendly inspector and other experienced old hands, who couldn't resist visiting any new mining enterprise, for it wasn't long before we heard the vibrating blasts from the mine they had named the "Three Sevens". Their casual attitude to the explosives caused Dad great trepidation. I was told gelignite needed a blow of forty pounds pressure per square inch to make it explode, but the detonators – commonly called dynamite caps – were a totally different proposition. Even the slightest knock could set them off, and many a gruesome tale could be heard about the consequences that befell those who mishandled them.

With Dad's concern, it was no surprise that when he discovered them practising the not uncommon, but potentially suicidal, procedure of clamping the detonators on to the fuse with their teeth (because it was said, unlike metal pliers, teeth could not cause sparks) he, metaphorically speaking, did exactly what he feared could literally happen to them – blew his top. To a degree his tongue-lashing was successful, they never again practised that folly – well, at least, not in Dad's presence.

Soon, to the sound of numerous explosions, things were

progressing at the Three Sevens Mine. By now we had all become familiar with dolly-pots. Dolly-pots are iron or steel containers in which pieces of quartz, suspected of containing gold, were pounded to dust with the end of a short, heavy piece of steel. Proper dolly pots were made of quite thick metal, and would virtually last a lifetime. Mainly however, for economic reasons – as was the case with Louis and Joey – they were more likely to be jam tins, that could only stand being used once. Often before the samples were pounded, we were allowed to admire the glittering traces of gold in the shiny freshly broken milky quartz. Louis at times would also entertain us with a non-spectacular fireworks display by burning small pieces of gelignite and short lengths of fuse that would hiss and dance on the bare ground.

It was around this time that Harry Williamson and his wife began to visit us. Harry was an ex-Wonthaggi coalminer, who several years earlier had taken over the small grocery shop that we patronised in Tuaggra Street, between the East Maryborough State School and the railway gates. He seemed quite an old bloke to me, but was probably only in his 50s. Although we later discovered that he had a finely tuned sense of humour and a wonderful hearty laugh, my first impression of him did nothing to raise such a suspicion. Only the bravest of kids from school would dare go into his shop alone, to spend their few pennies on lollies. If making a selection from those large jars with the ground glass stoppers or from the glass display counter was made with lots of finger tip twisting against the pane, and a drawn-out undecided "I'll have three of those, an-and-t-o-o-wo of those an-an-and . . ." continued for more than a minute or two, Harry's patience would snap. With arms gyrating in a shooing gesture, he would thunderously roar, "Get out, get out, get out . . ." until the terrified lollyless youngsters cleared the precincts of his shop. It wasn't long before Harry's lolly sales dropped drastically.

Because Harry's shop was by far the closest, Dad and Lloyd, who did most of our shopping, purchased most of our groceries there. It lessened the drudgery of lugging the heavy items home from the main street some twice the distance.

Strange though it seemed, Harry and my father clicked, so Dad soon became his friend and confidant. Sometimes I would accompany Dad on his shopping excursions. Often, in a state of indignation, Harry would point to a much depleted three bushel bag of flour, wheat, or potatoes, or a 70 pound bag of sugar, and agitatedly rave "Look at that Courtney – look at it – I only got it about a week ago and it's almost gone". I could never understand his attitude; I vaguely thought the more a shopkeeper sold, the more money he would make. Even Dad would laugh about what a strange attitude it was for a shopkeeper. Over the years, the story was always good for a laugh, at times of reminiscing. But it was 25 years later, when I met and married the daughter of a struggling country butcher of those times, that the reason for Harry's distress was made apparent. "Lyle!" Eileen responded, "Dad had the same problem, most of the sales would have been booked up." Realising the unworldly stupidity of my family was embarrassing. Of course, if so much of his stock had been sold on tick, there would not be enough cash to buy more.

Having been a coalminer for most of his life, Harry's lifelong recreation was something of a busman's holiday – he was a fervent gold prospector and miner. The mere mention of gold could spark a blended narration of fact, dreams and theories. There were anecdotes of promising finds he had made at various locations that were now securely locked away in his head. Places to which he would one day return and prove his conviction that the colours in those dishes he had long since washed, were merely the tips of golden icebergs.

Harry took a keen interest in the prospecting activities of my family. Dad and Lloyd never visited his shop without the subject being raised. Harry was very impressed with Lloyd's diligence and interest in the finer points of gold seeking, which he so willingly offered. Meanwhile, Lloyd was still at school. He was an excellent student, who had obtained his Merit Certificate at the age of twelve and a half. But in spite of his scholastic ability – probably due to Harry's tales of gold – he was eagerly awaiting his birthday in four months time, when he would reach the minimum school leaving age of 14, and would be able to also try his luck on the almost worked-out goldfields.

It was not long before Harry and his wife Lil – whom Harry mostly referred to as "she" – began to visit us on a more regular basis. It was usually in the early evening. Lil was moderately deaf, which made conversation with her difficult. Nevertheless, she obviously enjoyed those visits to our humble abode and in a quite loud voice, always had something to add to the conversation, even though at times, because of her hearing problems, her contributions were out of context. We mostly entertained them in the small clearing between the kitchen and the little quarry, where we would all drink generous quantities of tea. It was during these visits that I first heard Harry's wonderful laugh and realised that away from the stress of running his shop he was a kind, good-hearted, jovial man. We soon began to fondly anticipate the visits from Harry and Lil.

I thought it was strange that Harry never called Dad "Tom"; it was always "Courtney". Harry had enormous respect for Dad's intellect, and (no doubt because he had heard of his work with his patented car wheel) simply revered him as an inventor. Ever expecting that something new and significant could be brewing in Dad's fertile brain, Harry would often inquire, "What are you working on now, Courtney?" Dad would answer "Oh, I've got something in mind". And of course he did, for there amongst the family worries, was the spark of hope fanned by new ideas for an even better suspension wheel.

It was Dad's continuing faith in his suspension wheel, and dreams of the financial rewards that it would bring, which attracted our second frequent visitor. He was the minister of one of the less popular religions. Even though his flock was small, he had a good car and was always extremely well dressed. He would have been in his 30s, and had a smooth personality that in later years I tended to associate with used-car salesmen. Later I discovered he had two preschool children and a lovely wife. The blossoming association between him and Dad was almost nipped in the bud when on one of his earliest visits, a friendly little Jacky-lizard began to run up the parson's exquisitely pressed trousers. With absolutely no thought of being kind to a harmless member of God's creation, in sheer panic he flung it off and desperately tried, unsuccessfully, to stomp it into the dust. I feel sure that Dad's spontaneous outburst would never have been forgiven, had it not been for the desire of a spin-off from what he perceived could be a wheel of fortune. Dad's anger soon gave way to one of his oft-uttered philosophies, "Let bygones be bygones", and he quickly forgave the parson for his "trespass". They continued to plan big things for Dad's wheel.

18

Bush Rambles and Sisters

With all the activity around our place, and my ever-growing love of the bush, having to go to school was becoming an even greater nuisance. I eagerly awaited the May holidays.

At last we reached the end of first term, and the holidays began. During those precious days, Keith even allowed me to tag along with him and Jack, on their excursions into the bush. Most of the trips were to tend Keith's tub of wash-dirt at the "yellow clay patch". Walking there, washing the soaked clay, refilling the tub, then walking home again, necessitated an early start, if we were to be home in time for (midday) dinner. When the job was left until after dinner, it was usually almost dark when we passed the cemetery, where the repeated drawn out penetrating "oom" of bronze-wing pigeons gave a hair-raising atmosphere to the twilight. But whether it was midday or evening, we were always famished on our return, for taking something to eat was never even considered.

I loved the bush around the yellow clay patch: it seemed so isolated. Yet just a few hundred yards away, we would sometimes stand in a little clearing amid the ruins of what long ago had been the Bluchers school, which served a substantial community. On such occasions, my imagination would run wild as I attempted to visualise those times. It was there that I specked my first colour of gold that shone so brightly on the flat freshly rain-washed yellow clay surface. It was also there, that I learnt how to pan gold, and I first knew the thrill of gently swirling a little clean water over the last few spoonfuls of the heaviest powder and grit, that fanned out from the front bottom edge of the dish. With each gentle swirling flush, my eager eyes watched the dross recede and leave the yield of gold gathering at the "delta's" tip. It was amazing, even in this relatively isolated spot, how often a ball of lead shot or a boot-tack would mingle with the colours at the leading edge.

I was also permitted to form a threesome with Keith and Jack on a couple of shooting ventures. One was to the Carisbrook Reservoir and Bluchers. The reservoir paddock was surrounded by what was more or less a typical stock fence of that era. Sturdy wooden posts, four or four foot six inches high, supported five strands of number-eight plain wire with a barbed wire on top, while evenly spaced heavy wooden droppers prevented the taut wires from spreading easily. Despite the fact that since the onset of the Depression, short lengths of its wire had been judiciously removed from this fence by destitute citizens who considered their needs justified that action; it was still a formidable barrier. On most of our extended excursions into the bush, it was usual to be confronted by a considerable number of these obstacles along our chosen route. In those distant days of strong community commitment and trust, it was the accepted thing that both adults and kids could, at will, wander through the private paddocks that were scattered throughout the bush, without any objection from the owners. Probably this attitude was due to the fact that vandalism to private property at that time appeared to be nonexistent.

I was overwhelmed by my perceived grandeur of the reservoir, especially its "awesome" pier, which thrust out high above the rock-faced embankment and water. There was no way I would follow my brothers the score or so yards to its end. The acorn trees – which I had not seen before – growing behind the reservoir bank also intrigued me, as did the long overflow race that was so beautifully lined with bluestone pitchers.

We didn't even see a rabbit or hare, but Keith did let me have my first shots with a rifle, while we were at Bluchers. The target was an old jam tin: I disgraced myself by missing it with both shots.

The second hunt was to Mosquito. As we walked across the cleared paddocks, Keith had a shot at a rabbit in the distance a couple of times, but even though I dearly loved roasted rabbit, and we all could have done with the extra protein, I totally lacked the killer instinct. I found it hard to conceal my delight when he missed both rabbits.

At the far end of the paddocks, there was a long, high, massive heap of sand from the battery that had crushed the quartz from the long-since-abandoned reef mines nearby. As we began to climb this steep embankment, I was cautioned to be quiet. We stealthily crossed the wide flat top of the heap and looked down on a small flat, which was almost completely encircled by the sand heaps. I was astounded. There on the flat, were the most rabbits I had ever seen – and all of them totally unaware of our presence. Although Keith had only a single-shot rifle, within seconds, the sound of two deafening shots assaulted my ears, and before the rabbits realised what was happening, with a sickening feeling I saw two of their number in death-throes, on their sides in the sand.

I immediately decided I would never go hunting again; it was horrible. But alas, my love of the bush slightly outweighed my hatred of killing and I could not resist going on other such excursions whenever I was invited. Thankfully, more often than not, the hunts were unsuccessful, and in time, my hunting instinct developed into the non-killing versions, such as bird watching or simply seeking and observing the intricacies of our natural world.

It was another couple of years, before I could be confident that I would receive an invitation to join Keith and Jack on their long walks into the bush.

Again there was the inevitable school holiday visit from Auntie Tot, with various other relations, but once again, no Yvonne. In spite of the numerous activities in progress to improve our lot, Auntie Tot was still unjustly critical of Dad and my older brothers, and her attempts to persuade Auntie Mag to desert us persisted, but thankfully for us, to no avail.

Keith turned 16 on the 10th of May, and now 18 days later on the 28th it was Lloyd's fourteenth birthday. This was a big day for Lloyd, he had reached the legal age to leave school, but in spite of his eagerness to leave, which for people on our social level was considered the natural thing to do, Dad decided he should continue on for at least a while. We were also aware that this same day was our sister Valma's eleventh birthday. Our thoughts were with her and our youngest sister June, on that far-away mallee farm in New South Wales.

My visualisation of that farm was based on the occasional letters from my sisters, or from Auntie Liz. They wrote of kangaroos, emus, goannas, and apostle birds, as well as riding horses on the two and a half miles to school, and hosts of other exciting farm activities that made me envious – it all seemed so wonderful. I felt sure that Valma's birthday would be a very happy occasion for them both.

Sadly, my mental pictures of Valma and June were not so clear. Half my lifetime had left them just a vague blur in my memory, and with no talk of them coming home, I childishly accepted that I might never see them again. Six days later on the 3rd of June everyone remembered, or was reminded, that it was June's tenth birthday. Again the latent sadness of being parted from our sisters stirred in our hearts.

Next morning, I was having another of my days off school; with stomach ache – mostly they were caused by just the thought of having to go to school. While I was engaged in some activity far more interesting than anything I would have been doing at school, I noticed four people approaching from the direction of Mr Chester's place. I always felt a bit uneasy when strangers came around, especially when I had a guilty conscience about not being at school.

As they drew closer, from my vantage point I realised that one of them was Auntie Annie, but I hadn't a clue as to who the taller lady and the two girls might be. I took it for granted they were just some of Auntie Annie's friends, but I was puzzled by her visiting us in the morning, she always came in the afternoon.

I informed Auntie Mag of the imminent arrival of her sister with others. She reacted the way she normally did on such occasions – became all flustered and exclaimed "Good heavens, it's awful them catching me like this, had I known they were coming I'd have put on something tidy". But there was no time for that, by now the visitors were upon us, and Auntie Mag had to suffer the indignity of going out to greet them in her working clothes, just as Dad appeared from somewhere.

Instantly a burst of voices raised in ecstasy by the excitement of recognition engulfed the camp. Although still somewhat bewildered by the rapturous exchange of greetings, slowly I began to notice the names that were being bandied about – Maggie, Auntie Mag, Dad, Liz, Annie, Valma, June – they were all so familiar. Suddenly, with a swell of intense emotion, I realised my two younger sisters had returned.

With my shyness subdued by desire to be part of the momentous occasion, I bashfully came from my refuge, and joined the gathering to be reunited with my long lost siblings, and the person so revered by Auntie Mag – her sister Liz. Apparently, without even a hint to any of their Victorian relatives, Auntie Liz, her husband Lem, his brother Jack and his wife, my two sisters, with my eldest cousin – Liz and Lem's son Jack – had left their farm near Lake Cargelligo in New South Wales, in their big car, around 3 am the previous morning. After a gruelling trip, they arrived at Auntie Annie's house in Maryborough, about 10 pm that evening. Knowing it would be horrendous to lob the two young girls at our unprepared camp at that time, it was wisely agreed that the whole party stay the night at Auntie Annie's house. It must have been a real problem for poor Auntie Annie, having to unexpectedly find places for them all to sleep.

After they had breakfast next morning, my cousin Jack had driven his father, with his brother and sister-in-law out to Stoney Creek, where the latter two were to stay with Lem and Jack's sister and her husband. That left it to Auntie Annie and Auntie Liz, to walk the girls to their new home. I couldn't remember having seen Auntie Liz before, but I immediately felt comfortable in her presence. Unlike Auntie Tot, she didn't even seem to notice anything unusual about our living conditions. In the pleasant atmosphere, I quickly lost my shyness and felt fairly at ease with my sisters. The kettle was quickly boiled, and with lots of lively talk, everyone shared the pot of tea.

Valma and June eagerly inquired as to the whereabouts of their other brothers. Lloyd and Jack were at school; Keith was out the bush, but would be home for dinner. Louis, however, was working over at his mine. The girls immediately became impatient to see our eldest brother and his mine. It was suggested that I act as guide for my sisters. I really felt smug, and could not hide my feeling of importance as I led them through the bush.

By now the mine looked quite grand. Even with the aid of explosives, it had still been necessary to extend the logs up to about four feet high, and the mullock from the mine had been banked up around them to form an impressive mound. On his visit after the last "rise", the understanding mining inspector – surely with a twinkle in his eye – asked them "Are you expecting an Indian attack?" Mystified, the partners replied, "No! Why?" "I was just wondering why you're building a fort," came the inspector's witty answer. To the relief of the shame-faced mates, he again measured the mine from the top of the logs.

My sisters were very impressed, although a bit wary of the gaping hole, and even though I was keen to impress them, I too stood well back. A call to Louis some 20 feet below, received a quick response, and moments later he appeared at the surface. Of course he instantly recognised his sisters, and greeted them with effusive affection. That was the end of his work that morning, he came home to join the gathering. The girls were also anxious to go to meet Jack on his way home from school for dinner, so at the appropriate time, the three of us set off down the track. I made sure that the meeting didn't take place too close to the school, in case I was spotted. My words are inadequate to describe the mix of emotions we shared, as Jack rounded Mr Harrap's corner, and so unexpectedly came face to face with his long lost sisters. As I witnessed their unbridled delight, I knew my time of glory was over. In the last few hours as an appointed guide, for the first time I had known the euphoria of leadership, but suddenly I knew I had been superseded. Later the reunions with Keith and Lloyd were equally joyful.

Before they returned to NSW, the Griffith family visited us several more times in their big blue car, which was admired and discussed. There was emphasis put on the fact that it was a Buick. I gathered this name gave it some prestige. As was always the case with any car that came around the place, Dad spent quite a while examining its wheels and tyres.

Like Auntie Liz, Uncle Lem and their son Jack were easygoing and friendly. What's more, there was no criticism. I liked Auntie Liz very much. She certainly lived up to all the good things I had heard about her; in many ways she reminded me of Auntie Mag. I sensed they shared the same goodness, and felt sure, that had the decision been left to her, she would have gladly let Auntie Mag cure a pig. Their departure was a sad occasion for us all, especially the girls, Auntie Mag and Auntie Liz. I hoped we would soon see Auntie Liz again.

The sudden arrival of the girls urgently demanded a major change of our sleeping arrangements. The first move was obvious: Valma and June would replace Jack and me in Auntie Mag's bed. Dad would give up his three-quarter bed in the most western tent for us and he would sleep on the old hand-me-down miner's couch in the "kitchen". The problem was solved.

By this time, none of our beds had more than a couple of old grey or white blankets, and years of having no sheets had left them worn and inefficient. One blanket was always placed over the old kapok mattresses, partly to protect the worn striped mattress covers, but mainly to insulate the sleepers from the kapok, which years of use had partly pulverised to a fine dust that continually escaped through the flimsy covers. The second blanket went next to us on top. As stated earlier, for warmth, every one of our beds depended on old handout overcoats – mostly ladies' – a generous supply of old newspaper, and a wagga "bedspread". That's how it was until the day we moved into Dad's bed. We still had the threadbare blanket over the mattress, but there wasn't one on top. Having been used to that luxury, it came as a bit of a shock to find ourselves in direct contact with an assortment of old overcoats – overlapped like shingles on a heritage roof. The coats were interspersed with lots of newspaper, which crackled to our every movement. Although the wagga overlay did, to some degree, keep the coats in place, its weight tended to cause restless sleep, so body movement would cause the coats to separate, and let in the cold. Several times a night, the cold would arouse us to a sleepy stupefied state that enabled us to rearrange the scattered coats and paper.

Dad's obsession with the health benefits of fresh air didn't improve matters either. Although every tent had a gap of a few inches between the sides and the ground, Dad – often while we were asleep – would regularly do a round of the tents to hitch up the sides to let in more fresh air. In summer this was appreciated, especially when there was a bit of a breeze, it cooled the tents quite a bit, although it did give the mosquitoes much easier access. However Dad continued this practice when the tents were damp and cold. It wasn't that he was a bit of a sadist, he did it to help dry out the tents and their contents, for like so many of his generation, he had a deep dread of wearing damp clothes and sleeping in a damp bed. Such convictions left him in no doubt that a short term of slightly increased discomfort was far outweighed by its contribution to our long-term interest.

In spite of the discomfort, I'm sure we didn't complain; having our own tent was considerable compensation, and over the years as we waited for things to improve, the bother of having to continually rearrange the coats became just a part of life. I can't remember what Dad's bed on the sofa consisted of, but because he always ensured we kids had the best available, it must have been awful.

On the following Monday, Valma and June fronted up to their old school for re-enrolment. When they left this same school three years earlier to enrol in a tiny out back one-teacher school in NSW, without any tests, they were demoted one grade. The more I think about it, ridiculous though it seems, I can only conclude that they must have been the victims of petty interstate rivalry. That demotion affected June more than Valma, for now she had to suffer the indignity of being in the fourth grade with Jack. I believe it was that blow to her pride that sparked the fierce competition in all things, between her and Jack. The competitiveness became so strong, that it actually brought them closer together, and left Valma – within the structure of our foursome – in complete domination of myself.

Regardless of the joy of having two of our sisters home again I wasn't used to having girls around. I didn't have the slightest clue as to how they differed biologically to boys, but I sensed it was more than just having long hair and wearing dresses. Although I had to wait many years to learn the answers to those questions, it only took a few weeks before I felt completely at ease with them. Within a short time we were a strongly united quartet, with unflagging mutual loyalty true to the motto of The Three Musketeers – "One for all and all for one". Of course that was in the case of hostile outsiders; within our group there was always a cordial three-way contest for leadership.

While she was away, June had taught herself how to whistle. Not just an ordinary run-of-the-mill whistle, but a loud ear-splitting shrill that under good conditions could be heard about half a mile away through the bush. The whistle came just from the mouth, with no help from fingers or anything else. Surprisingly, June was keen for Jack and the rest of us to learn the art so that we could communicate with each other over a distance, but in spite of extensive lessons over the years, none of us succeeded in producing even a feeble version of the whistle.

Shortly after the girls re-enrolled, our school arranged for an afternoon at the pictures during school hours. At first, the school's promotion of the film had no effect at all on me: the fact that it would cost seven pence each put any idea of going well into the realms of fancy. Although I – like so many of the pupils of 2828 – had never seen a film, I had no feeling of being "hardly done by".

I was resigned – as happened on other occasions with school concerts etc. – to be herded with a score or so of other "financial rejects" from the school's six grades, into a single room to sit the time out under the guard of one usually disgruntled teacher. I was content to accept that as a retribution for being poor, even as I waited to accompany my three siblings home for dinner on the day of the film. When they met me at the school gate, they were exuberant, for Valma, June and Jack had each been given free tickets. Suddenly my attitude drastically changed, the injustice of that started my very last – and probably the greatest – performance of what had brought me renown in my first six months: I howled and howled and howled all the way home.

Everyone at home did their best to console me, and immediately started a whip round to raise the money so that I could go too. The money slowly rolled in, as my family searched hither and thither for stray coins. Moved by their efforts, my howling had subsided to deep sobbing by the time the tally stalled at five pence. Minutes passed, and in spite of frantic searching, not even another halfpenny could be found. With our school dinnertime quickly drawing to a close, there seemed little hope of reaching the financial target. It seemed that my spirits had been lifted only to be dropped into even deeper depths of despair, and Dad's usual consoling words for such occasions, "The birds will sing again", didn't help at all. It wasn't missing the picture that was so upsetting; it was the thought of being left out.

Although disappointment was no stranger to Auntie Mag, she was obviously upset about my plight. When she placed her hand gently on my shoulder, I thought it was a gesture of comfort and confirmation of defeat, so the tears began to swell again; but instead it was a guiding hand coaxing me to follow her. On reaching her tent, she lifted the pile of things off her tin box, and opened its lid. Somewhat perplexed, I watched as she removed her treasures, which I thought were so wonderful, and carefully placed them on the bed. Near the bottom of the box, with a flash of disbelief, I saw her reach for the aged ornate chocolate box that contained her meagre collection of old coins that bore the portraits of several generations of English monarchs.

Auntie Mag had often let us fondle those coins, as she explained the royal lineage, and even though the score or so coins were of low value, they meant a lot to her, and I knew she would not lightly part with a single one. With that knowledge, my disappointment turned to guilt, as I guessed her intention as she intently examined the condition, date and monarch, of each penny. At last after considerable indecision, two pennies were selected for sacrifice. I knew the image of the undistinguished looking elderly man was the likeness of Edward VII, who reigned for only nine years after the death of his mother Queen Victoria in 1901.

That afternoon I saw my first moving picture, but the pleasure of the occasion was somewhat tainted by the guilt of having imposed on Auntie Mag's generous nature.

I completely forget the name of that film and its contents, but the poignancy of that scene around Auntie Mag's treasure chest that afternoon remains untarnished by the ravages of time.

I suspect the two old coins may have been mentioned in discussions among the teachers, for the next day the teacher who had handed out the free passes apologised to Valma for having overlooked me.

* * *

The girls being home caused quite a few changes around the place: it wasn't long before Lloyd – who, in the absence of a night-man calling, mostly took it upon himself to perform the unpleasant burial – despairingly complained that the lav-can was filling a lot quicker.

We also began to socialise a bit more with the neighbourhood kids. At first, mainly with the Hill kids: Betty, Muriel (who was always called Mooie), Wilma, and preschooler Billy. There were also two younger ones, but we hardly knew them. The two eldest girls were roughly the same age as June and Jack, while Wilma was in my grade at school. They were all harmless poor kids and less worldly than we four.

The young Hills soon became frequent visitors to our camp. The girls were always wide-eyed and as timid as mice, while Billy was a quiet little fellow, with an unfortunate runny nose, which demanded lots of deep sniffing, and he always looked sad. They were also extremely trusting and believed everything we told them.

With shame I recall how at times we took advantage of that trust, and would "have them on". Our "Whirthingham" sewing machine, with its teak cabinet, was still with us, mainly because no one wanted to give it storage space, due to it being unusable because the needle holder was missing. At that time, I had heard about wirelesses, but didn't know anyone who had one, and neither did our newfound friends. With that knowledge, we decided to play a hoax on them. Although I was quite tall for my age, my three youngest siblings prompted me to climb into the small space between the treadle and the folded down machine head. Being both skinny and supple, we found I could squeeze in enough to allow the front door to be closed. There was no danger of suffocation, because the back of the cabinet was perforated. After the trial run, we smugly awaited the next visit from our friends.

At the first hint of their impending arrival, I snuck to the tent and took up my position in the machine. Soon our expectant visitors were being escorted into the tent to see our "new wireless". At the arranged signal of someone fiddling with the wooden doorknob, I commenced to speak. I was never much of an actor, so heaven only knows what I said. Nevertheless, they did not suspect it was a hoax and continued to pester us for permission to listen to our wireless until I quickly outgrew the cabinet, then we told them our wireless had broken down – they were really disappointed.

With more mouths to feed, Auntie Mag had to increase the size of the batches for our many meals of pancakes and fried scones. These were usually served straight from the pan in turn to those standing around the stove – it was reminiscent of a mother bird feeding her nestlings.

The Hill children – especially Billy – also loved Auntie Mag's frying pan delicacies, and would frequently enlarge the usual group of hungry "fledglings" around the cook. Although economics dictated they could not have an equal share, Auntie Mag could not ignore their appealing looks, so every now and then our family would be short changed when a pan-full came off the production line. At times over the next year or so, "us four kids" (as we called ourselves), for what we thought was a harmless bit of fun, would play what I now realise was a sadistic trick on poor little Billy. We would place small pieces of pancake in a tree, just too high for Billy to reach; telling him it was for the birds. We would then retreat, to watch his frantic efforts to retrieve the morsel. He always succeeded – mostly with the help of a stick. Even though I only played a minor part in that despicable act, just the thought of it, still fills me with shame. In spite of all our horrible behaviour towards them, the young Hills must have enjoyed our company, for they spent a lot of time at our place.

At that time, their father Bill was working on the railways, which necessitated him having to rise very early. Unfortunately, he was a heavy sleeper, and what made things worse, they had no alarm clock. Fortunately, none of my family needed to rise particularly early, so in appreciation of their neighbourly good will in providing us with drinking water, Dad offered – with my consent – to allow them to look after our much prized Big Ben overnight each work day.

After dark each night that the clock was needed, we would hear the scared voices of the older Hill girls, raised in what could roughly be called song, approaching. On arrival, their communication was always short and unvaried, "Daddy wants the clock". Grasping the clock, and without another word, they would head for home, with their voices again raised in song.

The clock was always returned early next morning, often by a single girl, and there was never the slightest hint of a song. It was obvious they were terrified of the dark, mainly we gathered, because they believed the bush between our abodes contained a sizeable population of "Boogie Men". When they were questioned about the perceived threat from those figments of their imagination, their total knowledge of their malevolent intentions seemed to be that "They'll getcha". "But", they assured us, "singing keeps them away".

* * *

Not long after Lloyd's fourteenth birthday, Dad relented and allowed him to leave school, and within days, he accepted Harry's invitation to be his partner, in a mining venture in the gully down below Chapman's paddock, where the shafts bottomed at around 12 feet. As was expected, Harry and Lloyd worked well together, and happily continued their partnership for a considerable time. At times they got a nice bit of gold; but when it was divided, once again, there was never enough to really justify the effort.

After their initial venture, they did some reef mining, but the only benefit Lloyd gained from that was learning, from Harry, the skilful art of digging the hard reef. After making a face a few inches high in the vertical north/south layers of sandstone, they would peel off slaty sheets in what seemed, to the casual observer, an effortless manner. It was fascinating to watch.

19

Managing the Goats and Playtime

It was surprising how quickly our goat flock had increased. It now consisted of almost 20 individuals of three generations. The number had grown despite the fact that our big black billy goat – on whom Keith had bestowed the noble name of Hore-Belisha after the then British Secretary of State for War – spent most of his time on the end of his 20-foot chain, circling the big ironbark tree to which it was attached. The tree at this camp was just inside the park reserve, close to the new goat house. The goats were only locked in their house for short periods during milking time, or when one of their number required some kind of special attention; normally they were free to roam the bush at will.

Valma and June had been milking cows in NSW and on their return were keen to transfer their skills to the goats. Their efficiency and instant affinity with the goats, plus Jack's competitive spirit and my desire to tag along, immediately began to free Auntie Mag and Dad from the chore of milking the goats morning and evening. Actually it went further than that, except for attending to Hore-Belisha – it was considered he was too formidable for us to handle – we quickly began to take over the day-to-day management of the flock.

Although some of the goats were quite strong, they were all placid, and we were slowly beginning to learn a few tricks in handling them. On the odd occasion when one was uncooperative, we discovered that by straddling their necks and holding their horns, we could mostly persuade them to do our bidding without too much effort – though at this stage I could only manage the smaller ones.

During the first few weeks of breaking in a new milker, in the absence of a bail, one of us would hold the goat like that while another milked. After a while, they would stand at ease without even a leg rope although at times they would get a bit restless and we would have to hold their right leg with our left hand, which slowed the job down by leaving only one hand free for milking.

We milked the goats into aluminium saucepans. Dad was very suspicious of aluminium and repeatedly warned us not to leave food standing in them for too long, for he suspected that they could poison their contents. Nevertheless they were very suitable for this purpose.

We felt good about sharing the responsibility of the goats, but at times milking became a bit monotonous, so to break the monotony of the job, we yielded to the temptation that comes to most country kids who milk cows or goats. It seems so natural to take a shot with a stream of milk at any of the numerous bush-flies that decided to rest on the rim of the milk receptor. A well-aimed torrent of milk would leave a fly soaked and flightless and easy prey to any meat ant hunting nearby. Often a partial hit would simply impede the fly's aeronautical skills, and send it crashing into the saucepan. Then like a hand of providence, a hooked finger would lift them from the drink, and flick them onto the ground, probably to meet a fate worse than drowning.

At times, usually when our minds were elsewhere, in response to some irritation – such as a bothersome biting fly or the like – the goat would unexpectedly lift its right hind leg and with an ominous splosh, sink the unhygienic cloven hoof into the saucepan. Our first desperate effort was to hold the saucepan firm, so that further foot movements would not spill the milk. Mostly, they didn't seem keen on the footbath, and would quickly remove the offending hoof, but sometimes it had to be forcibly lifted out. In any case, we would have to remove the bulk of dirt from the milk. This we did by letting the milk settle for a few minutes, and then pouring the bulk into another saucepan, before tipping out the concentrated dregs. Even when the milk was clean, Auntie Mag would carefully strain it through a clean piece of calico flourbag to remove the odd hair or speck that may have fallen off the goat. But on days when the foot affair occurred, it was always an awkward time when the milk was being dealt with. "Good heavens! The milk's dirty today, whatever happened?" Auntie Mag would ask. Nevertheless, she always seemed to accept our silent gawks at the soiled strainer, to be a declaration of puzzled innocence.

We also maintained our silence on the frequent occasions when extending the hospitality of a cup of tea to visitors. If the subject of goats' milk came up, someone would be sure to bring up the then popular belief that goats' milk lacks many of the potential health hazards of cows' milk (which at that time was unpasteurised) because "It was pure". I'm sure we must have blushed when we heard that statement. However, in spite of our undesirable milking habits, we never suffered school sores, and had fewer bad tummy upsets than most of our cows' milk drinking school contemporaries.

Auntie Mag would have been horrified had she known about our milking practices. When it came to food and its preparation, despite our living conditions, she was unfailingly diligent in her efforts to maintain a high standard of hygiene. What's more, even though the ambience of our dining facilities was well below the accepted standard of polite society, Auntie Mag was a stickler about us adhering to the table manners appropriate to such a society. Witnessing even a minor indiscretion of good table manners, such as licking a honey dribble off one's finger, was sufficient to prompt another rebuking rendition of the verse we all knew so well:

The Goops they lick their fingers,
The Goops they lick their knives,
They spill their broth on the table cloth,
And lead untidy lives.

I hadn't a clue who or what Goops were, but it was clear that Auntie Mag didn't regard them as ideal role models and I always tried to please her.

Although the goat house was straight in front of our kitchen, it was on the other side of the two quarries and a steep-sided channel about 15 feet wide and six or seven feet deep that connected them. This was quite an inconvenience; we either had to scramble down and up the steep banks of the connecting "neck", or triple the distance to the goat house by skirting the little quarry. Once again Keith came to the rescue: he constructed, out of un-barked ironbark saplings, a quaint little footbridge complete with a handrail. Not only did the bridge add a touch of rustic charm to our humble estate, it also took us a bit further along the road to easier living. But we still had a long way to go.

Our degree of comfort was still virtually at the mercy of the weather: if the weather was cold but calm, it was wonderful to sit around a campfire outside at night. On cold wet days, it was miserable in our draughty kitchen, and sitting in the wet tents was even worse, for they acted like Coolgardie safes. At weekends, on school holidays, and after school on such days, the only sensible thing to do was to retreat, usually with hot bricks, to the layers of assorted fabrics that constituted our beds, and when night came, the lack of lights did nothing to raise our spirits.

Preparing meals was a big problem under those miserable conditions. Food that required the minimum of preparation was popular on those days. Perhaps a pot of porridge or toast and dripping, but if things were particularly unpleasant at teatime, we would make do with bread and honey washed down with lots of tea.

For the second winter, the edges of my ears were encrusted with itchy chilblains. At times most of us had chilblains to some degree on our ears, feet or hands, but Auntie Mag suffered the most, and got them badly on all those extremities.

Not only was it miserable at home in cold weather, the schoolrooms were not much warmer. Admittedly, in school, we were not subjected to the chill factor of the wind, but each classroom's only heating was a frugal open wood fire behind the teacher on the platform at the front of the room. For the pupils in the body of the room some eight inches below and behind the "barricades" of heavy wooden two-children desks, the fires were about as warmth-giving as moonlight in snow.

It was even worse on rainy days. Mostly we could keep our ordinary clothes reasonably dry on our way to school, thanks to sugarbags that we folded into long "pixie" type hats, and any old overcoats from the donated rag bags, but our footwear always seemed to be leaky, which would condemn us to hours of sitting with icy wet feet. Our school was considered the most socially deprived in our town, so the few offspring of professional people were given elitist status by most of the school staff. It was from those well-dressed strata of pupils that most of the teachers selected their "pets" and on freezing mornings, it was amazing the variety of minor endeavours that could earn those chosen few the reward of a turn on the special chairs by the fire. In justice to even the worst teachers, it was not completely unknown for that privilege to be extended to the inadequately clad, barefooted, or even just sockless pupils from the lowest social strata – provided they were suffering hypothermia.

Some of the more compassionate teachers – especially those in the lower grades – would let everyone in turn be part of a small group to have a short warm by the fire.

On non-school days, when the white frost-coated gum leaf litter crackled beneath our morning steps, we knew it was the promise of a glorious winter day, and we didn't mind the cold so much, especially in August, when the dazzling sunshine gave brilliance to our forest's clouds of golden wattle blossom, which filled the air with its glorious perfume. On those frosty mornings, we would play with the sheets of ice from the puddles until our hands were blue with cold that numbed the soreness of our chilblains, but when we warmed them again the pain was excruciating.

* * *

Since her return from NSW, an insensitive teacher had been giving Valma a hard time. Although Valma was a bit overbearing with me, generally she was quite timid and submitted meekly to authority, which made her no match for her somewhat tyrannical teacher. June on the other hand, would question authority if she thought it unjust, so without encouragement from anyone, away from home she became the fearless advocate for our foursome. Valma's teacher had adopted the practice of keeping her class in at dinnertime for the most trivial reasons. Traditionally that was looked on as a complete no-no at our school, because most of the kids went home for dinner during the one-hour midday break, and many had a fair way to walk.

My three siblings and I would wait for each other before setting off for home together, so Miss Clarke's action affected us all. After several consecutive days of being deprived of twenty minutes of our precious home time, it became too much for June, so faithfully followed by Jack and me, she ascended the steepish ramp and faced the "dragon" in her lair and politely, but firmly, stated our case. I felt that our action would get us into big trouble, but strangely, Miss Clarke seemed to have suddenly had an awakening, for she henceforth abandoned dinnertime detention. Perhaps she was from a different community, where the kids didn't go home for dinner, and had just been thoughtless.

Another monotony-breaker at school was that a photographer was coming to photograph every grade in the school. Pre-ordered photos would be available in two sizes, a simple plain one, and a deluxe version mounted on stiff thick brown cardboard with a decorative frame-like border. I'm pretty sure the lesser one was to cost sixpence, the deluxe one was considerably dearer, but as it was well outside our reach I was not interested enough in its price to remember. To my surprise, we kids were given permission to put in an order for the economy version.

On the day of the "shoot" June togged me out in my best clobber selected from a particularly good bag of cast-offs and took considerable time before school grooming my hair. At this time I had become attached to an old overcoat from one of the donated bags of clothes. I realise now that that coat had become what these days would be called a "security blanket", for I was loath to take it off in public. Notwithstanding that, June allowed me to wear the coat to school, but ordered me to remove it before the "shoot", to reveal the most attractive shirt I could ever remember having.

In excited anticipation we awaited the arrival of our five and a half by three and a half-inch "snaps". As soon as she saw mine, June was stunned with exasperation, for there I was in the middle of the back row towering above the other members of my class, with my shoulders dragged down by the heavy drab overcoat. That episode still rankles her to this day.

* * *

Soon it was September and the school holidays at the end of second term. It was wonderful having our sisters home to share our adventures. At first, our free and easy daily forays were only into the nearby bush, where together we joyfully discovered or revisited the places we thought were special. We dug the chunky bullets from the target mound of the old, deserted rifle range or, half spooked, ventured into the gloomy depth of an old mine tunnel nearby. We even ventured a little further on towards Mosquito, where a huge red box tree, with a tangle of wide spreading limbs, turned a small secluded gully into a natural fun park. Spurred by an ever growing fierce sense of rivalry, June and Jack negotiated its foliage like possums, while even non-competitive Valma and

I would venture into its lower branches. There was also another smaller but similar tree with an even more fascinating entanglement of branches, in the gully below our original bush camp, which June and Jack quickly christened the acrobat tree.

In the 1930s, puddling machines were at the apex of our local mining technology, and owning one carried considerable kudos. Bush puddlers in plan, were that of a huge reverse doughnut – that is, the normal hole was solid, while the doughnut-ring was a trench about four feet or so wide, some fifteen or twenty feet in diameter, and around three feet deep. The floors of the trench were concrete, while the sidewalls were mostly lined with timber, usually logs that had been split in half lengthways, with the flat side facing out. A hefty balanced pole, which extended on either side to the outer edge of a solid gravel track that skirted the trench, was pivoted on a sturdy iron or steel axis in the centre of the island.

When the owners weren't around, playing on puddling machines was probably the biggest bush thrill, for kids in our neighbourhood.

At first, we played merry-go-rounds on Marshall's puddling machine, which was situated between our home and the cemetery. Later, when we extended our roaming, we discovered we had a choice of three such machines, Marshall's, Murray's and the one at Davies' eucalyptus plant.

For best results several kids would hop into the trench and balance their combined weight on either end of the pole. It usually only took a short run to accelerate the pole to an acceptable speed, then we would all lift our feet and flop our bodies over the whirling log, when, with a bit of luck we could suffer the discomfort of several revolutions before reactivating was required.

Puddlers were always built close to the bank of a dam, from which water was pumped by means of a simple lift pump, made from a long piece of galvanised downpipe about five inches in diameter. The pipe had a simple leather valve at the dam end, and an equally simple cone shaped leather bucket (piston) attached to one end of a long sapling pole. Usually there was a cross piece of round bush timber at the top for a handle. All the puddler pumps I saw had a shallow funnel shaped metal flange at the delivery end of the pipe. At first, I thought this was just for ornamentation, but later realised it was there to strengthen and ensure the opening maintained its circular shape. The pumps were placed at a low angle into the dam, and a race made of channel-shaped sheet-iron guided the water into the puddler.

To operate the machine, several dray loads of cloddy-clayish surface wash (wash is the material most likely to contain gold) were tipped into the trench, and water was added by means of the pump. A horse was then yoked to one end of the hefty pole, from which two harrows – usually just spiked logs – were dragged behind the pivoted pole at opposite sides of the trench. During puddling, the horse would monotonously plod the small circular track for hour after hour, pulling the harrows through the slurry of water and earth in the trench. As the clods and clay were broken down by the harrows, the heavy gravel and gold sank to the concrete floor, while the lighter sludge rose to the top. The sludge and other dross was skilfully released through a sliding gate on the downhill side of the puddler, this was then replaced by fresh water from the dam.

20

Failing Finances

Notwithstanding the good winter rain in June and July, which made the work unpleasant, Keith's new quarry bank was coming on fine. Dad never missed an opportunity to proudly escort anyone who came around the place, on an inspection of the site.

With the first quarry dam full from the good winter rains, we were all disappointed at not getting the vegetable garden going in the spring. But with all the other activities, there just wasn't time, and besides we would have to find the cash from somewhere to buy a coil of wire netting to keep out the goats and other stock that often strayed onto our unfenced blocks. So fresh vegetables continued to be rather scarce. Occasionally, someone would give us something out of their garden, and sometimes – when we were "flush" – we would buy a few cheap good fresh vegetables from two of the several market gardens scattered around the town, that were worked by the few Chinese still remaining from the thousands who came to our goldfields in the 1850s. Two of these gardens were within easy walking distance of our place, and occasionally I would accompany Dad on his errand.

Mostly we went to the closest one, which was situated next to the showgrounds in Gillies Street. Two placid elderly gentlemen, who lived in a quaint little hut, with a chimney and fireplace made of sheet metal at one end, operated this garden. The garden was about an acre, and one would rarely pass there between dawn and dark, without seeing the gardeners diligently attending their vegetables, often carrying two four gallon cans of water balanced on a pole across their shoulders.

Dad was very respectful of the Chinese and sympathised with them about the Japanese invasion of their homeland. Even though it was in complete contrast to his own nature, he was always impressed by their innate philosophy that seemed to enable them to accept the injustices of life without anger.

* * *

We decided that this year, we would build our bonfire on the other side of the track at the bottom end of Dad's block, where there were lots of suckers and dense Chinese scrub, which Dad said we could thin out. One morning while Valma, June, Jack and I were busy knocking suckers, a man passing along the track stopped and severely rebuked us. He said we could get into serious trouble with the Forestry Commission, but if we stacked the bushes into heaps he would collect them for his eucalyptus plant, and he wouldn't take the matter any further. Although we were all too intimidated to utter a single word of explanation in our defence, as soon as he had gone our knowledge of the true situation boosted our bravado sufficiently to ignore his instructions, so we continued to do it our way.

Two days after the Melbourne Cup, was bonfire day and preparations were virtually the same as those of the previous year. This year we did have a few more crackers and fireworks – though nothing as flamboyant as skyrockets. Our genial friend Mr Chester unexpectedly donated a modest quantity he had bought for us, on his last fortnightly visit to the town centre.

Not being on a hill this year, put our bonfire at a disadvantage, especially in view of a big combined neighbourhood one on the hill at the top of Loch Street, only some 400 yards away.

But that fire was something of a mixed blessing, for they had an abundance of fireworks, including lots of skyrockets, which by the standards of those days, were spectacular, especially from our prime viewing position. Nevertheless, it didn't seem fair competition. We were adamant we wouldn't have ours at that spot again.

There were also a number of loud vibrating explosions at various points around the town, which, I was told, was the work of reef miners with their subsidised explosives. In fact, my eldest brother was the chief suspect for a couple of the deafening blasts in the nearby bush.

Our fireworks display was not an indication of improved prosperity. Probably, to a degree, due to the extra expense of having the girls home, as the year progressed our financial position became desperate. Auntie Mag showed no hint of the disappointment when it became obvious early in December that she would even have to forgo the fondly cherished tradition of making the Christmas puddings and cake.

For the first time Dad was talking about selling Doll, but the stumbling block to that notion was that we hadn't sighted Doll since that day the circus came to town. Louis had made several forays on a borrowed pushbike to the Dunach area in search of her, and Dad constantly sought information of her possible whereabouts from people who might know, but it was all to no avail.

For several years more, in spite of the failure to find any trace of her, Dad looked upon Doll as money in the bank, and whenever we faced any really desperate financial crisis Dad would reiterate "I'll have to see about getting Doll in and selling her". But luck was on her side, and it remained, that the last we heard of Doll, was the sound of her terrified whinnies and pounding hooves against a background of intimidating roars and moans from the circus lions.

Then we suffered another quite distressing event. Our old faithful German collie dog that had run so excitedly to meet us the night we arrived at our first camp, and had been around far longer than me, became critically ill. Even if we could have afforded one, there were no vets in town. However, there were people around who had more than an average knowledge in such matters, and from the symptoms it looked like a case of ground-glass "poisoning", and the prognosis was hopeless. Soft hearted Dad had a hard choice, but he could not stand by and see poor old Sharp suffer. With Keith's help, they carried him to a suitable burial spot on the bush side of our block, where, with a single shot from Keith's rifle, Dad released Sharp from his sufferings. Knowing that there was someone around who could do such a callous thing to our inoffensive dog, was not a nice thought, what's more, it incited suspicion throughout our neighbourhood.

Soon after poor old Sharp's demise, to our delight, Danny Ryan's family, with whom we had become friendly and occasionally visited, offered us a small pup, which we eagerly accepted and Keith immediately named him Caesar. When we youngsters were around, our new pet spent most of the time with us. However, the somewhat domineering motherly nature that Valma had exclusively reserved for me now encompassed Caesar. While she fondled the cuddly creature at will, when June, Jack or I attempted to do the same, she would chastise us with, "Leave him alone, he doesn't want you mauling him all the time". Notwithstanding his domination by my protective sister, Caesar grew to be a faithful companion of the whole family, and for the next few years he never missed a chance to join any of the family on their jaunts into the bush.

In the second week of December, Edward VIII, the King of less than a year, shocked royalists of the British Empire by what they saw as shameful – the relinquishing of his birthright for an American divorcee. His decision was also the subject of much discussion among his less loyal subjects, and their opinions differed widely. Nineteen thirty-six had certainly been the year of British Empire Kings. The appointment of George VI brought the tally for the year to three – and still no new King coins.

Over the past few months, our minister friend had been visiting us several times a week. On a number of occasions, Dad and he set out in his car for the day on business to do with Dad's wheel. I gathered they were going to see potential new backers, or were visiting some of the well-to-do members of his now dormant Goeben Wheel Company, in the Boort/Wychitella area.

We also began to overhear comments that cast doubt on the parson's integrity. It was rumoured that he was ingratiating himself with some of his lonely old widowed parishioners, from whom he was receiving quite valuable gifts, and in some cases cash they could not afford to give. Dad never took much notice of gossip, and contemptuously dismissed the tales about his helpful friend. Keith however, was a bit more sceptical and to Dad's disapproval, christened the reverend "The Pilfering Parson".

Although we had all been christened Presbyterian, the minister was concerned about our lack of religious training, so he persuaded Dad to send Valma, June, Jack and me to his "foreign" – to us – Sunday school. So we set out on a different path to salvation. The most ardent converts were Valma and me – Valma by choice and me because of her domination. Occasionally when June and Jack decided to give Sunday school a miss because there were more interesting things to do, despite my desire to stay with them, I would be – sometimes literally – dragged to gospel lessons by my "born again" sister.

We did learn a few rousing songs though. My favourite was *Build On The Rock*, which was sung at every session. I thought its words,

Build on the rock,
The rock that ever stands,
Build on the rock,
And not upon the sands,
You need not fear the storm,
Nor the earthquake's shock,
You're safe forever more,
If you build on the rock

seemed to be good advice, but I thought building instructions were a bit out of place at Sunday school. Mostly though, it was simply boredom, especially when it meant wasting a lovely sunny afternoon on those hard long seats in that austere little hall. It did little to stir my spirituality, I always felt closer to God on our wanderings through the bush, where my insatiable infantile curiosity revealed wondrous earthly things that nourished my soul.

However, just before Christmas, one event made me realise that the weekly inconveniences might be worthwhile after all – I was invited to the Sunday School Christmas Party. At first I was reluctant to go and spend a whole afternoon without my siblings, with a mob of kids I barely knew, and with whom I believed I would have nothing in common. But from our first meeting, I had been a fan of our hostess, the minister's wife. I thought she was lovely, both in looks and manner. In spite of my misgivings, it proved to be most enjoyable, and gave me my first insight into the social behaviour of some of the more prosperous members of our community. I was undoubtedly the odd pea in the pod.

There was a reasonable quantity of delicious raspberry cordial – which I had never even seen before – heaps of buttered bread adorned with hundreds and thousands, some assorted little cakes, and a small ice-cream in a cone for everyone.

After we had partaken of the feast, there were lots of games on the fresh green lawn of the parsonage. That lawn was something special, I wasn't used to green grass in summer. The game I liked best, probably because I excelled in the pursuit and won first prize, was searching for peanuts that had been hidden around the garden. It was a really memorable afternoon.

For the next twelve months I anticipated attending a similar event, but the dream was not to be fulfilled. I never discovered if I was simply not invited, or if the cost of putting on such a "do" was just too prohibitive. Nevertheless, there was a degree of heavenly delight for us youngsters in the form of an abundant crop of berries on the mistletoes that heavily infested the box and ironbark trees around our camp. This summer was my first introduction to these sweet-sticky fruits that were commonly known to bush urchins as "snotty gobbles". The slippery fruit of our common mistletoe is encased in a yellow skin, which is broken midway, before the jelly coated oval seed is popped into the mouth. That is the easy part, the trouble starts after the pleasant jelly is sucked off. While connoisseurs of these fruits can spit the inedible seed out with the skill of a wine taster, the uninitiated find themselves in an embarrassing predicament. As the seed is ejected from the mouth it creates a somewhat elastic silk-like anchor thread, which causes it to rebound and attach itself to one's face or clothing. The novice snotty gobble eater can expend considerable energy before they excise themselves from the seed. At times, we – mostly June and Jack – would take a quantity of snotty gobbles to hand out at school, where their introduction to the unaware was always a cause of merriment.

* * *

With Christmas 1936 only a few days away and the exciting expectations of the school holidays, it was clear that this year our Christmas celebrations would be really austere. However, with a few days to go, it was realised that our finances could manage either a cake or pudding – but not both. Making such a decision was too hard for me, but because of the general feeling that they were more traditional, a pudding was the popular choice.

At last it was school break up day. June's and Jack's teacher in grade four was Miss Sears. Although she did teach me in a later year, my main memory of her is a tallish, slim, dark-haired person – at this time, probably in her mid 30s. Daily she walked beneath an unfurled black umbrella the short distance between the school and her home opposite the local showgrounds in the same street. She invariably carried that umbrella in all seasons and weather: it was generally presumed that her skin was sensitive to light.

I cannot remember her expressing emotion of any kind, and although she had a pleasant face, she was dignified to such a degree, that it made her look severe. Looking back, I believe that shyness may have been the cause of her perceived starchiness – that made her something of the stereotype of spinster schoolteachers of that era. But an event on this break-up day gave a hint of the compassionate kind heart that sheltered beneath that somewhat stern exterior. Just before dismissing her class for the Christmas holidays, June and Jack were mystified when Miss Sears quietly asked them to remain behind. As soon as the other pupils had gone, with unassuming graciousness, she personalised the general wish she had given to her whole class, of a happy Christmas and a prosperous New Year, and then presented each of them with a gift suitably wrapped for the season. I wonder if she guessed the endless happy hours June's game of Snakes and Ladders and Jack's book *The Arabian Nights* would give us youngsters during the holidays and for long after they had passed.

Miss Sears continued to take those short weekday walks until she retired a score or so years after my time at that school.

In spite of our increased poverty we were again all very much imbued with the magical spirit of Christmas and there was much to be thankful for this year. We were celebrating on our own blocks and Valma and June had returned home. Even without a cake for morning tea, there was still a special joy in the bustle of preparing our humble, but wonderful Christmas dinner.

After dinner, in an atmosphere of good fellowship, the retelling of old stories and general reminiscing continued all afternoon, and with the familiar whiff of smouldering cow dung, late into the night.

Again at midnight on New Year's Eve, we heard the whistles from the trains and the knitting mill above the sounds of bagpipes and the sound of revelry from the now closer main street.

This year Louis and Keith had both obtained a paid job with Andy Murray's yearly enterprise of supplying boiling water to the huge crowd that gathered at Princes Park for the annual Highland Gathering on New Year's Day. From a battery of wood-fired coppers placed in an allocated area the boiling water was ladled into the customer's containers – usually billies – at three pence for a pint dipper full. In spite of the number of people required to man the operation, it was enviously considered to be "a real money spinner" for the proprietor.

On the 7th of January, Auntie Annie and Sis again paid us a visit in honour of my birthday, and again Auntie Annie presented me with another decorated birthday cake, which in view of us not having had a Christmas cake, was especially appreciated.

Although I was excited about turning seven, for me a cloud of uncertainty had taken away the wonderful carefree feeling of my sixth birthday. Over the last few months, whenever any well-meaning visitor mentioned my birth, and its tragic consequences for my mother, dark suspicions began to make me feel uneasy. During the chatter and reminiscing of the elders of my family and our visitors, Auntie Annie would again repeat the sentiments I had heard so often. "It's a pity Flo didn't live to see her family grow up, she would have been so proud . . ." usually followed by, "it's sad Lyle never knew his mother". As was often the case, such statements led to further discussions concerning my mother's untimely death. As I listened with an empty chilling feeling, I felt sure my suspicion that I was responsible for my mother's death was confirmed. Being ashamed to mention the subject to anyone – not even my beloved Auntie Mag or Dad – left me uncounselled and allowed that secret guilt to haunt me for more than a dozen years. Whenever the subject of my mother – or even mothers in general – came up I would, as inconspicuously as possible, quickly remove myself from the scene.

Dad restricted our excursions into the bush during Christmas holidays because he feared we could be bitten by snakes. However, that loss was more than compensated for this summer, we had our own swimming pool – the quarry. At every opportunity on suitable days, the five younger members of the family still at home, would take to the water in makeshift togs. Lloyd was a terrible tease; he seemed to get more pleasure from splashing, and generally tormenting his juniors, than from the actual swimming. When Louis was home, he would often join us in our frolics, but Keith, who by constructing the dam was responsible for making this recreation available, denied himself the pleasure.

Now that we had a dam, it was deemed appropriate that we should get some ducks, mainly for aesthetic reasons, but also in the hope that they would supplement our egg supply. In due course, a setting of Khaki Campbell duck eggs was obtained from Mrs Ryan, the garbage man's wife, and placed under one of our "clucky" Black Orpington/Rhode Island Red, White Leghorn cross chooks. The name "clucky" comes from the fact that when domestic hens go broody, they forgo their normal vocal repertoire and, usually with their feathers fluffed out, strut around repeatedly emitting clucks.

We knew it was a bit of a risk putting duck eggs under a chook,

Thomas Courtney (Dad)

Margaret McCully (Auntie Mag) and Florence McCully (Mum)

The McCully sisters relaxing at the Talbot Reservoir – Evansford. L – R Annie, Deb, Auntie Mag, Mum, Alice and Tot

Grade 1 – Back Row from left: ?, Ray Watson, Frank Chaplin, ?, Ivan Letisser, ?, Lyle Courtney, Bill Marshall, ?, Les James, John Peters.
Middle Row: Valerie Stoneham, Margaret Cook, Marie Hubble, Amy Manton, Valma Duncan, Maud Chaplin, Ray Turton, Bill Hawke, Alan Maas.
Front Row: George Turner, Beryl Stevens, Jeanette Williams, Wilma Patterson, Margaret Wouda, Betty Jones, Marj Thatcher, Fred Hornsby, Norm Crossley, Colin Clarke.

Grade 111, 1939 – Back Row from left: Mary Pascoe, May Chaplin, Maud Chaplin, Bill Marshall, Ron Barnes, Bill Hawke, Lyle Courtney, Albert Greenwood, Horace Greenwooa, Ivan Letisser, Alma Trickey, Valerie Stoneham, Val Howard.
Middle Row: Jean Allen, Pearl Baker, Lorraine Wilson, Marie Hubble, Marj Thatcher, Margaret Wouda, Margaret Cook, Beryl Stevens, Jeanette WilEams, ?, Esther Peart, Thora Foster.
Front Row: Norm Crossley, George Turner, Keith Freeman, George Freeman, Colin Clarke, Ray Watson, Fred Hornsby, Kevin Rowe, Ray Turton, David Sing, Don Hanning, Max Stewart.

Before the crash: L – R Keith, Louis and Lloyd

L – R Valma, Lyle, Yvonne, Jack and June

Valma, Yvonne, June and Jack with Sharp the dog and Gipp the cow.

Dad with one version of his wheel

Jack and Lyle in their new suits

A few members of our goat flock with Donk on far right – 1939

Jack with his boat on the quarry

Auntie Mag's revered wood stove complete with flat iron, kettle and fire shovel.
The stove, although not used is still installed and in pristine and operational condition

Paddling in Keith's boat

Jack and Lyle in their "susso" clothes at the blackberry dam

Dad on the verandah of Lloyd's house

Lyle and Jack at home – 1942

June, Jack, Lyle, and Valma with Evelyn at far right

Eileen O'Grady becomes Eileen Courtney – 1965

as they usually give up the job soon after their normal incubation period of three weeks, and duck eggs take four weeks. Fortunately our mother hen didn't have a keen sense of time, and persevered with the required extra week, when most of the dozen eggs hatched. The new mum seemed quite pleased with her brood, and they responded to her "henly" tittering of encouragement when she found a tasty morsel for them.

All went well until a few days later when us kids, anxious to see the ducklings swim, decided it was time to allow her to take them to the quarry. Even before the fluffed-out formidable mum had clucked her way to the dam's edge, her fluffy "offspring" had hastily waddled and/or rolled down the steepish slope into the water. Words could not convey "mum's" distress at the behaviour of "her chicks", suffice to say, her emotions far exceeded those expected of a chook. Still, in spite of their weird behaviour, she continued to be a faithful mum who would patiently wait by the water for her wayward family to emerge.

21

Trauma in the Schoolyard

All too soon the Christmas holidays were over. Not surprisingly, it was affirmed that I would spend another year in grade one. Valma and June again suffered the consequences of having left Victoria, and would remain in grades five and four. Despite the NSW school's claim of having a higher scholastic standard, their education had fallen hopelessly behind while they were away.

Jack, of course, would join Valma in grade five, which did nothing to stimulate the self-esteem of our youngest sisters. It was particularly humiliating for June, for this meant that scholastically Jack had eclipsed her, which was very demoralising. But there was even more embarrassment in store for June. It came by way of Bob, the happy larrikin of our new contemporary friends, the Cooks.

Having recently obtained a fairly large mirror, Bob was keen to put it to some mischievous use. Conveniently for Bob, the windows of grades one, two, three and four faced the Cooks' house, some 300 yards away. It wasn't long before Bob discovered – much to the annoyance of the teachers concerned – that from their house he could reflect the dazzling sun onto the school's windows. However, the worst part for June was that when he focused on the grade four windows, he would shout out – in a raucous voice that was clearly audible from the school – "June Courtney".

Bob missed even more school than me, which gave him more time to exercise his talents as a community irritator.

* * *

Less than a year before we left our home by the school, we had witnessed the Cooks triumphantly arriving from Red Hill on the Mornington Peninsula. Their arrival was somewhat reminiscent of those timeless tales of wandering outcasts reaching their Promised Land. Somewhat blurred by the mist of years, my memory sees a pack of excited unruly noisy dogs circling the "caravan" of a covered wagonette and a couple of other horse-drawn vehicles, as it skirted the school side of the Prisoners' Dam, and stopped at their chosen site. They were a big family, consisting of the parents and, at that time, 12 offspring ranging from adults to a baby.

The unexpected arrival of the Cooks caused a flush of uncertainty around the neighbourhood: some timid individuals expressed their incorrect conclusions that they were gipsies. Thankfully for those fearful individuals, their minds were soon set at ease, for instead of soliciting tinkering jobs, fortune-telling and having their palms crossed with silver, they promptly began to fence their one-and-a-half acre property, and build a substantial mud-brick house.

When we first started to pass the Cooks' house, I was a bit scared of them, partly because there were so many of them and because they had lots of big fierce looking staghound-type dogs. But as we got to know the younger ones by meeting them on our way to and from school, we discovered they were as inoffensive as we were, and that went for their dogs too.

To me, their father looked pretty old. He was well over six feet tall, wiry and except on the very rare occasions when he got a bit tipsy, he was quite dignified. Mr Cook was also a keen gardener and with the advantage of having the town's reticulated water, he grew lots of fine vegetables. Often when he was in the garden while we were passing, he would call us over and give us some of his crop, which was appreciated by my family. We enjoyed our chats with him across his garden fence, so as one would expect, before long there was a good rapport between our two families. Mrs Cook seemed much younger than her husband, but that may have been because even I could see that she was heavy-handed with the make-up. Although polite, she made no attempt to nurture our acquaintanceship. I suppose having a dozen kids of her own was quite enough.

* * *

Although my joyful expectations of school had long since faded by this time, I was totally unprepared for the demoralising horror that was to come.

At our school, an imaginary east/west line divided the large playground. The southern (bush) side was designated for students up to and including grade two, while the town side was the domain of grades three to six. There was – supposedly – a strict rule regarding this segregation, which most of the pupils abided by, but during my second year in grade one, three big arrogant bullies from grade five decided to flout that regulation. Each playtime, they would cross the line with impunity, to terrorise the little kids.

Strange to say, their leader was always well dressed, and a universal favourite with the teachers, who saw him as a well-mannered young gentleman, instead of the sneaky, foul-mouthed cowardly bully that he was. Although soft and podgy, this baby-faced brute was a popular hero among the older kids, especially the girls. The source of the courage that allowed him to make the forays into the infant side of the playground to bully and repeat the foul-mouthed obscenities that festered in his sick mind was two puppet-like oafs who chortled in sadistic delight behind him.

Being so tall, skinny, and not having made any close friends at school, made me an ideal target for "Tony" and his leering entourage. I soon found that I could at least escape their pushing and pulling from all sides, by backing into the corner where the tank-stand and tank jutted out from the school's brick wall, and facing my tormentors. While neither Tony, nor any of his family, were close acquaintances, he seemed to know all about our poverty and the details of our family's affairs, and seemed to be particularly obsessed with the events surrounding my birth. His revolting torment, coming on top of the recent realisation of my perceived implications in Mum's death, made it particularly excruciating. Using words I had never heard before, he said my mother and father had bred like rabbits, and spoke of sexual matters of which I had no understanding, but which I instinctively knew were horrible. Because the torment was entwined with my secret sense of guilt, I did not dare mention it to anyone, not even to my younger siblings, or Dad and Auntie Mag. Finally, to complete my humiliation, he nicknamed me "titty-bottle".

Then things got even worse. Evidently some of the little kids in the "Bubs" had aspirations to take over from Tony when he moved on, for when he wasn't there, they filled in for him. Half a dozen or so would stand beyond my reach, yelling "titty-bottle". At times I would lunge from my corner to grab one of them and gently smack his backside, but on release they would all laugh as the victim ridiculed me further with such as, "You couldn't hurt a flea". It wasn't long before these annoying little kids became a constant support group for Tony and his mates.

During playtime one morning, their combined torment became so great, I could stand no more, so I sprang from the corner and ran for the ramp at the "infant" entrance. Tony and his mates did not follow, evidently fearing I was going to dob them in, but the little louts followed like bush-flies, right to the entrance door. Quietly I went to my deserted classroom and sat in my desk, but remaining in class without prior permission was an offence, and an authoritarian male Headmaster had spotted me. I dared not truthfully answer his interrogation as to why I was there, and was not crafty enough to say I was sick, which could have justified the "crime". So though I feared the consequences, I just sat mute. In view of having no excuse, I was promptly ordered to "Follow me!" and in the Headmaster's intimidating unfamiliar office, I received the cuts. It all seemed so unjust.

On hearing of this assault on me, Valma bristled with indignation as her mothering instincts were aroused. With the fearless courage of a mother magpie defending its chicks, she – with me in tow – immediately sought out the offending teacher and severely berated him for his treatment of me. "No one is allowed to hit or upset Lyle," she warned him, then further added to my crushing embarrassment with "he has a bad navel".

I was now totally dejected and desperate, so in view of June acting as our "rep" in Valma's case with Miss Clarke, I gathered the courage to vaguely tell her about the way I was being tormented. The details I gave were vague, because I could not bring myself to repeat the repulsive words of torment, but I did mention that Tony was the chief perpetrator. Mentioning Tony's name was a bad mistake, June was clearly shocked at my allegations, and her total disbelief made me feel a liar. It was obvious she too considered that Tony was incapable of perpetrating even my minuscule account of his misdeeds. Sadly, I realised that June, like most of the older girls at our school, thought Tony was a real heartthrob.

My last ally now was time. Eventually the tormenting of me became a bit of a bore for Tony and his mates, for after a while they left me in peace, and even the less obnoxious "human bush-flies" became less persistent and more tolerable, and when I progressed to the third grade in 1939, the tormenting ceased.

22

Pride Lost in the Honey Pot

Even though we didn't have much in the way of furniture, our kitchen/living room was somewhat overcrowded. Our two tables along the south wall, left just enough space for the narrow kitchen dresser that had turned up from somewhere to serve as storage for our crockery, cooking utensils and cutlery. Dad was very proud of that stainless steel cutlery, branded Dixon – Sheffield England. He often told how he had pre-ordered it from Dunklings (a Melbourne jeweller), when he was told they were expecting the very first shipment of such cutlery from England.

The old leather upholstered miner's couch that served as Dad's bed ran along the north wall with its head against the west wall. A few feet from the foot of the couch, there stood an old perforated-zinc-sheet meat safe, which provided storage space for much of our food. When not being used for cooking, our oval cast-iron boiler was stored under the table, where it housed our bread and scone supply.

An old wooden form, about five feet long, occupied the space between the wall and the back of the tables, while a number of wooden boxes – mostly kerosene cases – that we used for seating, were usually placed at random in the centre of the room.

Besides being a haven for bush-flies (which in summer still received their daily morning scorch) when no one was in the room, it was also a popular spot for the chooks; this situation caused us no end of bother.

Keith now had several hives of bees, which he kept between the quarry and "Noor" Davies' paddock. Unfortunately, they were within a network of meat ant nests, so when the heavily-laden bees dropped exhausted in front of the hives, they were easy prey for the ants. This problem really worried Auntie Mag. Daily, often for several hours at a time, she would patrol the apiary, continually rescuing bees from the marauding hordes of ants. In spite of her efforts on their behalf, the bees gave her no immunity when it came to stings.

In order to harvest the honey, Keith made a simple, rudimentary extractor from a piece of half-inch pipe, a couple of pieces of secondhand two-by-four-inch timber and a topless 44-gallon drum. The two baskets that held the frames of honeycomb were made from the light timber of old kerosene boxes, and wire netting. It worked reasonably well, but with just a simple handle at the top and no gears, it was difficult to reach the required spin-speed for the centrifugal force to throw the honey out of the honeycomb.

Storage tins for the honey were always in short supply, so often when extracting, a saucepan would be used to store any small quantity that wouldn't fit in the tins and this overflow would be used first. On one such occasion, a large saucepan almost filled with honey and covered only by a small piece of flimsy cheesecloth was left on the table in the deserted kitchen.

On entering the kitchen later, Auntie Mag was confronted by the unexpected sight of our fine proud rooster, completely drained of his usual pomp, and hopelessly bogged to his breast in the deep saucepan of gooey honey. Despite the loss of the valued syrup – which was later fed back to the bees – Auntie Mag, who was normally distressed by the waste of any food, burst into hilarious laughter at the king of the fowlyard's predicament. Everyone around was summoned to witness the rooster's fall from grace, before he was rescued, washed and returned, somewhat bedraggled and humbled, to his harem.

23

Moving On

Some months earlier, at a depth of around 30 feet, Louis and his mate decided to change direction, and began to follow the gold bearing reef by means of a drive (a drive is a horizontal tunnel branching out from the vertical shaft). Evidently their skills had improved, for they were maintaining the required progress in spite of having lost the fallback strategy of extending the shaft skyward.

From time to time Jack and I would go down the mine to see the progress. They would lower me down the mine in the windlass bucket, but with help Jack was able to negotiate the rough makeshift ladders and steps that were cut into the side of the shaft. It was terrifying approaching the edge of the void and manoeuvring with assistance into the bucket. But once I was in the bucket with a tight grip on the attached rope, I had total trust in my oldest brother's hands on the windlass handle. The descent, though exciting, was always scary for me. But once I reached the bottom, it was a different matter.

It was a big adventure entering the drive at the bottom of the shaft and to see, in the light of the steady candle flame, the vein of milky quartz – which they called a lode – that coaxed the miners with its glittering traces of gold, to laboriously follow it further into the hill.

One day, without warning another family set up an even more primitive camp than ours, about 400 yards away on the crest of the hill between our blocks and Louis' mine. We did not encroach on their privacy, nor did they on ours. Nevertheless, we did feel a bit cramped and inconvenienced by them just being there, for it necessitated plotting a curved course to the mine. We soon learned they were another branch of the Marshall family, and it was said that they had 10 children.

Then there was another threat, another mining claim had been pegged perilously close to the one held by Louis and Joey. Their mine was on the very edge of a bush track that ran at right angles to the reef they were working. Now directly opposite, only 20 feet away on the town side of the track, two mates had started a shaft on a claim they had pegged. Being much older and more skilled miners, their shaft progressed rapidly – without the need to build a "fort".

Strangely, that didn't cause any animosity, although there was a hint of indignation when it was discovered that their neighbours had started to drive under the track towards the impressive eminence of the Three Sevens. It was also rumoured that they were getting much more gold than Louis and Joey, which may have been so, although one can never be sure about such matters, for as Mark Twain once wrote, "A miner is a liar with a hole in the ground".

As things turned out it didn't matter much anyway. Louis and his mate were gradually becoming thoroughly disillusioned with mining in general, and after spending the first month or so of 1937 in fruitless toil, they decided their hopes for the Three Sevens would never be realised. Sadly they abandoned the mine and dissolved their partnership. I was particularly saddened by their action; I felt that closing the mine was a further blow to our family's already humble standing.

Their decision gave the other miners a free go: they began to work both mines, and eventually connected the two, deep under the track.

Louis at last accepted that mining had proved not to be the pathway to his prosperity. He immediately obtained a temporary job assisting a recently widowed woman to run her dairy farm in the vicinity of Clunes.

On his return to Maryborough, he again obtained a not terribly rewarding job at Pascoe's dairy.

Meanwhile Keith was getting a bit of work with various members of the Rich family. I never got to know either old Mr Rich or his first name, for my brothers always referred to him by his nickname – "Sticky". He had several sons, most of whom were also involved with bees. I never did quite work out just what the business set-up between the family was, but they did seem to work harmoniously together. As well as being involved with bees, one of "Sticky's" sons, Eddy, made extra use of the apiary truck by collecting cream from the district's scattered dairy farmers for the local butter factory. As it was considered a two-man job, Louis, being big, strong, and healthy was sometimes recruited to assist with the operation. While Louis was doing that job, there was sometimes a spin-off for all of us, in the form of a bit of cream to go with our scones and honey. Because of Louis' busy social life, Eddy found him a bit unreliable, so he enlisted Keith for the job, which unfortunately for us, dried up our cream supply.

Lloyd also tried his hand as an apiarist, mainly with Mr Phillips and his son-in-law Herb, but it was only for a very short time. From the first day, he had a very nasty reaction to bee stings, and with each day on the job the allergy grew worse, until one night after a particularly bad day he came home in a dreadful state. He was swollen virtually all over, and his face was hardly recognisable. Dad was desperately concerned about Lloyd's condition and stayed near all night, to watch over him and attend his needs. Even I realised Dad's concern was justified, and over the long days it took Lloyd to recover, we all were aware of how fortunate he was that the only long-term harm was that it ended his career in the apiary business.

24

The Parson Flaunts His Goodness

By the end of autumn 1937, Keith had finished the quarry bank. With all the difficulties encountered along the way, it was generally accepted that the structure was built in an amazingly short time, and that it was an excellent job. The finished bank was 36 yards long, and at its most massive portion in the centre of the gully, almost 20 feet wide at the base, and over six feet high. The top of the bank was some four or five feet in width. It was a remarkable feat for a lad of Keith's age.

With this major work completed, Keith resumed his equally physically demanding pre-dam task of making mud-bricks. After much discussion and disagreement with Dad concerning the positioning of the building and the nature of the foundations required, he began to build two connecting rooms, each 12 by 14 feet, directly behind our kitchen-shack. Dad was still suffering the back injury so wasn't able to give much assistance and Louis and Lloyd, who had other commitments, only offered spasmodic assistance. Nevertheless, the whole family looked upon the project as a major leap forward.

It was soon discovered that the hot summer days produced the best quality mud bricks; they would dry quickly and were very hard. Even so, it was necessary to protect them from the goats for the first few hours, for the young kids found the closely spaced freshly made bricks an irresistibly attractive dancing stage. In spite of our diligence, many a brick was permanently branded with deep cloven imprints of the playful young goats. But only on rare occasions a brick was damaged beyond repair.

Dad's previous horticulture experience in Gippsland, proved to be of great assistance when he and my three older brothers turned their attention to preparing the site for the dreamt of vegetable garden. With the prevalence of wandering stock, let alone our goats, it would have been futile to start a garden without a secure fence. Louis had accumulated a few pounds from his job on the dairy farm near Clunes, so was able to come good with the 30 shillings required to buy a hundred-yard coil of three foot high wire netting.

After much consideration, it was decided the ideal configuration of the enclosure would be about 15 yards wide and 35 yards long. Such a strip would incorporate not only the best soil below the bank, but also the lowest, which would make it ideal for syphoning water from the dam. Most of the posts for the fence were sorted from the remainder of the firewood block that had been cut out the year before. What's more, the three strands of number-eight fencing wire required to support the wire netting, scarcely reduced the efficiency of the multi-wired fence, around a certain government paddock deep in the bush, from which they were surreptitiously removed.

Then came the enormous job of preparing the ground for the actual garden. They didn't just dig it deep enough for the vegetables: Dad insisted that it be trenched. This operation entailed digging out the clay subsoil to a depth of about two feet, so that lime, lighter soil and leaf mould could be mixed with it to make it more friable. Moderate rain in the earlier half of the year had, to some degree, softened the ground, which over a long dry summer could bake as hard as a brick.

According to local legend, our new garden site had been one of Maryborough's first rubbish dumps. Even if that claim was questionable, the evidence that it had been an early tip was beyond dispute. When we first occupied the blocks, this particular area was littered with a variety of ancient "floating" rubbish, which Dad, Lloyd and Keith later collected to fill in the two 80-foot shafts on our town-side boundary. The garden trenching produced lots of collectibles, which included a number of old coins, some of which were thin copper-based discs about an inch in diameter, with a square hole in the centre surrounded by raised Chinese writing. There were also lots of bottles, most had been broken, and the much-prized greenish-glass alleys (which were known as *bottolos*) from the sealing valves of the early aerated-drink bottles, were there by the score. There were also a considerable number of these bottles – some still intact with the marble and the rubber sealing ring – found at the spot where Keith had excavated the material for the quarry bank. At that time the alley in the bottle was considered more valuable to kids than the now prized entire bottles, so they were quickly broken.

* * *

With my three younger siblings, I was still plodding a popular American evangelistic pathway to salvation, which would bring us all the wonderful things, which I was not conscious of not having. Our leader, the young energetic minister was still a frequent visitor to our humble home, or strictly speaking, the ground around it, still eagerly assisting Dad in his endeavours to reactivate the Goeben Wheel Company, with high expectations of sharing in the wealth they perceived it would bring.

In view of those facts, it's hard to explain the following event. The kindest explanation I can muster is that our minister had a subconscious realisation that had our Saviour performed His great Christian acts in secret, a wonderful enduring faith would never have eventuated. Therefore, he considered that an impelling reason why good works should not be hidden under a bushel.

When Valma and June were summoned from their respective grades and escorted to the Headmaster's office one morning, the question "What have they done?" swept through the minds of their respective classmates, and broke the monotony of schoolwork.

With no hint of explanation, the girls were in a state of apprehension by the time they reached their destination, but that was nothing to the cold dread that clenched their hearts, when they entered the office and were confronted by our friendly parson and his sweet subordinate wife. Surely when their paths crossed so frequently elsewhere, nothing short of a family tragedy would cause this man of God to seek them out at school. But no, thankfully, the good man was simply there on a mission of charity.

Suddenly their trepidation turned to excruciating humiliation, as in the presence of Mr Noonan, the respected but stuffy Headmaster, their eyes were directed to a box of somewhat scungy secondhand clothes – dresses, shoes and basic underwear. With due decorum, the Headmaster and parson left the office, while the minister's wife supervised the girls in trying on the outer clothes, which were then paraded before the parson, to judge the suitability and size of each garment. Thankfully, the suitability of the undergarments was decided by the wife, without the necessity of the girls trying them on.

After the "models" finished the parade, the selected articles were dutifully bundled up by the minister's good lady, and with due reverence, delivered into the hands of my sisters, who – in accordance with our instilled commitment to good manners – despite the humiliation expressed their thanks. Then the girls were instructed to return to their classes, while the minister remained to illuminate Mr Noonan's office with the glow of his goodness. Valma immediately distanced herself from the humiliating parcel by thrusting it into June's care. June, always ashamed and oversensitive about our family's poverty, was distraught at the impending humiliation of taking the hated parcel back to her classroom, where it would cause no end of inquisitive speculation. Such was her anguish that it exceeded the possible adverse consequences of disobeying the Headmaster's order to return directly to her grade.

The door of Mr Noonan's office was little more than the width of the bell-tower base from the school's front door, which led into the sizeable fenced school garden. Except when rostered grades were escorted through it to spend an hour or so of happy diversion tending the garden, students were strictly forbidden to use this entrance, and were not even permitted to step into the garden unsupervised. It was therefore with considerable courage, born of desperation, June chose that means of escape. With her long legs, scaling the garden's gateless back fence was of little hindrance before her scurried flight across the gravelled playground to the school's back fence, where she found a nook to hide the bundle, which she knew she could furtively retrieve on our way home for dinner.

Although some of the other kids at school were worse off for clothes than my sisters, it seemed strange that they were not summoned to try on the remaining garments. But who am I to question who should have been chosen?

Dad was really upset about the public humiliation of the girls, and mentioned that he'd have a few words with his reverend friend about the matter. I never heard any details of that discussion, but Dad was greatly disappointed by our parson's sanctimonious airing of his benevolence. Dad's forgiving nature again prevailed and their congenial association continued to flourish.

A considerable time after that event, in an atmosphere of mystery, Dad's parson friend quietly left the town for a distant parish. Perhaps Keith's nickname for him was apt, for years later, a Melbourne newspaper reported that in a distant town he was convicted of defrauding a lonely old parishioner.

* * *

During the warmer months, our bed had shed its wagga, newspaper and most of the old overcoats. Most nights the lightest overcoat was more than enough, and on really hot nights the lightest garment of any description that would preserve our dignity by extending the length of our oversized flannels, was all we desired. As the cooler weather approached, we would gradually reassemble the assortment of fabric that constituted our winter beds. It was only years later I realised that our bed was a sign of deprivation. At the time we accepted it without complaint.

Around the middle of the year, a wave of anticipation swept through the community with news that the arrival of the long-awaited State Electricity Commission power to our town was imminent. It wasn't that an electricity supply would be new to Maryborough. In 1923, the Maryborough Knitting Mill installed generating equipment and the town's first power supply line, but the arrival of the SEC was seen as a huge step forward.

The construction of the powerlines had passed through Carisbrook, and was quickly progressing along the last four miles to Maryborough. Many locals – including my eldest brothers – who had seen the construction, were aghast at the size and uniformity of the poles and exclaimed how they dwarfed anything our local forests could produce. Unlike the rest of us, Dad wasn't the least surprised by the description of the poles. He simply said "They'd be from Gippsland," but he was enthusiastic about the ingenious scheme to supply the whole of Victoria with electricity from the enormous brown-coal fields of Yallourn, and he praised Sir John Monash for his great vision.

Jack and I were very keen to see these massive poles and construction work, so Keith offered to take us to see them. At the first opportunity, the three of us set off with our faithful dog Caesar, down the long bush gully below the cemetery, for the two-mile walk to the settlement of Flagstaff, where we believed work on the line was in progress. To me the sight was awesome: instead of the stunted, often misshapen poles that supported our local electrical system, these SEC poles were huge and virtually identical. Each pole had been crafted by skilled adze-men into a ten-sided column of artistic perfection. As well as being astounded by the height of the poles, we were also aghast at the distance between them and by the extended insulators that anchored the stout cables. It was indeed an amazing sight for a country kid of that era. Although that power and the easy living it could bring was so close, it would take another 16 years to reach our house, eventually completed on the edge of the quarry.

* * *

By the end of winter, the good rains over the preceding months had filled the enlarged quarry. We all felt proud, and a little smug about the fine body of water. Someone discovered that by standing in a particular spot on the high cliff near the kitchen where both ends of the long boomerang shaped lake were obscured, it wasn't hard to imagine you were standing on the bend of a beautiful tree flanked river. Of course, it was necessary to overlook the fact that a river lined with red ironbarks would be a bit of an oddity, but that little problem never aborted my flights of fancy to some exotic riverland every time I stood at that enchanted spot.

The quarry being full also stimulated our imaginations into conjuring up new forms of amusement. We soon noticed that when there was a heavy frost, a large sheet of thickish ice formed over its back portion. This stirred memories of the stories we knew about skating on frozen lakes in foreign parts and what fun it was – that is, when you weren't being chased by a pack of bloodthirsty wolves. Though we weren't stupid enough to think of venturing onto the ice ourselves, it did seem a waste not to let something enjoy the fun. Our chooks were the obvious choice.

They were an interesting lot. Over numerous generations, the breeds had been thoroughly blended, but because most of their descendants inherited more prominent aspects of one particular breed, this was enough for Auntie Mag and at least us kids to classify them into that category. The few that were unable to display any particular affiliation were conveniently dismissed as cross-breeds. This enabled us – with considerable pride – to inform friends and acquaintances that we had three different breeds of chooks. We also possessed a few bantams.

Auntie Mag usually fed the chooks, but on these frosty mornings, she was often relieved of the job by Lloyd and/or us younger kids. We discovered that by strategically spilling a frugal trail of wheat in front of the hungry chooks, we could lead them all the way to the edge of the quarry, and then tempt them to eat their morning meal off the ice-sheet. Although we didn't dare tell Dad or Auntie Mag about our new-found entertainment, we thought it was hilarious watching them in a state of confusion as they slithered about like novice skaters, and at times with a desperate flurry of wing-beats, escaped the crumbling ice beneath their feet. It must have had a profound effect on egg production.

With September came the frogs, and by Jack's birthday on the sixteenth, the sound of their croaking from the quarry at night was loud and continuous. By far the most dominant were banjo frogs, which like most people around here, we called bullfrogs. Another large species, which was quite plentiful, was locally known as "the big green frog". I later learned it was the growling grass frog. We particularly loved this frog's distinctive, long, quivering calls: it was undoubtedly our favourite frog.

Added to the calls of those two, were the voices of several smaller species. Of these the most outstanding was the ear-splitting shrill from the myriad of what I now know as Ewing's Tree Frog. Blended together their voices created a timeless symphony, that could coax my fertile imagination back to the mystic swamps – which my older brothers had so graphically described – of giant ferns and mosses, where dragonflies a yard across skimmed the water amid a variety of lumbering dinosaurs.

In the years that followed, it became our expectation that each year the frogs would again gather to celebrate Jack's birthday – and they seldom let us down.

25

Euphoria and Fear

Our day-old *Age* continued to be our window on the world. Although I had by no means advanced to reading the news portion of the newspaper, I could not help hearing my elders discussing the terrifying details of the civil war that had broken out in Spain and the more pessimistic predicting it could lead to a second world war. Even though I didn't have a clue about where Spain was, or what the war was about, I was horrified by the talk. Fortunately, on being told it was all a long way away, once the talk ceased, in the security of my family and happy home in the bush, the horror of those events quickly faded to an intermittent ghost.

Dad had never discouraged us youngsters from partaking in any discussions, which covered topics from family matters, local and world affairs, to philosophising about life and the universe. The views on the universe were mainly based on a couple of well-worn books that had come into our possession, written by the popular English physicist Sir James Jeans. At times our opinions must have been unusual or amusing, yet we were never scoffed at or ridiculed.

As far back as I could remember, long before I could comprehend it, politics and world affairs were a major topic of the conversation at our place. Dad never missed an opportunity to passionately lecture his offspring – or for that matter, anyone else he could "corner" to listen or argue with – on these subjects. Considering that, I would have been particularly dumb, even at my tender years, if I had not started to get a slight inkling of how Australia was governed. For instance, Dad had told us that the Prime Minister was the "head man" and that he received a salary of four thousand pounds a year, which seemed outrageously generous to me. I was also familiar with the names of a few prominent politicians of that time and the past.

Dad always seemed proud to inform people he had never belonged to a political party. However, his strong sense of the social injustice that he said divided the Australian population so cruelly, insisted that he could be nothing but a socialist at heart. Frequently Dad would passionately instil into us the evils of "foreign banks" and the "financial system". He claimed that those institutions were responsible for the situation where, in a land of plenty like Australia, food was literally being destroyed while people starved. He insisted there was a shortage of nothing but the means of exchange – money.

* * *

1937 seemed to be a year of extraordinary events. Early in the year, the disappearance of an airliner on a flight between the vague names of Brisbane and Sydney, caused wide concern that is hard to imagine in today's hardened society. As the fruitless search, with the most aircraft ever involved in such a venture in Australia, continued over many days, Dad repeatedly reminisced about another airliner, the *Southern Cloud*, which had disappeared without trace a few years before. After a week, there seemed little doubt that this would be a similar case.

Then several days later, after the search had been more or less abandoned, a wave of astonishment rocked the nation. It was reported that a bushman from a remote property in Queensland's McPherson Ranges, acting on his profound knowledge of the mountains, and thoughts of the plane's possible flight path, decided to spend a few days on a personal search. After negotiating many miles of hazardous mountain terrain and near impenetrable jungle, on meagre rations, he miraculously came across the dreadful scene of the plane's wreckage, and the terrible plight of two survivors amid the dead. But it wasn't until many years later, when I read that bushman's account of the event in his book, *Green Mountains*, and visited the area, that I fully appreciated the bushmanship and endurance of that remarkable man – Bernard O'Reilly.

Then, only a few months later, the horrifying news of another air disaster encircled the globe when the huge German zeppelin, the *Hindenburg*, exploded while preparing to dock at an airfield in

America. The disaster caused much discussion and speculation as to whether the death of the 36 people was really by accident.

* * *

By the spring of 1937, it seemed that we had begun the long slow climb out of our abyss. Looking back, it seems that our tumble into the pit of financial despair bottomed out around Christmas 1936. It wasn't that things were much better, but Keith had almost given away the fruitless job of gold prospecting, and was doing part-time work helping Eddy Rich with his cream-collecting contract with the local butter factory. He was also getting a bit of work with Eddy and his brother Claude on the bees and getting the odd day with another of the town's beekeepers. Those employers were also finding the going tough, so the pay was pretty poor.

For some time Louis had been working for a minimal wage at Pascoe's dairy, but suddenly, much to the family's distress, in early spring he decided to leave town and try his luck in Melbourne. I gathered that Dad had given Louis a few contact names, and one of them who had known Dad in more prosperous times, out of loyalty, gave my brother a job in his small engineering works.

Lloyd was also in luck. Auntie Annie's son Burnie Patten, who owned a dairy, offered him a job doing a milk round. Although this was a seven-day-a-week job, each delivery run only occupied a few hours each morning, so he was still able to continue his gold-seeking activities with Harry Williamson, but that seldom added much to his regular wage. Soon after, our cousin asked Lloyd if he would also do the evening round, for fifteen shillings a week with full board. Lloyd accepted the offer, even though it would mean he would no longer be able to continue his prospecting adventures with unworldly but lovable Harry.

* * *

Another thing that bucked our spirits was the spring planting of the first seeds in our new vegetable garden. Dad really let his head go, for cheap as they were, I was surprised we could afford such a variety. The whole family joined in to attend to the watering and weeding as the plants progressed at a speed beyond our wildest expectations. Within just a few weeks we were relishing tasty sandwiches – mostly made from pan scone – of soft beef fat with radish or mustard and cress.

Our food was still mainly humble, but there always seemed to be enough to banish our hunger and the importance of pan scones and pancakes in our daily diet had not diminished in the slightest. Except when the weather was very nasty, there was seldom a day when Auntie Mag did not spend time over the big arch-handled frying pan on the stove, producing the choice morsels just slightly slower than they were consumed.

Our slightly improved circumstances allowed Auntie Mag, on occasions, to again bake things that I could remember us having before we moved to the bush. The most appreciated were the big dried-fruit buns that she called "dripping buns". I thought they were delicious although she always explained, "They're not as good as the ones we made at home: Grandma always used butter".

As the years passed and we became more affluent, those buns became regular and popular accompaniments to our cups of tea. In time those buns also became popular with both relations and friends and were looked upon as a symbol of Auntie Mag's cooking prowess. Years later, when the next generation of our family came on the scene, the buns were no less appreciated and, even though by then our Aunt had followed Grandma's example and was making them with butter, they were still called, somewhat affectionately, "Auntie Mag's Dripping Buns". Anzac buns – made with dripping and rolled oats – became another rediscovered delight.

* * *

As November progressed, there was scarcely a cloud in the sky, and our ever-growing smugness about the thriving garden, was enhanced by the knowledge that the quarry could supply all the water it needed. In those early days, the quarry water was too muddy for washing clothes or ourselves, so we still depended on the limited supply from the sandstone walled "spring".

As this month closed, a threatening cloud of another kind quickly dulled our euphoria. An epidemic of infantile paralysis – now known as poliomyelitis – was sweeping Victoria and isolated as Maryborough was, the first case here was confirmed in early December. When it came to the perceived welfare of his kids, Dad displayed a fearless disregard for the law, and forthwith decided to keep us home from school. This time the authorities were not far behind, and they quickly decided to close the schools and to begin the Christmas holidays early.

Dad forbade us young ones from going into the town, but that didn't bother us much: we always preferred to spend our recreation time in the bush. We were a bit disappointed though, about not being able to see what was reported to be a fascinating animated display of electrically-operated model animals in the large windows of the newly-opened SEC office. Fortunately, the display outlasted the infantile paralysis outbreak, so we were able to witness this marvel of the 1930s.

As the warm days of summer began to dry the soil of our vegetable garden, it became something of a family social gathering each evening, as we all gathered to water the precious plants by means of a variety of containers. Dad had a bit of an obsession about children, or even young adults, carrying heavy loads, ". . . while your bones are soft". For that reason, I was restricted to using two seven pound jam tins with wire handles and when my older siblings filled their four gallon kerosene-tin buckets or other large containers too full, they would be unfailingly rebuked with his homespun philosophy. "Only lazy people try to carry too much at a time."

These watering sessions soon became the ideal venue for pooling the various snippets of information that members of the family had gathered during the day. At this particular time – as would be expected – the latest news on the situation with the infantile paralysis outbreak was the main item, and in particular, the latest on its development in our town. Everyone was worried, and like me found it hard to clear the mind of the frightening threat to our wellbeing.

In spite of that, I think we were all still looking forward to Christmas, and an added joy was that Louis had returned home. I have often wondered over the years if the epidemic had anything to do with his return at that time.

I don't think our feelings – a mixture of euphoria and fear – could be more graphically portrayed than in a surviving letter, written by Auntie Mag to her sister Auntie Liz. (Auntie Mag always made a verbatim copy of any letters she wrote and these were always kept.)

Maryborough
21/12/37

Dear Liz

I have been going to write for some time and as Valma has written, I will write a few lines and put it in with hers. We had a nice fall of rain recently, which came at a good time to save carting water for washing, (We get our drinking water over at Hills) so I will have plenty for a few weeks again. It is only two months or a little over since we started the garden & it is wonderful how the vegetables have grown, we have been using lettuce, onions, radish, silver beet, & mustard & cress for some time now. The peas & French-beans are just ready for picking, so we will have our own vegetables for Xmas this year. We also have growing, Tomatoes, Parsnips, Carrots, Sweet Corn, Beetroot, Potatoes, Pumpkins, Marrows, Rock Melons, Jam Melons, Squash, Mint & Parsley.

Isn't the Infantile Paralysis a terrible disease, & now that it is in the town & surrounding districts, I can't help worrying a little, especially when any of the children show signs of being sick.

One Sunday a few weeks ago, the children took their dinner into their tent & sat on the bed to eat it, and in the middle of it, they noticed a hen under the bed fighting with a snake.

Jack ran for Tom & after the snake dodged him around the tree at the back of the tent, he managed to kill it.

Andrew has been living at Alice's this good while, he has taken an interest in gardening he has put in some vegetables at Alice's, Tom went down and did some digging for him.

Sis and Maud Severino are also at Alice's. They are working at the knitting-mill & are renting Alice's outside kitchen. (It was actually a very basic flat.)

The letter then goes into several paragraphs giving respective details concerning the deaths of several old Evansford identities; then continues – with a hint of hurt and indignation – with a paragraph about a favourite cousin she had not seen for many years:

Jim Adair was over from the West a few months ago, I believe he looks well, he wanted to come and see me, but they put him off.

The remainder of the letter is of little consequence.

Auntie Alice and Uncle Andrew – Auntie Mag's siblings – had stayed on at the old home in Evansford after Uncle Will married in 1934. However, right from the start, Alice and Mona – as Auntie Mag put it – "couldn't get on", mainly, I gathered, because Auntie Alice was a bigoted Presbyterian, and Auntie Mona was a Roman Catholic. The situation quickly became intolerable, and after a year or so, Alice bought a small weatherboard house, about two miles from us on the other side of Maryborough. Later, Uncle Andrew, who suffered constantly from severe eczema, which was exacerbated by him working among the allergens on the farm, was granted an invalid pension. This allowed him to move into the more eczema friendly environment of Maryborough, where his sister Alice was happy to accept him as a boarder.

Since then, Uncle Andrew's visits had become increasingly frequent until now, weather permitting, they were virtually on a daily basis. We all liked quiet, inoffensive, unworldly Uncle Andrew, who even us younger ones could joke with, and occasionally tease. He always seemed to have news of the scattered members of the McCully clan, which was of keen interest to Auntie Mag. We all looked forward to his visits.

Once again I was enchanted by the magic of Christmas. Once again it was a busy morning, gathering and placing suckers around the camp, and preparing the dinner. Unlike the previous year, our 1937 Christmas would again be celebrated with the traditional cake and pudding.

Auntie Mag's letter's forecast of having our own peas and beans for Christmas dinner was in fact an understatement. There were also tasty tender thinnings from the carrot beds, and smallish but delicious waxy new potatoes, that had been bandicooted somewhat prematurely from the plants. Likewise, Christmas tea was enhanced by a variety of salad vegetables the likes of which I had never partaken of before. Added to the variety that Auntie Mag had mentioned in her letter to Auntie Liz, was tender young beetroot pickled in vinegar and sugar, which like the potatoes, had been pulled before maturity for this special day. We were all indeed proud of our garden's tasty and bountiful produce and there was a promise of more to come. Half a dozen or more rounded bed-mounds were blanketed by the healthy big leaves of three types of pumpkins, Turks Caps, Triambles and Queensland Blues, all showing promise of a large crop as we approached autumn. On a few smaller mounds, rock melon plants thrived and after the exuberant descriptions from my elders of their delicious fruit, I eagerly anticipated a new taste thrill.

26

Time On Our Hands

Auntie Tot with an entourage of relations paid us a visit over the Christmas period.

When our relations arrived on this occasion, we were literally caught in the act of swimming and frolicking in the quarry's muddy duck-fertilised water. Scandalised, our relations stood atop the quarry face near the "kitchen", while Auntie Tot expressed her disgust at our behaviour. She berated Dad for allowing us to swim in the unhygienic water and wrongly – though perhaps not entirely unjustifiably – predicted that we would contract virtually every pestilence short of the bubonic plague. Had her predictions been correct, the threat from the infantile paralysis epidemic would have been insignificant.

With not the slightest supporting evidence, unless our poverty was damning, Auntie Tot announced that my sisters ". . . will come to no good and end up on the streets" and that us boys ". . . will end up in gaol". Our formidable aunt's predictions never came to pass.

Once again the longing to see Yvonne was unfulfilled. But Auntie Tot insisted my sister's every whim was taken care of, and how happy she was with her family. I wondered if she was: surely she wanted to see us as much as we longed to see her?

There was never any acknowledgment from Auntie Tot of my family's earnest endeavours to drag ourselves out of our economic deprivation; instead the condemnation of my father and older brothers continued, as did the futile pressure on Auntie Mag to leave us.

Dad put few restrictions on our swimming with the ducks, but he would only allow us to go swimming while he was at home and never before two hours after a meal, for it was generally accepted that that time slot was very conducive to bringing on the cramps.

* * *

Again faithful Auntie Annie and Sis paid us their customary visit to deliver the cake Auntie Annie had made to mark and brighten the occasion of my eighth birthday. In this, the first week of January, the number of infantile paralysis cases in our town had grown to more than a dozen, and concern about its ominous threat occupied much of the afternoon's conversation.

As summer progressed, our vegetable garden became more bountiful than we had dared hope. I had never known such an abundance or variety. They lifted my enjoyment of dinner to new heights, and the delicious salad vegetables for tea on those hot nights, gave gastronomic delight beyond my wildest dreams. We even had more than we needed ourselves, so we were able to pass on some of the excess to others.

Uncle Andrew – who even in the heat of summer walked almost daily the four-mile return journey to visit us – greatly admired our extensive garden and praised the quality of its produce. However, while he would gratefully accept offerings of peas, beans, pumpkin, melons, marrows, tomatoes and all the leafy greens, he would awkwardly decline the offer of any root vegetables – beetroot, carrots, parsnips, potatoes, onions, radishes, etc. This strange rejection of produce that we knew he really liked, caused much conjecture among my elders, but no one came even close to the reason why he declined the offerings. It was not until many months later, that he confessed the reason.

As stated earlier, our garden was on the site of an early rubbish tip, and the soil in which the vegetables grew was liberally littered with broken glass. Our cautious uncle instantly observed that fact on his first visit to the garden. Having had first-hand knowledge of the terrible sufferings of dogs that had been callously "poisoned" by bait impregnated with ground glass, he perceived there could be a similar risk with our root vegetables, and no one could convince him otherwise.

* * *

By now, Lloyd's salubrious brick-floored tent, where our recently returned stately, tall, black "His Master's Voice" gramophone was installed, had become the most desirable location in our camp. Although normally only a chook game enough to tackle a snake would dare risk the consequences of entering his tent, lately Lloyd's benevolent tolerance of our constant invasion of his private domain seemed somewhat out of character. The main attraction of Lloyd's tent was of course the gramophone. I suspect that it was the reason for Lloyd's new tolerance towards us, to act otherwise could have jeopardised the prestige of having the gramophone under his "roof". However, just to be on the safe side, we always tried to closely adhere to his strict protocol of behaviour during our visits. Occasionally some minuscule infringement would kindle his wrath.

We still had a good collection of the brittle 78-rpm records of the 1920s, which I gathered were purchased by Mum during our family's more affluent times. These records were a varied lot, ranging from *Building the Chicken-house* – a one man sketch occupying both sides of the record, which although we played it regularly never ceased to tickle our imaginations – to the majestic voices of Melba and Caruso. Between those extremes, was a variety of songs and music that could conjure up a smorgasbord of human emotions.

Dad revered the voices of Caruso and Dame Nellie Melba. He had seen Melba perform in Melbourne, and whenever her name was mentioned, he would eulogise about the magnificence of her performance, and when I listened to our recording of her singing *Home Sweet Home*, I tried to imagine how wonderful it must have been to actually see her sing.

There was a heart-wrenching series of records concerning prisoners – most victims of injustice, of course – and the terrible deprivations and conditions of life in gaol. There were also a number of recordings where the male singers extravagantly expressed love for their mother. I was very moved by both those subjects, with the former it was the thought of being deprived of my loved ones and the beauties of nature, with the latter it was an overwhelming feeling of guilt.

There were many other songs, some happy, some sad. There were hymns; songs of love and songs of death. The latter included *The Letter Edged in Black*. We were a bit reluctant to play that one. Sid Murray claimed it was an omen of bad luck and even went as far as saying that every time he heard it, someone close to him died. Although it had never had those disastrous consequences for any member of my family, there was always an anxious few days after someone dared to play this song, which otherwise could have been something of a favourite among us youngsters.

Contrary to what one might expect, the saddening effect of the mournful songs only lasted for the duration of their playing and in no way dimmed the usual happy atmosphere within our camp. Perhaps the tragic plight of the suffering souls in those "open-heart" songs made us realise just how fortunate we really were.

There were also symphony orchestras, pipe and brass bands, and a particularly stirring recording of *Land of Hope and Glory* on one side and *The Soldiers Chorus* on the other side. The label proudly boasted that they were "Performed by a Chorus of 2000 voices". In sharp contrast to *The Soldiers Chorus*, *The Dream of the Big Parade* was a graphic portrayal of the horror of war. This song subtly, yet boldly, censured the then popular belief that the glorification of war was synonymous with patriotism. Surely it must have been a forerunner to the popular protest-songs of a later generation.

But my favourite song by far was *When the Lovebird Leaves its Nest*, which went:

When the lovebird leaves her nest,
Does she fly to the east or the west?
And when she flies above me,
Does she love me, as she used to do?
Is she winking, is she blinking,
At somebody new?
When the lovebird leaves . . .

At the time I was quite sure the subject of that song was ornithological, and didn't even dream that it could be the verbalisation of a rejected human male's pondering. But by the time I started to wonder if the song was really about budgerigars, it had instilled in me a lifelong interest in avifauna.

We also got mixed up about another record called *In the Garden*. We thought it was the expression of the ecstasy a young woman felt while strolling in the garden with her beau Andy. Joining in the chorus, we would sing along with our interpretation of the words:

Andy walks with me,
Andy talks with me,
Andy tells me I am his own,
And the joy we share as we tarry there,
No other has ever known.

Perhaps if the singer had not slurred the words, which were actually –

And He walks with me,
And He talks with me,
And He tells me I am his own,
And the . . .

then maybe we would have realised it was a hymn in praise of God, not a song about a swain called Andy. It would have at least cleared up our perceived contradiction of the opening lines of the song: "I walked in the garden alone" – so how could she have been with Andy?

Many of these brittle old 78-rpm records still remain with members of my family, and are tangible symbols of my fond memories. Recently, I heard again the crackling emanations from their tortured grooves, and was wafted back through the long years to those wonderful happy hours we spent in Lloyd's tent.

Playing the gramophone was always accompanied by a touch of trepidation, for there was always a fear that the spring would break. To the point of monotony, we were regularly warned not to overwind the machine. As a result we usually did the opposite, so at intervals over the record's three minute duration, a decrease in the revolutions would send the performance spinning towards the base end of the scale before it would be revived by a few hasty turns of the winding handle.

On a few occasions the spring did break, but thankfully, not when we were using it. Luckily, the end of the springs appeared to be their weakest part, for that was where they usually broke, so it was possible for someone to fashion a new end. Nevertheless, when the spring did break, it was usually some time before anyone could muster the fortitude to dismantle the machine and evaluate the damage which thankfully, was never as serious as it could have been. When the spring was broken, with a little extra effort we could still access the contents of the recordings. We would achieve this by placing a finger near the centre of the record and manually spinning the turntable. Doing this actually gave us extra entertainment, for we found that by varying the speed we could change baritones into sopranos and vice versa.

Gramophone needles were another problem for a while. We always used "His Master's Voice" needles, even though they were the most expensive, which supports my suspicion that in spite of our social degradation, there was still a hint of latent snobbery in my kin.

The needles came in a delightful little tin with rounded corners and an over-fitting hinged lid, which was beautifully ornate with an illustration of the company's logo – a sitting terrier dog, named Nipper, with his ear tilted to the large horn of an Edison phonograph.

I visualise the tins as being about $1\frac{1}{4}$ x $1\frac{1}{2}$ inches and about $\frac{3}{4}$ of an inch deep. Each tin contained 100 needles and they cost the exorbitant price of one shilling and three pence. Those golden-varnished tins issued the warning that to avoid damage to the records, each needle was to be used only once. Indeed after being used once the points of the needles showed considerable signs of wear, and there was no doubt that to continue to use them in that condition would soon have gouged and distorted the record's track. However, if we had had to adhere to that dictum, financial reality would have deprived us of this culturally uplifting entertainment. My family was never found wanting when it came to innovation, so thanks to a piece of a broken oilstone, the problem was soon solved. Even I soon learned the art of turning a needle while dragging it across the oilstone at the appropriate angle to rejuvenate the point. Although the manufacturers may not have approved of the new point's geometry, it virtually ended the need to buy new needles, and they didn't seem to damage the records.

With lots of time on our hands, as the Christmas holidays extended into the early months of 1938 because of the infantile paralysis epidemic, the gramophone was a welcome supplement to our other recreations of bush wandering; playing tipcat, swimming, cricket, alleys, snakes and ladders and a wide variety of card games.

Even though Dad was always justifiably concerned about the high risk of eye and other injuries from this inherently dangerous game, tipcat was my family's most popular "field-game". All members of our family except Dad and Auntie Mag would readily participate. I consistently enjoyed playing this game, for it was the only one in which I had any chance of competing with my siblings. In spite of the danger associated with this game, thanks to the whims of "lady luck" none of us received any injury of consequence. Tipcat was not only popular with my family: it was possibly the most played outdoor game among the downtrodden families of our district and far beyond. The main reason for its wide popularity was almost certainly due to the low cost of the equipment required. No more than an old broom-handle and a sharp knife were required to produce the essential components. The cat consisted of a short piece of broom-handle – usually about four inches long – whittled to a pencil-like point at both ends. The tip was also a piece of broom-handle, mostly about two feet six inches long, with a similar point to the cat at one end. The rules of this game were quite intricate and scoring complicated. Put simply, the basic requirement was to tap the cat at either end to make it rise into the air, then hitting it as far as possible with the body of the tip.

Another popular competitive "sport" with the neighbourhood youths and kids, was skimming the abundant slate flakes from the reef mines across the surface of a suitable expanse of water. These competitions were always unplanned; they would spontaneously develop whenever a group of potential competitors found themselves on the edge of a suitable dam. The aim of this contest was to see who could skim the flat piece of slate the furthest and achieve the most skips, before it sank. A few years later Jack and I played a more difficult version of this game, which involved skipping rounded quartz stones, fired from our shanghais across the water, in the manner of Barnes Wallis' bouncing bombs that destroyed the German dams during WWII.

Keith, who was always making things, would produce "longbows" and a score or so of arrows. The bows were hewn from suitable ironbark saplings or the springier stems of golden wattles. To form the bow the flexible sticks were then strung with a length of fine steel cable that had been salvaged from the long gone "production line" of Dad's Goeben Wheel factory. The arrows were split from the deal of kerosene or fruit cases. After being rounded with a sharp knife, each shaft had three dressed tail feathers from our chooks bound to one end with cotton, and sealed with bees' wax. At the other end of the shafts, he fitted a potentially lethal point, fashioned from pieces of galvanised iron. Looking back, I cannot understand why Dad allowed us to play with such dangerous equipment, with nothing more than repeated warnings to be careful with them, yet he would be outraged by any of us leaving a shovel turned face up on the ground, or if we carried an axe incorrectly. Nevertheless, the target tournaments we had with these weapons were highly entertaining – and injury-free.

My brothers also created a source of amusement in the park reserve. Some halfway up the hill between our camp and the new rubbish tip, stood an ironbark tree. Its very long limbless trunk and mop-like crown made it look something of a freak among its more normal multi-branched and bushier kin. Evidently, the simple fact of this tree being there was a challenge for my brothers to put it to some use. The upshot was the establishing of a "swing-tree".

There was always plenty of ropes around our place. As far back as I could remember, one of the most popular creative activities of my brothers, was manufacturing ropes of various sizes, from hay-band. Discarded hay-bands were always freely available from either of the two hay and corn stores in the town. These bands held the sheaves of hay together, and were removed before the hay was cut into chaff. The bands were about a yard long, and consisted of multi-hemp fibres, rather loosely held together in a single ply twist. As every hay-band contained a knot, it was desirable to use only the bands that had been cut near it. Because the hay-bands had to be tied together, often in lengths of hundreds of yards, as the first step in making a rope, the finished product was a very knotty affair.

Once sufficient lengths were tied together to produce the desired strength and length and thickness of rope, it was doubled and one end was tied to a suitable anchorage. Then a device made from a length of strong fencing wire, with a hook at one end and a crank handle at the other, with a single cotton reel as a hand-held bearing mid way, was attached to the other end of the doubled twine. Then the long tedious winding process commenced. Having formulated plans for the swing tree, the manufacture of a very stout rope well over thirty feet long began. The thicker the rope, the knottier it became, which in the case of the rope for the swing tree was a distinct advantage, for it enhanced the ease to obtain a firm grip.

A couple of years later, Jack made a major advancement in the production of our hay-band ropes: he hit on the idea of plaiting the hay-band, instead of just tying the strands together for the initial twist. Although this entailed a lot more work, it produced a much higher quality rope, with the complete absence of knots.

As soon as the rope was completed, Keith climbed the tree and securely attached it to the first branches some thirty feet from the ground. The ground around the tree had a considerable slope, which was paramount in making the swing the outstanding success that it was. The idea was to hold the rope as far out from the tree trunk as possible on the high side of the hill, then to put every ounce of effort one could, into a short sharp sprint, before lifting the legs off the ground. My older siblings and most of our friends soon became skilled at this activity, and could "fly" around the tree several times until the rope was fully wound around the trunk. The swing gave enjoyment to all comers for many years, and during its existence wore out quite a few ropes. The distinctive tree still stands, scarcely changed.

We also found time to engage in more passive pastimes. Often we would make whips from homemade rope and would have whip-cracking competitions. Bullroarers and boomerangs, both Aboriginal inventions, were a very popular toy among the youngsters of my generation. While any similar piece of wood could be used for a bull-roarer, the one-foot wooden school rulers were ideal. All that they required was a small hole inserted near one end, to which a length of string was attached. By spinning them around one's head, it was easy to produce a loud wavering roar. The fortunate thing about using our school rulers was that by removing the string, they could be again used for their intended purpose. Boomerangs were quickly made whenever someone managed to find a scrap of three-ply sheet big enough to cut and shape them from. Making and flying kites was also popular with us. There was never any trouble obtaining the sticks for the cross, newspaper to cover it, or flour paste to stick it on and old rags for the tail, but finding the few pence to buy a ball of string was always a problem.

* * *

Our older brothers Keith and Lloyd had somehow obtained two 44-gallon petrol drums, which they had lashed together to form a raft. They had also scrounged enough secondhand boards to cover the top to form an acceptable seat for those who "sailed" her. This decking was especially appreciated on hot days, when the drums got hot enough to burn the skin. For a short time this craft seemed safe and reliable as with great pride we lumberingly paddled or punted it to every extreme of our water-playground. However, it wasn't long before inherent design shortcomings became apparent. The worst defect was that when under the load of several bodies shuffling to stay aboard with a tolerable degree of comfort, without warning the drums would suddenly do a complete flip that spilled its load into the murky water. After several of those uncomfortable and potentially-dangerous events, the raft's designers saw the need for structural alterations.

Without much argument, it was decided that the easiest remedy would be to fit the craft with an outrigger. This was made by wiring two four-gallon kerosene tins at one end of a couple of bush-spars which had their other end securely wired to the body of the craft. With this addition, all considered our craft achieved the desired degree of "seaworthiness". When there wasn't much demand for leisure cruising, it served as a desirable platform on which to relax. Sadly it was also Lloyd's preferred summer retreat to read his Westerns, so because of his higher pecking order, we kids were not afforded many opportunities to enjoy this much-desired relaxing pastime.

Valma, June, Jack and I were now responsible for milking the goats each morning and night. But at times when due to dry conditions and lack of food conducive to milk production, or when Auntie Mag made something that drastically depleted our milk supply, we would often have to round up a goat prematurely to squeeze out a few stopgap drops. One day around afternoon teatime, while we were engrossed in aquatic frolics, Lloyd appeared at the top of the quarry face and informed us "There's no milk! And it's cup-a-tea-time". The news that Lloyd had so kindly passed on to us, hardly registered, as we continued our activities.

After a short time Lloyd again appeared and again gave the news headlines, "There's no milk!" We nonchalantly accepted the confirmation of his earlier report, and continued with the pastime we considered was most fitting for such a hot day. From a strictly legal aspect, Lloyd, being the purchaser of the flock's ancestors, would also be the owner of all their descendants. Notwithstanding that fact, apart from assisting in the construction of the goat house, his association with them had always been somewhat estranged. I cannot remember him ever trying to milk them, and if he had tried, it was obvious that his endeavours were fruitless. Apparently the news of us not having any milk was of more significance to Lloyd than it was to us, for he persisted. Finally he got through to us what we had chosen to overlook – he required us to leave our recreation to scour the scorching, glistening quartz-strewn hills for the goats; catch a milker and prematurely strip her meagre lactation.

Our ensuing backchat soon conveyed to Lloyd our reluctance to do his bidding and he became enraged at our blatant rebellion. Suddenly he was at the water edge, and then with a determination to put down the mutiny that would have been worthy of Captain Bligh of the *Bounty*, he launched himself fully clothed into the water. Then in the manner of a killer whale among baby seals, he was in our midst. Three of us were lucky and managed to flee the pond, but whether by Lloyd's design, or just by chance, Jack fell victim to his rage. With great alarm, we watched as Jack was roughly ducked several times beneath the waves. Jack was one who always hid his emotions, so we never knew just how traumatic the event had been for him, but two results were undisputed, Lloyd did enjoy his cup of white tea that afternoon, and the occasion strengthened our quartet's alliance against Lloyd's persistent tormenting and bullying.

One of Lloyd's favourite torments was to spin me around until I was thoroughly giddy, then gleefully watch me stagger and grope as I felt the ground violently tilt and sway. Another of his favourite teases was to hold me around the waist and swing me, screaming with terror, over the high quarry wall. His unusual ability of being able to turn his eyelids inside-out to produce a hideous red-eyed visage was a particularly potent element of his tormenting kit, which never failed to make his younger siblings squirm with horror. His verbal tormenting was also persistent – especially for June and me.

After strict instructions concerning their potential danger, and the need to be frugal with their use, at the age of eight, Dad entrusted me to carry a box of matches. I suspect that after he considered the dangers and the advantages of doing so under our primitive living conditions and the scarcity of lights, it was justified.

This was the time when no bush boy worthy of that title was without a shanghai (ging) though the quality range of the finished products was enormous. Because my brothers – especially Keith – took great pride in their workmanship, my family's gings were always in the Rolls Royce class. All my brothers had a shanghai and now, at the age of about nine, they considered I was responsible enough to possess one, so the search for a suitable prong began.

During the weeks of searching that followed, we seriously considered several possibilities, but after the pros and cons of each of the forks was thoroughly assessed in situ, they were all eventually left to continue as part of the structure of the tree. Then at last – just when the search seemed hopeless – there hidden in a thicket of ironbark regrowth, was the object of our quest. Using a sharp knife, the fork was quickly collected, and on reaching home, it was barked and sculpted to the desired shape, which included a suitable groove just below the apex of each fork, to accommodate the laces that would connect it to the flexible parts of the weapon. Then began the preservation process. It was necessary to dry the wood slowly to prevent it from splitting. This was achieved by frequently "massaging" it with mutton fat. After many weeks of this treatment, the prong took on the appearance of polished wood and would be pronounced "cured".

Over the next few years, except during school hours or when I was using it, that shanghai seldom left my pocket. Later when Jack and I – and later still, I alone – took over the day-to-day management of the goats, it would have been completely impossible to round up or control the ever-growing flock, without our shanghais, and in the process we became highly skilled with this implement.

That same prong, with the rest of my old shanghai, still remains in good condition, tucked away in a cardboard box.

During these holidays we had an unexpected visitor. Keith's old mate Reg Hovey reappeared for a few weeks holiday. Not long after his mother had died in 1935, Reg left home and went working with his brother somewhere "up north". Reg's long-held dream was to go droving in Queensland, for he loved horses and cattle. But because we had not had any contact with him for a considerable time, we had no idea until now, if his dream had been fulfilled. Although he was a bit vague about where these events actually occurred, Reg had plenty of tales to tell. Wide eyed I listened as he drawled on about his conquests over supposedly unrideable horses and how – much to the displeasure of various side-show owners – he stayed in the saddle until he broke the spirit of their most notorious buck-jumpers. For hours he kept us entertained with similar accounts of his other achievements and adventures – I was really impressed. The other members of my family were more sceptical, for they were more aware of Reg's fanciful imagination and a little more than doubted the authenticity of his stories. However, there was one thing we agreed on – Reg could tell a good yarn. All too soon, Reg had returned to who knows where to experience more exciting "adventures". Over the next couple of years, he would unexpectedly turn up – always with vivid accounts of his astonishing experiences. I loved those visits from Reg. He was one of my favourite people, and his tales did wonders for my imagination. After the war started, Reg joined the army, and I can't remember seeing, or hearing much about him again, until after the war.

Before school started, I was introduced to another taste thrill. With Keith as our snake protector and guide, we ventured on an excursion down below the cemetery, to Jukes' paddock, the old dredge dam, and to a dam in Hargreaves' paddock, which was surrounded by a healthy growth of blackberries. I had never tasted these delicious berries before and was astounded that the abundant crop was ours for the taking. Even though we gobbled more than we collected in our containers, we still took home enough for Auntie Mag to make a few jars of the most delicious jam I had ever tasted. We made several more trips to that fruity spot over a few weeks and for the next few years it became an annual event.

By the end of January 1938, there was every reason to believe that the infantile paralysis epidemic had peaked and as summer drew to a close the trauma of its ever-threatening presence subsided. As much as I hated school, being released from that persistent threat more than compensated for the termination early in March of our extended school holidays.

The new school year brought good fortune to Valma, June, Jack and me. Valma and Jack were rewarded for their efforts the previous year, and moved to grade six, and at last June advanced to grade five, while I, after a year and a half in the "Bubs" and two years in grade one, was rewarded for my years of "study" by being promoted to grade two. This was a big relief for my family, who felt that even though I was slow off the blocks, I was now on my way.

27

Dust and Departures

During our extended holidays, there had been quite a few very unpleasant dusty days, but they were nothing compared with one particularly nasty dust storm that occurred soon after we returned to school. On that afternoon, the sun appeared as a reddish smudge in the brownish sky, while an unrelenting hot gale, such as I had never known before, blasted every exposed thing with fine mallee sand. I was terrified and had secret thoughts that it was the beginning of the end of the world. For the first time in my years at school, I was happy to be confined within the walls of my classroom and I dreaded the time when we would be ejected.

All too soon the school-bell sounded and within minutes I met with my three youngest siblings in the schoolyard and began the terrifying journey home. The landscape was bathed in unreal reddish "twilight" as we gingerly headed up the path past the adjacent houses for the scant protection that our home would give. As the track began to pass through the wind torn trees and the hot gritty tempest lashed our legs with leaves and other forest litter, we saw Dad and Louis hurrying towards us – they had come to shepherd us home. I cannot speak for my three companions, but I instantly felt relief and reassurance.

On reaching home, it was obvious that the tents and even more so our kitchen, were more a hazard than a haven under the prevailing conditions. Over the previous few months, mainly due to Keith's endeavours, the mud brick walls of the two-roomed building under construction had grown. Despite the fact that they had progressed only to a height of four or five feet, the safest and most comfortable place in our camp was within this enclosure. As we crouched against the stout windward-wall, for the first time since we left the school, I felt relatively safe. As the evening approached, the traumatic conditions abated and it was reasonably safe to leave our mud-brick sanctuary and return to our normal abodes and activities.

But nature had more nastiness in store for us: on returning home from school one afternoon shortly after that dusty day, we were astounded to find our settlement in something of a shamble. During the afternoon a mini-tornado of astounding intensity, but only a chain or so wide, had swept through our camp and blown the roof off not only our kitchen, but also our stately lav. The storm also caused minor damage to our tents and tore branches off some trees in its path. We were pleased we had missed the event; it must have been terrifying for those at home. Thankfully, there was no long-term damage; within a few days my brothers had restored our rustic camp to its normal state.

Keith had been making good progress on the building, and there was the exciting prospect of soon having a two-roomed solid mud-brick building gracing our predominantly calico camp. It was therefore a big disappointment when soon after those storms, a change in circumstances made it obvious that further work on the building would be delayed indefinitely, or even aborted completely.

It was a shock to us all when Louis suddenly broke the news that he was returning to Melbourne. Even though his hectic lifestyle allowed him little time to spend at home, his happy carefree presence always brightened the atmosphere around the camp. But what really shattered us was that he had talked Keith into going with him to try his luck in the "big smoke". We were somewhat relieved to learn that Keith had no long commitment to his change of address, he stressed his future plans depended on how he adapted to the "alien" environment. Although Louis appeared to earn slightly more than Keith, Louis smoked and tended to have more expensive tastes. For that reason, it was no surprise to learn that Keith had been persuaded to finance the train fares. As insurance against the uncertain prospects of the venture, and to ensure his means of retreat if things went really bad, Keith bought himself a 3-month return ticket. Louis on the other hand, was prepared to cast his future on the winds of fate and purchased a single ticket. For a while, the absence of my two oldest brothers cast a shadow of gloom over our household.

Some time later a letter arrived from the obviously homesick Keith. They were sharing a single room with Sid Murray's brother – and Louis' long-time mate – Don, in a boarding house run by an apparently kindly old couple called Mr and Mrs Ball. No meals were provided, but they were able to cook meals in the room.

Louis had not succeeded in finding a job, but Keith had found uninspiring work in a fabric factory. Keith didn't say much about the job, but enough to enable us to read between the lines that he was not really adapting to the drudgery of the work. Dad astutely stated that it was obviously a "sweat shop". It was also evident that Keith did not enjoy the hustle and bustle of city life and was suffering from being deprived of the freedom of the bush.

Further letters from Keith unintentionally imparted a hint that times were pretty lean for our brothers and their mate. Louis had still not found work, and the letters implied that things would have been unsustainable without the generosity of their friend Don, who by all accounts was lucky enough to have a slightly better paid job.

As the weeks without our brothers slowly passed there was no hint of their plans for the future, and time was running out for Keith's return ticket.

Then unexpectedly, a few days before the due date, Keith arrived home. It was only then that he told us – with a touch of humour, now that it was over – about the horrible working conditions he had endured and of their struggle to keep financially afloat. It became obvious to me that living in an indifferent city was far more demoralising than poverty amid a caring small-town community. Even so, Louis decided to stick with city life.

Jack and I in particular were delighted at Keith's return, for he brought with him our first introduction to the mysteries of wireless. It wasn't actually a wireless: it was the makings of a crystal set. What's more, he had the plans of how to put all the parts together.

Among the fascinating parts was a small glass cylinder, about an inch and a half long and an inch in diameter, with a metal cap on each end to which mounting brackets were attached. This component held the vital parts. The statically mounted crystal was in the centre at one end. At the centre of the other end, the cat's whisker – a small coiled, supposedly silver, spring with a straightened short length at its extremities – was attached by means of a tiny chuck on one end of a small shaft; at the other end was a tiny Bakelite knob handle. The shaft was held about midway in a limited-sliding grip by a universal ball mounting, which enabled the cat's whisker to be "tickled" over the crystal's surface in search of a sensitive spot.

I was also fascinated with the shiny condenser. This consisted of two sets of several interlocking, semicircular aluminium plates. One set was fixed with mounting brackets attached. The other interlocking – but not touching – set was attached to a movable shaft, which could be rotated on the common centre of the two semicircular sections. Keith explained that the purpose of this fascinating device was to allow one to "tune in" the various wireless stations by turning the Bakelite knob at the top, which varied the proportion of interlock between the two sets of plates. There was also a cardboard cylinder about four inches long and three inches in diameter, wrapped with a considerable number of cotton-insulated copper wire winds, all precisely touching in a single layer. Keith told us it was called a coil. Completing the kit, was a long length of several strands of twisted shiny new copper wire and a number of porcelain insulators of a shape reminiscent of sheep's knucklebones: these parts, Keith informed us, were for the aerial.

The most impressive components though, were the two fine sets of second-hand earphones, complete with adjustable metal headbands.

In an atmosphere of urgency and with less than adequate tools, Keith constructed a dainty little wooden box with a three-ply lid. The coil and condenser – except for the turning spindle, which protruded through the lid and was topped with the Bakelite knob, were attached to the underside of the lid, where they would be protected by the box. The small glass-barrelled crystal and cat's whisker holder, was mounted on the top of the lid. This position made it convenient for the operator to watch while twiddling the tiny knob of the cat's whisker to find one of the crystal's elusive sensitive spots. Finally the aerial wire was strung out as high as possible, and anchored at each end with porcelain insulators. A rubber insulated lead wire connected the aerial to the crystal set in Keith's tent.

Throughout the remainder of the daylight hours, Keith twiddled the cat's whisker and turned the condenser knob, but all was to no avail. With tireless tenacity and hope undaunted he continued that procedure until after sunset, when lack of light made considered manipulating of the cat's whisker almost impossible. Suddenly, there was an excited "shh" from Keith. Even in the dull light the deep concentration on Keith's face told the story – a faint whisper was emanating from the innards of the earphones. Our apparatus had at last snatched a whisper from the ether. We soon discovered the elusive waves came from the transmitter of 3AR Melbourne. At first the reception was poor, but over the next few weeks, further adjustments greatly improved reception, particularly in the later evening.

Keith's departure from Melbourne was a forerunner of a change of fortune for Louis, who had continued to reside at the same address and room as his friend Don. Unexpectedly, the aged, well off proprietors of the boarding house where they rented the room, bought themselves a new car. But neither could drive, and it was apparently evident that the possibility of either of them learning was positively remote. This situation proved to be most advantageous for Louis.

By all accounts, right from the first, Mr and Mrs Ball were charmed by Louis' friendly, carefree demeanour and they were aware that he possessed a driving licence and was also unemployed. Under those circumstances, it was a natural progression for them to offer him the job as their chauffeur, which he eagerly accepted. The arrangement proved to be beneficial for all concerned, as the wheels of the car hardly stopped turning. In total harmony and enjoyment they toured the not-too-distant countryside. Those excursions created an environment that nurtured a firm friendship based on mutual respect.

28

"High Noon" on Marshall's Run

By this time, all attempts at animal husbandry in regard to the goats had been abandoned. Indeed, to all intents and purposes, the management of our flock was now in the hands of the four youngest members of our family.

Hore-Belisha had long since been released from the chain on the ironbark tree, because in our barren landscape, keeping up the food supply for him was virtually impossible. As a consequence of this, plus the somewhat resented assistance he received from several of his young male offspring, the flock was expanding at a most astonishing rate and at that time numbered about 50. Because of the aforementioned scarcity of food, their ravenous appetites, and not having any food fads, our goats were quickly becoming a nuisance to our neighbours and even ourselves.

Although the new wire-netting fence around our vegetable garden permitted them to only drool at the tasty morsels within, the makeshift barriers and guards fashioned from scraps of wire and sticks, that protected Auntie Mag's meagre collection of flowers and shrubs, often failed under the assaults of plundering goats. Despite the frequent disappointments and the occasional tear over the mutilation of her treasured plants, our self-sacrificing aunt continued the struggle to maintain her favourites. Most were from the old world gardens of her more salubrious past, with a few newer varieties that she had grown with miraculous ease, from the specimen flowers that relations or friends would bring to show her.

A more threatening problem was the goats' disrespect for the property rights of our neighbours, especially in regard to the several divisions of the Marshall family. One particular member of the family was universally known as "Old Joe", to distinguish him from presumably younger Joe (he didn't seem that much younger to me) who occupied a property of similar size, at the extreme bush end of the combined Marshall "estates". Rightly or wrongly, because of his seemingly advanced age, I regarded Old Joe as the patriarch of our neighbourhood Marshall clan. The eastern boundary of his sizeable paddock fronted our western boundary across the unformed future Poole Street. Unlike our fenceless property, a substantial four-foot-six-inch-high fence of five strands of number-eight wire and topped with a two-strand twisted barbwire, defined his boundary. Although such a fence was adequate for common stock such as horses, cattle and sheep, it had not been built with the penetrative powers of goats in mind, for they entered his land with little more effort than it took them to leave ours.

Old Joe's house and garden were situated in the far corner of his property and were separately fenced. Between the house enclosure and Poole Street, were several acres of well-grassed pasture, which was lightly grazed by a few cows. Evidently this grass was well fertilised and sweet, for our goats never bothered to venture further to sample the more exotic herbage of the house garden. Notwithstanding this compromise by our goats, Old Joe was not at all conciliatory, and strongly complained to Dad and my older brothers about this assault on his property. We had no way of restraining the goats, nor could we educate them to respect the legal aspects of the situation, or instil in them the common knowledge that was often brought to our attention: "There is no law for goats or geese, they can be shot on sight".

Maybe that was so, but after all we were more than a third of the way through the twentieth century, surely Australians were more civilised than that. Besides we were doing our best – we would chase them out of his verdant pasture whenever we saw them there.

One pleasant Saturday afternoon when most of us were at home doing our own thing, suddenly the sound of loud gunfire broke the silence. Several of us quickly assembled at a spot on the town side of the camp, where a cleared strip afforded us a clear view down the several hundred yards to our neighbour's property. The sight of Old Joe, standing with gun in hand on the rise near his house, as he oversaw our panic-stricken goats vacating his pasture, and Dad's somewhat immoderate outrage at our neighbour's action, chilled me with fear and seared the scene forever on my then impressionable mind. Quickly our eyes scanned the paddock for fallen members of our flock, but there were none to be seen. With relief I surmised that Old Joe must be a rotten shot. Nevertheless, as Dad strode down the length of our block towards the slowly approaching man with the gun, my terror was increased by my outrageous thoughts of the possible consequences.

With the same spine-chilling anticipation that I knew a score of years later, as I watched the climax of the Western film *High Noon*, I saw Dad and Joe meet in the midst of the pasture. In this case – unlike in the film – the drama was not sustained, for it soon became clear that the two adversaries were engaged in – more or less – cordial conversation. I never heard any details of that conversation, but on his return Dad said that, "Old Joe wasn't a bad sort of a fellow" and that he had only fired the shots to frighten the goats. I think the goats got the message, for I cannot remember them bothering him again after that episode.

* * *

Often over the years, I have thought about the flock's sustained loyalty towards my family. Admittedly, when we first got the goats, it was a bond of mutual benefit. The goats supplied us with milk, and in return we supplied them with food and shelter. But after a few years we ceased to provide those benefits and the association became one-sided, we were the sole beneficiaries.

In view of that, it's hard to understand why the goats maintained their allegiance to our camp and us. It must have been the result of having been shackled to humans by the servitude of domestication, for thousands of goat generations. The first hint of any threat from dogs, electrical storms, heavy rain, etc. would literally send them scurrying for home.

Admittedly, in the case of a storm or heavy rain, the first couple of goats to reach our dunny achieved probably more comfort than my family did in our assorted shelters. And they would usually stay there until some unfortunate person unexpectedly pulled back the wheatbag curtain to enter. Even though we were all conscious of the possibility of goats being there, the outward rush of escaping animals never ceased to cause us some degree of fright, especially at night. Then as one entered the establishment, invariably one would feel fresh baubles squashing underfoot, for our goats did not use our toilet in the accepted way. There was also room for some goats to shelter against the quarry face, or against the fence of the goat house, but the comfort those things provided was of little consequence. Several of the luckier ones would acquire shelter under the several square yards of gum leaf-thatched roof in the goat house.

Usually the goats could be found within half a mile or so from our camp, but on rare occasions when food was scarce, they would go much further and at times they would venture the four miles through the bush to Craigie. They always seemed reluctant to cross bitumen-sealed roads, so they mostly kept to our side of the nearby Carisbrook and Majorca roads. Sometimes they did venture across the main sealed Carisbrook road, in order to graze on the often-lush pastures of the town's sanitary depot, which was over a mile or more away.

The goats had also found that the nearby Council rubbish tip was a fairly reliable provider of gourmet goat fare. They would spend much of most days extracting enjoyable morsels from the general household rubbish, or patiently standing back as Danny Ryan unloaded the latest delivery from his quaint custom built horse-drawn "state of the art" garbage collecting vehicle. But feasting on the leftover delicacies from the kitchens and dining room tables of our fair town was not achieved without the risk of discomfort or even mortal danger to the four-legged diners. The biggest danger to both humans and more so the goats, were the fires that frequently smouldered for weeks in rubbish that had been covered with earth as the tip proceeded on a face down the steep gully. At times these slow chars would intensify and burn with the fury of a furnace that made glass drip like melting ice, but little evidence of that danger beneath was evident above the overburden. In spite of its potential to cause human fatalities, the carefree Council of those virtually litigation-free times did nothing to minimise the danger.

Looking back, because Dad seldom went near the tip, he didn't know about the underground fires that at times raged. We, however, were always very aware of the potentially fatal consequences of breaking through the foot or so of earthen crust above these "furnaces", and to a considerable degree, so were the goats. Nevertheless, although we never actually lost a goat in these death-trap fires, it was not unusual to see one with singed legs limping among its fellows.

At first, my three youngest siblings and I would only visit the tip in order to collect the goats for milking. Later, if the tip was deserted – and with more daintiness and propriety than is usually associated with such activities – we would scan the tip for things discarded by more affluent members of the community which could be of use to us. We were only permitted to bring home metal or glass items that could be thoroughly sanitised. Anything in the clothing, or similar line, was avoided like the plague. Empty kerosene tins were highly prized, and indeed the older male members of my family would visit the tip specifically to search for these rare and extremely useful articles.

We loved to collect the beautifully made, but of limited use, tobacco and cigarette tins of the numerous brands, which were there in abundance. Often we would make decorative "water wheels" from tobacco tins. This was done by pushing the edge opposite the hinges of one tin, into the body of another, then opening the lids out and pressing them together to form a paddle. This process was continued until the multi-paddled wheel was completed. Tobacco tins were also used to test the penetrative power of rifle bullets. A number of tins would be placed one behind the other, then a bullet would be fired into the cluster. With something of a thrill, the lead bullet would then be found "exhausted" in one of the tins down the line.

We also highly prized the hand pump insect sprays we often found in perfect working condition: these we used as sophisticated water dispensers during our summer frolics. At times a real gem in the form of some piece of household cutlery that had obviously been accidentally discarded would be discovered. Paring knives would often be found near vegetable peelings. Auntie Mag would thoroughly boil such items before we put them to use. Sometimes we would find the odd alley, broken toys, and old alarm clocks which I would dismantle with glee in the hope of fixing them. I cannot remember completely achieving that objective even once.

A more prevalent though less serious hazard for our tip-grazing goats, was due to a common practice of those days. When opening a tin of jam or the like with a hand-operated tin opener, a small section of the circumference would be left intact to act as a hinge, so that the lid could be opened and closed at will, while the contents were being used. When such tins were discarded, the lids were usually pressed further into the tin as a safety measure. Often as the goats foraged amid the rubbish, a foot would penetrate the opening of the tin and press the spring-like lid further in, when like the barb on a fishhook, it would grasp the animal's leg and prevent the foot from being extracted. Often the jagged lid would cause a nasty cut in the goat's leg, so it was always considered a priority to remove the tins as soon as possible. This didn't cause us much inconvenience with the tamed members of our flock, such as the milkers and pets, but it was often a real problem with the unhandled members.

With difficulty – that often involved all available members of our clan – we would muster them into the small goat-house yard. However, it soon became clear that all the sheep dog-like instincts of our family were in the care of its four younger members. The inept "help" from our elders was in fact a hindrance; they always seemed to be in the wrong place to prevent a breakaway. There was always less shouting and running when we four were left alone to do the job. Later, by pure accident, we discovered that by inciting the wilder animals into desperate flight, the lid would be bent further in and the tin would fly off. Admittedly, this procedure usually exacerbated the injury to the goat's leg, but for our convenience, we decided that in the long run it caused the wild members of our flock less trauma than being unceremoniously herded into the dreaded yard.

With moderate frequency, another version of the above occurred when a goat inserted its head into a larger tin to retrieve some tasty morsel. In such cases it was usually the goat's horns that acted like fishhook barbs, and the victim of its own folly would have to crash around the terrain until it was noticed by some member of the family. Even when wilder members of the flock were in this predicament, it was usually quite easy to catch them and "restore" their sight.

Invariably the goats would spend their nights on the camp-side slopes of the low hills that surrounded three sides of our settlement. Already the goats had scraped, with their front hooves, shallow bedding holes in the hard ground, in quite a few places around this natural amphitheatre. Superficially, they seemed to use the various sleeping grounds at random, but perhaps if we had studied their pattern of behaviour more closely, we may have discovered the choice of the bedding site was linked to the weather conditions at the time. Because of our camp's close proximity to these goat "dormitories", we soon became familiar with the sounds that emanated from them during the night. When the air was still and the goats were restless, we would clearly hear the loud rheumaticky cracking from the knees of the older members. When any of the females were in season, throughout the night there would be a chorus of the loud distinctive blubbering – interspersed by the sound of crashing horns – from the randy males as they tirelessly trailed the reluctant females around the current sleeping site. Although such nights were common, they never so much as raised a comment from any member of my prim-and-proper family. With profound dignity, we chose to ignore such earthy behaviour.

The eagerness of the young males to assist Hore-Belisha with his duties resulted in many spectacular battles when a young would-be successor challenged the old master. Standing almost toe-to-toe, the combatants would rear up on their hind legs, then in unison, drop to a resounding crack of horns as they crashed their heads together. These fights would sometimes continue for hours without either animal giving much ground, so the battles were confined to a very small area. Strange to say, there never appeared to be much visible damage, yet invariably, the younger goat – I suspect due to having a lower level of tolerance to headaches – would eventually turn and trot away, usually followed for a few paces by the victor. Although, for various reasons, over the next few years Hore-Belisha's young rivals came and went, they all stuck faithfully to the Marquess of Queensberry Rules for billy-goat stoushes, and the old warlord remained happy and supreme.

That is until a couple of years later when we obtained three orphan baby lambs – two females and one male – which were wholeheartedly accepted into the goat flock. Because I belonged to a softhearted family, these lambs could have confidently expected to roam the hills and gullies around our home until they died of old age, and indeed the ewes did, but the ram struck a bit of trouble.

In the fullness of time, the ram grew into an animal worthy of being the subject of a Wool Board logo. It was clear by his bearing, that he believed that old erroneous nonsense, which implies that goats are intellectually inferior to sheep.

From observations over the years, it seems to me that the males of each particular species fight to their own set of rules. The Marquess of Queensberry Rules to one species would be considered Rafferty's Rules to another. Under natural conditions this doesn't matter, for mostly, the males are only interested in fighting over females of their own kind. However, among animals that have allowed themselves to be domesticated, unnatural circumstances can cause trouble.

In due course the ram fathered a couple of lambs (being female, they also died of old age) and at least two sheep/goat hybrids – both stillborn. The behaviour leading to that latter indignity seemed to really upset Hore-Belisha, and led to what I think would be a rare thing among mammals in the wild – fights between males of different species.

Well that's not quite right. They desperately wanted to fight but nature had made it impossible for them to do so. For the Creator, in His great wisdom, decreed that rams attain their headaches by a different set of rules. Unlike billy-goat fights, which are straightforward slogging matches, ram fights seem more formal – somehow reminiscent of the days of Redcoats and gentlemen officers. The rules for ram "punch-ups", which were securely locked in the genes of our fearless animal, demanded that after appropriate "formalities", which bring the combatants face to face, they must slowly back off for a considerable distance. Then to some signal – yet unknown to science – they accelerate towards each other until with a violent dissipation of energy they come to a sudden halt as their horns crash together.

Now perceptive readers will have already visualised what a farce it would be when our ram and goat attempted to engage in mortal combat. The ram would begin to slowly back off in preparation for his charge, but instead of doing the same, Hore-Belisha moved forward but no matter how often he reared up on his hind legs, before he could crash down the ram was out of reach. Likewise the poor ram had no hope of achieving the space necessary for his charge. I feel that had he been able to make just one good charge, it would have been curtains for our old billy, but that was never to be.

As time passed, these encounters became a bit of a local curiosity. In those entertainment scarce times passers-by of all ages would stop to watch the poor frustrated ram slowly backing up hour after hour, between the ironbark trees, on the grassless quartz strewn hills. Probably many observers unjustly thought the ram was a coward but nothing could have been further from the truth. It's just that all living things are in many ways the prisoners of our genes.

Our ram wasn't around long enough to sire a second crop of lambs the following year: he died prematurely – probably due to frustration and loss of self-esteem.

29

Schoolyard Squabbles and Rivalry

Squabbles among the boys – and on rare occasions, girls – at our school would often lead to the mutual resolve "I'll see you in the plantation after school". The plantation of several acres was on the southwest border of the playground. It had been planted with pine trees years before, in the hope of one day being harvested for the benefit of our deprived school.

The trees in the plantation were then a considerable height, and provided a dense screen around a small clearing where for some unknown reason the trees had failed to grow. This secluded clearing provided an ideal place to resolve the rights and wrongs of serious disputes, by physical combat. These "adjudications", based on the assumption that right was synonymous with strength, always attracted supporters of the combatants and a few unaligned spectators. The number depended on the prominence of the adversaries or the bout's expected entertainment rating. Occasionally we Courtneys would attend these bouts, to give tacit moral support to some acquaintance who invariably was the least affluent. Irrespective of the substance of the disputes, the most popular combatant seemed to be always the most pugnacious and have the largest band of supporters, who – in the absence of a referee – would ensure that the Marquess of Queensberry Rules were of no consequence. Pushing and even trying to trip the underdog were commonplace.

Over the previous couple of years, June, Jack and I, and to a much lesser extent Valma, had established friendships with the younger members of the Cook family, who were roughly around our ages. Although his three younger brothers, Artie, Alan and Jim, were more in tune with our subdued temperament, we got on best with Bob. We were also friendly with their two younger sisters, Jean, about June's age, and Maggie, about my age. They were quiet, intelligent and dignified, but because of their financial deprivation, they were often the brunt of derision from the more affluent, catty girls of our school.

June, who never had a lot of friends at school, got on really well with Jean. Valma, on the other hand, had become very popular at school: she created her own little world and seemed to float above our humble social status. This disposition allowed her to be a popular member of a clique of haughty fluffy-headed young misses, who discouraged her from associating with the likes of the Cooks. June, Jack and I, however, also had an affable acquaintance with their parents as well as their two older brothers, Ted and Walter, who still lived at home. By this time, Dad and my older brothers were also well acquainted with the members of the Cook family, who had recently obtained a wet-battery wireless set. For people not connected to mains electricity, there were two alternatives in the choice of a wireless. Dry-battery sets were by far the cleanest, and when their non-offensive battery-packages went flat – as they frequently did – they could literally be changed without getting the hands dirty, but by the standards of those days, these batteries were very expensive.

Wet-battery sets were far more economical to run, but the heavy bitumen cased, lead-plated, car batteries filled with acid and distilled water were very heavy. They had a habit of exuding their fluid content, which had an obnoxious acrid smell. There was also the inconvenience of having to have them recharged every week or so. However, the fact that they could be recharged for a minimal cost made them a desirable option for the poorer people, that is those who could manage the luxury of a wireless at all.

Some time earlier, the Hills had purchased a dry-battery wireless, and on a few occasions Bill (Mr Hill) had invited Dad, Keith and Lloyd to their place on a Saturday night to listen to the wrestling. Dad was quite amused by the extravagant descriptions of the bouts, which he enjoyed but obviously did not take seriously. Keith, on the other hand was very impressed by the skill of the various contestants, most of whom had fanciful names. However, the Hills seemed to be somewhat reluctant to share this product of their radio, for invitations were sparse.

In contrast to the Hills, the Cooks were eager to share their wireless, and most Saturday nights the male members of my family would be invited down to listen to the wrestling. Even to timid me, the wonder of the wireless pouring forth the colourful description of the torturous gymnastic bouts at the West Melbourne Stadium was spellbinding. We soon learned the colourful names of the regular combatants, and sorted our likes and dislikes. At play we even endeavoured to apply the classical holds that were so excitedly described in minute detail by the commentator.

Keith later managed to obtain a small booklet, which with line drawings illustrated the various holds in fine detail. Now on moonlight nights, when the grass was green down on the clearing of the old market garden below our camp, we would practise the often-brutal holds on each other. The pain from Big Chief Little Wolf's "Indian Death-lock" – even when moderately applied, as was always the case with us – was excruciating. Many of the other holds were almost as painful. Mostly, June would also join in the "fun", but Valma was always the self-appointed, though largely ignored, referee.

The Cooks were our only neighbourhood contemporaries with whom we exchanged home visits. Of course the Hill kids visited us, and we went to their place for water – but we never went inside their house. We were also on friendly terms with a few other kids we would occasionally meet away from the school on neutral ground.

Soon after the Marshall family abandoned their campsite on the adjacent hill, another Marshall family set up a similar camp to ours, in the bush behind the old rifle range, just outside "young" Joe's bush-side fence. On occasions we would meet the two youngest members of the family, Billy and Laurie, who were roughly Jack's and my age, in the bush between our respective camps, when inevitably we would play marbles. Billy was a marbles fanatic and by far the best player in our school, so in spite of him not having the wherewithal to buy any, he always sported a large, bulging bag of assorted alleys. The kids at school who were further up the financial ladder – short though the ladder was – never seemed to catch on that affluence was not necessarily synonymous with skill. Even Jack and June who were the undisputed best marble players of our clan soon learned the folly of "playing for keeps" with Billy, and any proposed tournament with us would not proceed without first securing an agreement – that "We're not playing for keeps." That never caused any hassles, for there were plenty of other kids around, with better alleys than we had, to be "skun" by Billy.

The competition between June and Jack now extended to almost every activity and at times they would dare each other to perform potentially lethal acts. Not only would they perform daring manoeuvres in trees, they would also dare each other to jump over diggers' holes where landing short would have sent them tumbling to certain death. The very worst of the mines was up past Louis' old claim. Admittedly all the earth had been removed from around it, which provided ideal run-up and landing conditions, but the shaft was reputed to be over 120 feet deep and went down to water level. We had no reason to doubt that statement, for when a rock was thrown into its void, the prolonged rumbling of the descending stone would end with the sound of a muffled splash. But for once luck was on our side, for in spite of themselves, they survived to become wiser.

30

The Man I Might Have Been

Although bread and dripping is the legendary staff of life that sustained the down-and-outs of the Great Depression, for my family the bread portion of that epitome of hard times was mostly replaced by the various end products of scone dough. I am yet to decide whether that put us more up, or down, the social scale.

On occasions over the years Dad, usually with the assistance of Auntie Mag, would make a batch of homemade bread. To me, it seemed to be quite a complicated operation, which I did not completely understand. The process seemed to take up most of the day, this was probably because – as was the case with most of Dad's endeavours – he never seemed to employ the simplest methods, even though he constantly impressed upon us that "Nature is pleased with simplicity". The process involved collecting water from boiled potatoes and mixing it with the "three-pen'eth" of yeast, he had purchased from the baker. I gathered that this procedure was for economic reasons, for it substantially reduced the amount of baker's yeast required. He would then let the mixture stand on the warm hob of the stove for the yeast to "grow". Enough flour was then added to make a soft dough. It was then placed on the hob to "prove", or in other words, rise. Sometime later, the dough – which by now had attained a degree of elasticity – would be tipped on to the table, and thoroughly kneaded before being rolled into balls of a suitable size for two to be placed end on into each of our two four pound bread tins. These were then placed on the hob for the balls to rise until they filled the tins, then they were placed in the oven to cook. Because of that ponderous process, it was usually well into the evening – often around nine or 10 o'clock – before we could sample the crusty result.

Due to a minuscule rise in our monetary position and because a batch of hot bread was an occasional and special event, it was usually possible for my family's combined financial resources to be stretched to allow the extravagance of buying a pound of butter. Its unvarying price of one shilling and eight pence, which made it unaffordable for our daily use, made the hot bread a real treat.

In anticipation of this delight, we would bide our time while the bread cooked. If it was a pleasant night, even when there was no moon, thanks to our good night-vision, we would temper our impatience by playing. Sometimes we would play on the clearing of the old market garden site below the camp, but more often we would vie for a turn to "fly" a few spins around our popular swing-tree. If the night was still, the smell of newly baked bread would waft up the hill to the swing-tree, even before we heard the long awaited call from the kitchen summoning us. As we hurriedly approached our goal, the ever strengthening, mouth-watering whiffs ensured that our digestive juices were well prepared for the gastronomic challenge of our overindulgence in a "feast" of hot bread straight from the oven.

In the flickering light from the open doors of the stove, the steaming hot bread slices that were sawn un-squashed by our elders, with our sharp, serrated bread knife, were then moderately spread with the luxury – butter. To us, this was indeed a highlight for our tastebuds. We all agreed that while the bread was hot, the addition of butter could elevate its scrumptiousness to its full potential. However, the next day it would still taste good with the more accessible spread of soft beef dripping, which was mostly so thoughtfully donated to us by our more affluent relations and friends.

With the cooler weather of late autumn, Lloyd resumed one of his long-standing pastimes, which was gathering solder and lead. In the 1930s, it was common for many residents of Maryborough to ignore our official rubbish tips in favour of the abundant and more convenient box/ironbark forest that closely encircled our town. In places, rubbish of every description was continually being scattered over several acres of bush. Lloyd would periodically peruse these areas of civic disgrace to find old galvanised water tanks or any other metal items with seams or patches, that revealed by the excess use of solder, to be the work of some incompetent plumber or handyman. Lloyd would make a mental note of where promising items were and periodically over the cooler months – usually with Jack and me in tow – he would return to the spot and make a suitable fire with the abundant sticks from the self-pruning eucalypts. He would then strategically manoeuvre the chosen articles over the flames until the solder had melted and trickled into the fire. After the fire had cooled, Lloyd would collect the ashes and wash them in a gold-panning dish to isolate the assorted lumps and droplets of solder. The booty was then melted in a jam tin and poured into a bar-mould of a suitable size, that he had chiselled in a dry hard mud-brick or a similar spot of ground. It was most important that the ground was dry, because the slightest wetness would cause a violent "explosion" that could scatter the molten metal over an area of several feet.

Lloyd was also ever on the lookout for scraps of lead, which he also cast into bars. Occasionally we would find a real bonanza in the form of an old lead/acid car battery. In complete ignorance of the potential health hazard, these batteries would be thrown into an outside fire to melt the lead away from the corrosion and other materials, including the battery's hard rubber-based case. He then collected the ashes from the fire, and washed them in the same manner as he did in the case of solder – often Lloyd would generously succumb to our pleadings and allow us youngsters to participate in this most fulfilling part of the process. The material in the "wash" must have really been a dreadful concoction of potentially lethal chemicals.

At times, us kids would either accompany Lloyd, or find our own way to the abandoned old rifle butts to dig in the target mound for bullets. The most eagerly sought were the hefty lumps of solid lead that had been fired from the old 450-calibre Martini-Henry rifles. Not so prized, but far more common, were the lead filled round-nosed nickel bullets of the more modern .303-inch rifles. The lead from both types of these historic relics was also melted into bars.

When Lloyd ceased the practice, Jack and I took up the non-profit "business" for the next few years. The metal was never sold.

I often wonder just how much lead was infused into our bodies and, in view of its propensity to cause brain damage, like the character in Henry Lawson's poem, I ponder about "the man I might have been" – a pluralised version of course.

Winter again brought the red ironbarks of our forest into full flower. This was one of the years when the cups of the flowers were so filled with nectar that the slightest breeze would send the overflow trickling down the leaves, causing them to glisten in the sunshine. In some cases the nectar was so bountiful that the major part of the tree's foliage would look as if it had experienced a recent shower.

As one might expect, such a flowering in a forest of thousands of trees would bring an influx of myriad lorikeets and other nectar-feeding birds into our bushland. I have never ceased to wonder how birds know – sometimes from hundreds, or even thousands of miles away – that such bountiful events are taking place. Such profuse nectar flows were not an annual occurrence. Although the ironbarks flowered each winter, some years the trees only exuded a dew-like coating of nectar on the inner surface of the flower cups. In such years, the hordes of parrots failed to appear – how did they know?

Thankfully, because of the slight improvement in our financial position, unlike in the winter of two years ago, the deplorable need to harvest some of the "keets" to supplement our diet could no longer be justified, in fact it wasn't even considered.

It was this year, by our own initiative, that we youngsters learned how to suck the nectar from the brimming cups of the flowers on the lower branches of the ironbarks with a hollow grass straw. That discovery added a new item to our list of tasty bush treats, which included snotty gobbles, cranberries, golden wattle gum, native yams and the seeds of the introduced onion grass, which the kids of the district called plum puddings.

31

Silence is Not Always Golden

We didn't get much rain in the first few months of 1938, and some of our older acquaintances were gravely predicting a severe drought. However, when we got over three inches in June and more than two inches in July it seemed that the pessimistic predictions of the weather sages were somewhat off target. Such a quantity of rain in our part of the country was generally seen as heralding the end of a dry spell.

In spite of the good rain, my family was forced to face a potentially more pressing threat to our domestic water supply. In June, without any preamble, the Hills informed us that they were shifting, and there would be no certainty that the new occupants would allow us to continue to get our potable water from their taps. Within a very short time, the Hills had gone, but for some time there was no activity around the house. In view of that fact and not having received confirmation of an embargo, we continued to make the usual daily collection of our consumable water.

It was rumoured that a young couple had bought the house, and soon a man of that description was spotted, apparently doing a bit of upgrading work around the house. Without delay, Dad paid him a visit on site to clarify the situation regarding our future access to their taps. The man's name was Bill Hardwick: Dad said, ". . . he is a nice young fellow". He told Dad he would be getting married in September, but until then the house would be empty. In the meantime he would be doing quite a bit of work on the building. Without hesitation, he gave us permission to continue to collect all the water we required. Because we mostly collected our water early each morning, we did not make further contact with either him or his future bride until they took up residence after their marriage in September, although occasionally from a distance, we saw them pottering around the house.

One evening we heard a loud cacophony of shouting, singing, tins and dishes being banged and a variety of other raucous sounds. I didn't have to be told that it was a tin-kettling. I could remember hearing several such neighbourhood commotions after dusk, before we left the house near the school. I remembered how on the first occasion, my fears had been quickly allayed by the explanation that it was a happy event, arranged by the friends of a newly married couple, to celebrate the first night in their future home after returning from their honeymoon. Unbeknown to us, the Hardwicks had married a short time before, and had moved into the house that day. From the din that night, we gathered they had lots of friends.

Most of our family soon got to know them, including Jack, June and I who were often allotted the job of collecting water in the billycart. We saw more of Mrs Hardwick than Bill and soon grew to really like her, she had friendly gentle ways. On the other hand, their solidly-built reddish dog, Ginger, who obviously had an ancestry mixture of any of several breeds – though all the self appointed "experts" in such matters agreed unanimously that he was "a good part Queensland Heeler" – could not be trusted. We always had to keep a wary eye out for him, for he had a reputation for nipping people on the legs.

* * *

Dad's health was beginning to be a cause for worry. Lately, at random, Dad started taking quite unpleasant "turns", the nature of which he was reluctant to discuss. He would brush these turns aside, saying they were nothing to worry about. I was consoled by his assurance, especially as after an hour or so, although obviously still pretty wonky, he would resume his normal activities. Nevertheless, my frequent standard silent prayer ". . . that we'd all live forever" now included a special mention of Dad.

After putting up with this situation for several weeks, Dad was reluctantly persuaded to visit a local GP, Dr Miller, called by long-time locals young Dr Miller. He had succeeded his father, who

I gathered, had been a long-time GP in the town. Dr. Miller's vague diagnosis was that Dad had heart trouble. He prescribed a pink bitter-tasting liquid and warned him that he "would have to take things easy". This news was indeed a serious blow to our household and for a while it left me with a numbing feeling of insecurity.

* * *

Our forays into the bush were becoming increasingly adventurous, and included visits on our own, to the relic townships of Mosquito, Bluchers and the Carisbrook reservoir. Especially during the cooler months, when there was no fear of snakes, Dad didn't mind, as long as we always told him where we were going and how long we expected to be. On one of our frequent visits to the Carisbrook reservoir, partly due to the stock proof fence that enclosed the reservoir and the considerable amount of natural bush on its upstream side, we were overwhelmed by the wildflower display. Auntie Mag loved most of nature's wonders, especially flowers and she found a special delight in the infinite variety of wildflowers, so we decided to give her a treat by taking her to see them. One delightful afternoon a few days later, the five of us set out on the four-mile return trip. Over the next few years, Auntie Mag accompanied us on similar walks in springtime, to see the wildflowers that adorned various parts of the bush.

As the distance from our place increased – and especially once we were beyond the normal range of our marauding goats – much to Auntie Mag's delight, in spots the floral displays were really impressive. But the full glory of the bush was only revealed after we squeezed through the tight wires of the reservoir fence. Auntie Mag was enthralled by the magnificent floral display that this area presented, it was indeed a showcase of our box-ironbark wildflowers; she was especially overcome by the sheer beauty of the mass of *Grevillia alpina*. Their prolific flowers ranged in colour from white through shades of yellow, apricot and pink, to brilliant red. Considering the dry year, the sight was indeed a testimony to the tenacity of our hardy wildflowers.

Sadly, as we wandered, Auntie Mag could not hear the harmony of the wonderful bush-sounds of those days. Despite the prevalence of youthful egg-collectors, our bush teemed with a multitude of bird species, mostly in such numbers that the recent discoverers of this area would find hard to believe. Most of the exquisite songsters of box-ironbark forests were present: we would hear the purest liquid notes of the white-throated tree-creeper and the rippling lilting songs from the abundance of crested bellbirds. With bellbird songs, after each rippling rendition that lasts several minutes, the birds pause for a short while, then give a repeat performance in a different key. Mingled with those sounds were the exquisite full-throated voices of abundant rufous whistlers and grey shrike-thrushes. At times we would also hear Gilbert whistlers rendering notes that appeared to be an enhanced imitation of a human whistling a dog, and the glorious extended song of the western warbler.

Inevitably, these wonderful sounds would be performed against a background of less assertive songsters. Often, those sounds lingered with an added enchantment – the distant intermittent mellow dongs from the rectangle-section tapered bells that hung from the neck of the leader of each of the few small mobs of cattle that grazed our bush. Over the years the bird sounds have drastically diminished and to the forest's benefit, the delightful muted dongs of the cowbells have long since gone.

* * *

For some days towards the end of October, a tragic air disaster became the main topic of conversation. Long before we collected our day-old paper, we heard the sad details of how an Australian National Airways DC3 airliner called the *Kyeema* had crashed into Mt Dandenong, killing the 18 people on board. As Australia's worst air disaster, it received prominent coverage in the newspapers and on the wireless. The magnitude of such a tragedy, that people around referred to as being "so close to home", sent a spasm of shock through our community.

I too felt deep sorrow about that tragedy, but as a child whose actual known world ended at Evansford, I had no feeling of closeness to that mountain over a hundred miles away on the other side of Melbourne. I never dreamed that soon, with feelings of horror and awe, I would actually touch part of that ill-fated plane.

Not very long after the tragic crash of the *Kyeema*, Louis unexpectedly arrived home on one of his infrequent visits somewhat triumphantly bearing a cardboard box about eight inches square and some three inches deep. In a state of excited anticipation, I watched as he removed the neatly fitting lid and revealed a torn distorted piece of aluminium. He quickly explained that it was part of the *Kyeema*, which he had souvenired from the crash site. He explained that when Mr and Mrs Ball heard of the crash, they – and possibly, with the full approval of their chauffeur – immediately left to inspect the scene. It seems that security in those times was rather slack, for Louis reported that the area was alive with sightseers, many of whom, like Louis, were collecting the scattered fragments at will. During Louis' short stay in Maryborough, his ghastly trophy was the cause of much interest and would be readily shown to indulge the morbid curiosity of many of his acquaintances. On his return to Melbourne, he left the box with its contents – that also included many newspaper cuttings concerning the disaster – with us. Over the next few years, to my ever-declining sensitivity and awe about its history, it remained an item of conversation and would readily be shown to interested visitors.

* * *

In the last week of November, I had my first conscious encounter with the trauma and grieving that comes with a death in the family. Late one afternoon while my three youngest siblings and I were behind the quarry mustering the goats into the goat house for the evening milking, we noticed Uncle Andrew arriving. Uncle Andrew usually arrived in the early afternoon, so this departure from the normal could only mean that he was the bearer of important news. Minutes later, we were called to the kitchen and informed that our Auntie Liz had unexpectedly died the previous day. Auntie Mag was devastated by the news, for although the barrier of distance had parted them for many years, Liz had remained her fount of wisdom and a paragon of culinary knowledge that placed her only second to "Grandma".

Valma and June were also shattered by the news of the motherly soul they had learned to love during their three years in her care. All members of my family were saddened by the news, but having had little contact with our eldest aunt, to Jack and me it all seemed a bit remote, so unlike our sisters, we mustered the fortitude to complete the evening milking without much effort.

32

Health and Water Concerns

As summer approached, Dad's health was becoming an increasing worry. His "turns" became much more frequent and severe and at times they would virtually confine him to bed on the sofa for a week or so. Dr Miller told Dad it was unlikely that he would ever again be able to even fulfil his Sustenance obligations, so that source could be cut off. In view of this situation, the doctor suggested that Dad apply for the Invalid Pension. However, a decision on this matter was postponed for the time. Doctor Miller impressed on Dad the importance of doing exercise in the form of regular walks on comparatively level ground at first, then gradually as he strengthened, progressively try to manage more undulating terrain. The doctor said that if he followed these instructions there was a good chance that over time his health could improve considerably, but he stressed it was most important that he not be impatient and try to rush things. Although Dad was not usually inclined to take advice readily, he implicitly obeyed the doctor's instructions.

During the time of being confined to his bed, Dad struck up an unusual friendship. A little Jacky-lizard that resided in the vicinity of our kitchen now began to actually come inside. At first it was obvious that the lizard was after the numerous flies that infested the open-fronted shelter. After a while – I suspect to relieve the boredom of being confined to his couch all day – Dad began to foster the lizard's friendship by having a saucer of milk placed on a bag close to the head of his bed. It didn't take long for the Jacky to respond to this friendly gesture. While he enjoyed the milk, the flies that the dish attracted seemed even more to his liking. It was fascinating to watch how with a lightning flick of the tongue the flies appeared to simply vanish from the edge of the milk dish, their whereabouts only being betrayed by the satisfied "munching" of the fearless little reptile that was giving us all so much joy. The only minus of this happy association was that we all had to be constantly careful not to stand on Dad's delightful visitor.

Another thing that gave Dad pleasure during this period was a young magpie we had found wandering between our place and the town. The unfortunate creature had probably escaped from someone who – as was common in those days – intended to keep it as a pet, for its wing had been cut. However, the person did not do what was the normal practice of merely trimming back the wing feathers so the bird could not fly until the feathers grew again, by which time the bird was a pet, they had actually cut into the flesh. This action had condemned the bird to being flightless for life, for the feathers would never grow again. With plenty of newspaper strategically spread for hygiene purposes, this magpie camped on the head of Dad's sofa, and appeared to desperately attempt to converse, to which Dad appropriately responded.

* * *

During August and September there had been scarcely enough rain to wet the ground, and the local population was alarmed to learn that the Evansford Reservoir, which was the source of Maryborough's water supply, was alarmingly low. The future of our town looked so perilous, that the brains of our civic fathers – figuratively speaking – turned to water, as they girded their loins and faced the impending disaster.

Nineteen thirty-eight was quickly drawing to a close, and we still had not received rain of any consequence. Something had to be done quickly, so in consultation with the Mines Department, the Borough Council frantically began to search for an alternative water source that would save our town.

By the end of November, it was decided that our town's saviour would be a long-since abandoned gold mine that bore the stately name of the Princess Royal. The selection, by association, gave us a touch of reflected pride; for it was situated at one of our favourite haunts – Mosquito. Without delay, what we youngsters saw as a great feat of engineering got under way.

Preparation work had to be carried out on the old shaft. It soon was common talk that the first job was removing the remains of seven horses and an unspecified number of other domestic animals from the mine hole. In view of the then convenient practice of disposing of deceased animals by dumping them down deep mines, this was no surprise to anyone. Even during our short time in the bush, I had become accustomed to occasionally seeing a horse or cow, being unceremoniously dragged behind some vehicle, towards its final resting-place at the bottom of some deep mineshaft.

By the time we chanced to find the work site unattended, and were able to closely inspect the workings, the sides of the shaft – presumably down to water level – had been completely lined with sawn timber. Blocks and slabs of concrete, the likes of which I had never seen before, were strategically placed around the mine. I was informed that these would be for engine mountings and the floor for a shed.

Soon a nine-inch cast-iron pipeline was snaking its way towards Maryborough along the Mosquito road, heading we were told, for the Settling Ponds, that were situated just out of town on the Ballarat road. At the time the progress seemed so slow to me, but in view of it being such a tedious task joining the relatively short lengths of the heavy pipes with lead, hemp and pitch, I now realise it was amazing how quickly it covered the journey of some two miles. The laying of the pipeline was also a bit of a bonanza for our lead collection: in the process of joining the pipes, it was not uncommon for some lead to be spilt on the ground, the majority of which would be retrieved for reuse. However, it was evident that the workmen either overlooked, or considered it was not worth the effort to retrieve, minute quantities. In any case, this practice – while significantly enhancing our chances of acquiring lead poisoning – considerably boosted our stocks of that heavy metal. Soon the onset of the school Christmas holidays would afford us the opportunity to keep a daily check on the snaking progress of this "great" waterworks project.

* * *

The 1938 school year was something of a scholastic watershed for my three youngest siblings and me, for the whole four of us passed. But with this happy event, there was a touch of sadness for June and me, for Valma and Jack would be leaving our humble old East

State School, for the more stately Technical School, situated on the "better" side of the railway line, across the road from the station. Mind you though, the Technical School was still not the top of the town's state schools. Most people, who were more conscious of their perceived financial/social superiority, almost invariably sent their children to the more prestigious High School.

It wasn't all bad for June and me. June was at last promoted to the sixth grade, while I, after four long years of insufferable torment and "study" in the "Bubs", first and second grades, would progress to third grade. For me, there was also the bonus of not having to carry a slate, for I had advanced to using an exercise book and pen and leaving the infant side of the school's playground, where I had towered over my contemporaries, to join the big kids – many of whom I still dwarfed – on their side of the school.

* * *

Again the similar Christmas rituals of other years prevailed. Our Christmas dinner was the best I could remember having, which no doubt indicated we were slowly but surely lifting ourselves from the depths of our financial pit. The toil of course, was interrupted by our traditional mid-morning break to sample Auntie Mag's Christmas cake.

As we relaxed in the afternoon and evening, enthralled I listened once more to the familiar stories of our family's better days. Fortunately, Dad was well enough to join in reminiscing, and again told us of his early years in Collingwood.

We heard the tales of his youth in Gippsland and of how he happened to leave there. As a favour for a good friend in financial difficulties, he volunteered to take a mob of horses to southern NSW, to avoid him having them confiscated for debt. But instead of returning home immediately after the task as he had intended, he decided to make a slow rambling return journey through North Western Victoria, with the intention of calling on some relations of his Gippsland friends. During this venture, he rode into the picturesque village of Evansford, while a casual mixed cricket game was in progress and one of the publican's daughters was proving difficult to dismiss. It appears that Dad accepted an invitation to attempt that task and succeeded in promptly bowling her out with the first ball.

That meeting caused him to linger in the district longer than he intended. He occupied himself in a variety of rural occupations –

including working on a thrashing-machine, woodcutting and inventing. In due course he married the female "batsman", who 13 years later, became my mother. As was typical of Dad's often-unorthodox behaviour, he simply abandoned his block in Darnum.

* * *

On New Year's Eve, we once more listened to the train and factory whistles and the sound of music and merriment wafting up from the town and Keith again spent the day engaged in the hot-water business at the sports in Prince's Park.

Faithful Auntie Annie and Sis again arrived bearing a decorated cake that Auntie Annie had made to mark the occasion of my birthday. Mostly, the conversation consisted of the reminiscing that I had heard so often, but this year it was interlaced with the threat of war with Germany. I gleaned from what I was hearing that such a war seemed inevitable. This left me with the chill feeling of terror.

* * *

Due to the dry spring and summer, most of Victoria's forests were akin to a tinderbox, awaiting a spark that would bring widespread death and destruction throughout the state.

A few days after my birthday, news of scattered bushfires became a subject of serious conversation. The area south-east of Melbourne seemed to be of particular concern. This caused Dad to speak of the devastating bushfires that had ravaged the state since white settlement, such as the terrors of "Black Thursday" in the tall timber forests of Gippsland. This day was generally accepted to be Victoria's worst bushfire-day on record. We did not suspect that in a few days, "Black Thursday" would lose that notorious title to "Black Friday", a day when fires swept the state, but were particularly disastrous along the hills south-east of Melbourne. Over the next two days, more than seventy human lives were lost. The situation remained desperate until rain eased the situation. Nevertheless, the fires remained a prominent topic of conversation for weeks, as new information and tragic stories added more detail to my terrible mental picture.

* * *

Auntie Tot and Auntie Deb, with an assortment of their family members, made their usual Christmas holiday visits – but still without Yvonne. They, too, spoke of the impending war, but that did not stop Auntie Tot from again expressing disapproval of my family's poverty, which she still perceived as our own fault – or at least Dad's and my older brother's.

* * *

Early in the New Year, the unpleasant liquid that was coming from the tap of our new neighbours confirmed the "salvation-water" from the Princess Royal mine had arrived. The quality of the water soon became a major topic of condemnation and humour. Some asked whether they had got all the dead horses out of the mine. Despite the quality of the water, it did save our town from disaster. During the summer months, on our high part of the town where the pressure was always low, most days tap water was unavailable from early morning until well after dark. On frequent occasions, when our usual collection of eight gallons of potable water was insufficient to see us through a dry scorching summer day, it was a thirsty wait until 9 or 10 pm, when our benefactor's tap began to flow again.

Often while we waited, we would sit outside in the company of Harry and Lil Williamson, who on balmy summer evenings would stroll up to our place – often three or four times a week. They were always welcome: their company was light-hearted and delightful, for it didn't take much of a joke to send Harry's inimitable rollicking laughter into the bush around our camp. The Williamsons had recently sold their grocery business to their next-door neighbour, Mr Mellow. Because his house was next door to the shop, he would not require the attached living area, so arrangements were made for Harry and Lil to remain in residence. Even so, Harry didn't have a very high regard for his benefactor.

At times as we sat outside on a stiflingly hot evening, we would hear a distant murmur in the forest to our south. Quickly the murmur would intensify to a roar, then to wild movement in the treetops and usually with a cloud of dust, we would be engulfed in the refreshing strong breeze of a cool change. Those cool changes would fill me with unbridled ecstasy. Even now, in moments of nostalgia I still relive the magic of those moments.

* * *

As soon as the festive season was over, Bob Cook and Jack decided to explore the realms of the rabbit-trapper. Several rabbit-traps were in our possession and Bob had access to a number that the Cooks possessed. So – with me tagging along, ever hoping we wouldn't catch any rabbits – began some three weeks of dedication to the venture. Each afternoon we would set forth for the hunting grounds around Bluchers and Mosquito. Although we jointly only possessed about a dozen traps, because most were the heavy older type and not the lighter Lane brand, it took quite an effort to carry them so far. On the first afternoon, by the time we selected "sure-fire" sites and set our traps, the sun had set. We made our way home past the cemetery in deepening twilight where the deep moans from several bronze-winged pigeons that inhabited that area, created a weird unreal atmosphere. In spite of Jack and Bob's bravado, I couldn't help being a bit spooked and invariably, each evening of our "hunting season" found us in the same situation. The next morning we were up at daybreak and with Jack and Bob in high hopes we set forth to attend our traps. As we staggered home under the weight of the heavy traps, unlike Bob and Jack, I was thankful that our adventure had been fruitless. My companions could not hide their disappointment, yet they were undaunted and as we trudged along, they identified numerous reasons why our venture had failed. Even after a week's effort with the same results, they were still finding reasons why we hadn't bagged a single rabbit.

One morning as we approached a trap they had set in a dry creek bed behind the cemetery, the distinct rattling of the trap's anchor-chain illuminated their faces – success at last. But as we neared the trap, we realised that there could be worse outcomes than not catching a rabbit. To our horror there, with a hind leg clamped in the brutal steel trap, hissing and snarling with a fury that imparted a threat that far exceeded its physical capabilities, was a huge, yellow, feral tomcat. Bob was not the least affected by the cat's threat or plight, and immediately intimated he would quickly dispatch it as soon as he found a suitable stick. But Jack and I were more compassionate towards the unfortunate creature, and after a tense few moments we prevailed upon Bob's usually dormant sensitive nature, to adopt the more difficult and dangerous task of releasing it. Without further ado, Jack removed his coat and with considerable difficulty, Bob and he managed to confine the teeth and claws beneath it. Once this was done, it was comparatively easy to release the furious animal from the steel jaws. In spite of his original intentions, I believe Bob shared Jack's and my relief when it was confirmed the cat's leg was not broken and had suffered only superficial damage.

Stubbornly Jack and Bob refused to admit defeat. With me in tow, not because of any hunting instinct, but because I would grab any excuse to go into the bush, they continued our morning and evening trips to the rabbit territory for another week or so with still no success. Dad was not a bit concerned about our fruitless efforts, in fact he was sympathetic, but I felt that while he admired our tenacity, he was also a bit amused. Bob's father on the other hand, lacked Dad's philosophic outlook – he expected tangible reward for effort. So after many complaints about Bob's wasted effort, during the third week he demanded that Bob stop wasting time and put his efforts to some more rewarding cause. So ended my "career" as a rabbit-trapper.

33

Illuminated Nights

It turned out that Valma and Jack being promoted to the "Tech" School wasn't all plain sailing, for pupils attending that school were expected to wear its uniform. Furthermore, there was the cost of the necessary books. For people in our circumstances, this was not an easy problem to overcome, especially as in our case, where two uniforms and sets of books were required at the same time. For some poverty-stricken parents with a number of children with a uniform scholastic ability, who attended the school, the burden was diminished somewhat, for some of the necessities could be progressively passed down the line, as the older students moved to higher grades. With considerable strain on our financial resources, a full uniform was obtained for Valma, but fully outfitting Jack was just beyond our means. Fortunately the problem was overcome when it was discovered that variations to the standard boys uniform were tolerated, but it was still mandatory for them to wear the official school cap with its embroidered school badge, which incorporated the school's motto – "Head, Heart and Hand".

Valma and Jack now had to walk more than twice the distance to school as June and me, so they had to leave home earlier. Because June and I were not so pressed for time, it was taken for granted that we would do a bit more of our allotted morning chores particularly milking more of the goats, which we didn't mind at all.

Valma and Jack always liked to be in the schoolyard well before going-in time so that they could mingle with their friends. Although June and I couldn't see any sense in wasting a quarter of an hour or so each morning, because of our strong sibling bond and the pleasure of the feeling of togetherness on our way to school, we complied with their wishes. But now, with that incentive gone, June and I adopted the "just in time principle."

* * *

Dad's failing health did not stop him being passionate about the welfare of his family, Australia and world affairs. He strongly condemned the current Australian government and the incumbent Prime Minister, Joe Lyons, for switching political sides and cowardly allowing the foreign financiers to inflict needless poverty upon so many Australians. It therefore came as a bit of a surprise to me early in April when, hearing that Joe Lyons had suddenly died, Dad solemnly remarked, "Poor old Joe wasn't such a bad fellow". It was evident that Dad did not carry his grudges beyond the grave. All the same, Dad quickly transferred his wrath to the two Prime Ministers that replaced Joe within a short time, for their policies closely followed those of "poor old Joe".

* * *

Since we moved into the bush, all the members of my family had kept pretty good health. Most of us had suffered a number of minor illnesses but until Dad's recent heart trouble, I can't remember anything else that was considered severe enough to warrant the services of a doctor, except for the time Lloyd was badly stung by bees.

Auntie Mag regularly suffered severe headaches. I realise now that they were almost certainly migraines. Although it was plain for anyone to see she was suffering severe pain, usually she would attempt to continue with her normal household activities, but at times the headaches made her so sick she was forced to go to bed. On these days there was always a cloud of gloom over the camp. It was distressing being unable to help her. Even on the occasions when Aspros were available, they were usually of little use.

At times we all got colds, which sometimes were considered severe enough to be called influenza. Like most kids of those days, we got bouts of measles, German measles and chicken pox. Although mumps and whooping cough were often rife at our school, none of us caught whooping cough, and only June contracted the mumps. With colds and influenza (no one ever abbreviated it to flu in those days) a few days being pampered in bed usually saw off the complaint. Despite the discomfort, I always considered that was better than being at school. In the case of measles and chicken pox, Dad insisted we stay in bed for up to a week, even after we began to feel all right. With measles there was great stress placed on the need to reduce the light to a minimum to avoid eye damage. As one would imagine, that was not easy to achieve in a tent. For me, there was one welcome spin-off from having any of those childhood scourges – compulsory quarantining forbade either the patient or siblings from attending school for a week or so.

* * *

From mid autumn, the weather conditions indicated that the winter of '39 was likely to make things unpleasant in our camp. We had over four inches of rain during April. The ever-deteriorating conditions of our ageing tents tested their ability to protect their contents from such an onslaught. Further substantial rain in May made it even harder to keep the beds completely dry. Dad would never have allowed us to sleep in wet bedding, but at times they became clammy. In view of that situation, I suppose it was not too much of a surprise that when Valma was forced to bed with a severe bronchial infection, despite Dad's constant treatment and loving care over the next few days, her condition deteriorated alarmingly. We were all worried sick about Valma; I had never seen anyone as sick as she was. I feel sure that Dad's memory of her life-threatening bouts of pneumonia in her first few years caused him grave concern about the prognosis. He decided it was time to arrange for Doctor Miller to make a house call. The doctor arrived mid morning and, after examining Valma, told Dad to continue the treatment and keep her warm, for he felt sure she had passed the crisis.

Dr Miller was very impressed with our selected land, he said it had great potential and he seemed in no hurry to leave. Despite his illness, Dad still dreamed of better things to come by way of his patented suspension wheel, so he brightened to the occasion and escorted the doctor around the property and passed on his extravagant plans for our selection. Soon they were squatting on a patch of clear ground on the side of the hill, both equipped with sticks, as Dad sketched on the ground his highfalutin plans for the healthy classic house he dreamed he would build. The house was to be round. The doctor was very impressed and would occasionally add a few scratches of what he thought would improve the futuristic plan. He seemed to share Dad's view of the importance of fresh air and sunshine. For more than an hour they talked as Dad unfolded his dreams for the house and the additional prestigious developments that would enhance our real estate.

Contrary to the doctor's opinion, as evening approached it was obvious to us all that Valma's plight was becoming desperate. Dad decided it was essential that she see the doctor again without delay; it could not be put off until the morning. Darkness had now set in, and efforts to find a suitable light for the doctor to examine Valma were to no avail. Until now, candles were unknown in our camp: I think they were two pence each, which put them beyond our reach. However in the prevailing circumstances, cost was not a consideration. With four pence trusted to our keeping, Jack and I set out for Crossley's grocery shop, which like all shops of those days, closed at 6 pm. And it was now about 7 pm. The grocery shop was about three quarters of a mile from our home, so when we arrived all was in darkness except for the light from a small window towards the back of the house. With feelings of uncertainty, we entered the side gate and made our way past their huge pomegranate tree and down the dark somewhat spooky unfamiliar path to the back door. As we neared the lighted window we could clearly hear the loud wireless, and although I had never heard the program before, I think they were listening to the much talked about wireless serial, *Dad and Dave*.

On reaching the back door, we timidly knocked. At that time the Crossleys would not have known either Jack or me, and we only knew them by sight. After a few minutes the door opened to reveal a lady, who asked us our business. We delivered our request and nonchalantly without further ado, she closed the door and moments later the window of the shop, situated in the front part of the house, emitted light. The light in the shop soon went out, and moments later the back door opened again to the increased sound of *Dad and Dave* in the background. With little more than the price from Miss Crossley and a "thank you" from us, we exchanged our four pence for two fine shiny-white Electron candles. It was kind of the Crossleys to even serve us, for everyone was aware that conducting such transactions after hours was against the law, which put them at risk of a fine. Luckily the doctor had not arrived by the time we got home. Soon a candle was lit and us kids gazed in awe at the clear brilliant illumination that – to our eyes – flooded the tent. Within minutes, despite the worry for our suffering sister, we were making weird shadows with our hands on the tent's walls and roof.

In a short time Doctor Miller arrived and instantly assessed the gravity of the deterioration in Valma's condition and proclaimed that the infection had developed into pleurisy. He immediately took her to hospital in his car. Recovery proved to be slow and for days her condition was considered to be serious. It was about a fortnight before she was well enough to return home. During her stay in hospital, our strong family bond ensured she was never short of supportive visitors.

Soon after Valma's illness, Louis, as was usual, unexpectedly arrived home from Melbourne, but this time it was not just for a visit. I gathered that some serious health crisis had struck Mr and Mrs Ball – I have a vague feeling that Mr Ball had actually died. In any case that worthy couple were no longer in need of a chauffeur, so Louis was out of a job. Fortunately he was able to once more obtain a job at Pascoe's dairy.

Evidently Dad's illness caused a bit of a stutter in our ever-so-slow financial progress. I remember on two occasions Dad sending me to see Louis at his work place, on our former property near the east school, to ask him for a desperately-needed couple of shillings. On both occasions he was able to fulfil Dad's request. However, things were about to improve.

It seems that during the doctor's visits to attend Valma, he again brought up the subject of Dad applying for the Invalid Pension. Dad agreed and an application was made forthwith. Now after some delay, Dad received notice that his application had been accepted and from a certain date, he would receive a fortnightly payment, which I gathered was a bit more than the Sustenance. This lift in the family income, via the pension, enabled us to indulge ourselves with a few "luxuries" that we had been deprived of for most of my life. Perhaps the most obvious improvement to our lifestyle was more illuminated nights. Only since Valma's sickness had I realised just how deprived we were in that regard – those candles had been a revelation. No doubt the thought of that recent "luxury", was a factor in the decision that candles were now within our budget and could be used daily – though sparingly and not in every tent.

The old oval-section quart whisky bottle that for as long as I could remember contained a quantity of kerosene which was reserved for the not often used dull hurricane lamp, and for medical purposes – splinters, nail spikes and the like – was now being filled at frequent intervals. This not only allowed the hurricane lamp to be used more frequently, but a couple of small glass lamps that had long since been set aside because of kerosene shortage, were now recommissioned. However because the normal clear-glass flues that caused such lamps to emit a brighter, smokeless yellow light were missing, and the cost of replacing them was still beyond our means, their light was of low quality – reddish, smoky and smelly – but it was still better than no light at all.

34

Living With Fear

As we entered the second half of 1939, increasingly the main topic of conversation was about the possibility of a war with Germany, with emphasis on how it now seemed to be inevitable. Such conversations imbued me with a ghostly nagging fear that swelled to sheer terror in moments of idleness.

The perfume from the glorious blossom of the golden wattle at the end of July; the influx of birds for the flowering of the ironbarks; and the birth of more goats to extend their numbers, was tangible evidence that nature was oblivious to the state of human affairs. We now had a sufficient number of nannies to allow us to be a bit choosey – especially in the flush of the milking season – so any goat that was hard to milk or had a bad temper could be – so to speak – put out to pasture. We no longer routinely gave each new arrival a name at birth, instead they would simply be referred to as so and so's kid. The honour of a name was now reserved for those that had some special characteristic, which often didn't become apparent until sometime after their birth. Of course all of our regular milkers were credited with a name. The name often only referred to some physical characteristic – such as only having one horn or its colour or colour-pattern – preceded by "the" and ending with "goat".

Valma, June, Jack and I assumed ownership of our favourite milkers. It was considered highly unethical to milk another sibling's goat without consent or good reason. Strange though it seems, this arrangement appeared to also suit the nannies, for a degree of bonding would develop between the goats and their milkers.

Occasionally this bond became so strong that some of the goats would vie for attention. This rivalry developed to an astonishing degree with two of June's milkers, named Doosie and Woomelang. If June began to milk one, the other would literally try to squeeze between them. If June gave in and began to milk the interloper, the first goat would adopt the same procedure to stop the milking and the job could only be completed by physically restraining one. This desire for June's attention was so strong that often outside normal milking hours, they would approach her in the yard and hassle each other in an attempt to present themselves for milking.

Sarah was now the universal favourite. She had a dignified personality that is not normally associated with her species. By this time she was the mother of several offspring and the grandmother of many more, but none of them shared her personality. Her twin Donk, was also an outstanding animal and was by far the largest member of our flock and had a placid nature like Sarah.

The other three wethers, though not quite as big as Donk, were also gentle and family favourites. I had been granted the ownership of Donk at his birth and soon after Burbler arrived he was given to Jack. When our sisters arrived home, the ownership of Siberia – a fine looking black-and-white animal with curled horns and "bells" under his chin – was declared to be Valma's. Blanko, who looked somewhat like his older brother Donk, but was smaller and always looked sad, was given to June. In fact his dull demeanour gave Keith the inspiration for his name. I think June drew the short straw.

On occasions, we would sell a goat – always young ones to which we had no close attachment. Although the going price was only ten shillings it gave a welcome lift to our household finances.

The original members of our flock were now getting quite old, so it followed that occasionally one would die. Disposing of their bodies was, at this stage, one of the few jobs concerning the goats that us kids were happy to hand over to the older male members of our family – usually Keith or Lloyd. There were plenty of shallow mines close to home to serve as graves for the deceased goats, which were always covered with a respectable depth of dirt from the mullock heap at the edge of the diggers-holes. Usually Jack and I would attend the "service" and offer whatever assistance we could, while learning the finer points of the job that would soon be handed over to us.

Usually at least one of each pair of twin kids born was a male, as were the majority of single births. Already the percentage of male goats in our flock had reached the point where it was obvious that something had to be done to at least cap, but preferably reduce, their numbers. On rare occasions Louis would assist, but because Keith possessed a rifle, he was almost exclusively conscripted to perform this unpleasant job. As soon as practicable after the birth of the kids – when we youngsters weren't around – most of the newborn males would disappear. At other times we would suddenly notice the absence from the flock of a particular young billy – invariably it would be an unimpressive poor creature that had been stunted due to the goats' inbreeding. But even so, there were always enough billys left to, on numerous occasions, serenade us throughout the night with their competitive amorous blubbering.

* * *

We were saddened to hear that the Chapman family were selling up and going to Western Australia. Since we moved into the bush, Mr Chapman was ever eager – notwithstanding his own difficult circumstances – to help make life easier for my family. Even as he packed to go, his desire to make our lives a little more comfortable was still apparent. He arrived with their veteran Coolgardie safe, which humble as it was, would give us new dietary thrills – we could now have almost cold food in summer. There was even talk of having jellies and Auntie Mag would at last be able to get her special occasion treat for us – Lemon Snow – to set properly. I was looking forward to the onset of summer. Though the Chapmans had really only touched our lives, I could not help but feel deprived by the loss of our true friend.

* * *

Each "new" copy of *The Age* brought more frightening news about the probability of another World War. With dread I would listen to the older members discussing this situation, which everyone seemed to accept as being imminent. I silently prayed that it would not happen, but sadly, unlike my persistent long-standing "Christmas pudding" wish/prayer, which so far was holding rock solid, this no-war prayer was not to be answered.

On 3 September, we heard that Germany had invaded Poland and that England had declared war on Germany. We were told that our Prime Minister, Bob Menzies, had announced it on the radio. We were told that his announcement ended something like – *. . . it is therefore my melancholy duty to announce that Australia is also at war with Germany*. I had not yet fully comprehended the vast distance we were from Europe and its troubles, so my terror of a war was somewhat exaggerated. I imagined that we would immediately be in its midst.

On first hearing the news, uncontrolled fear sent me scurrying over the hill to the vicinity of our old camp, with my mind racing with thoughts of how we could escape the impending doom. For a considerable time I sat with my back against one of the old ironbark trees that had provided shade for us on our first Christmas dinner in the bush and childishly assessed our situation. Then with a glimmer of comforting relief, I perceived a strategy that was even more out of touch with reality than my "lion defence plan". I decided the best thing we could do, would be to go further into the bush, and in times of extreme danger we could hide up trees.

The Age told of terrible land and sea battles but to my relief, as the days and weeks passed, for us things didn't change at all, except that the war dominated every conversation and we were hearing more names of young men who had enlisted. As I began to comprehend just how far from us the war was, my horror of it diminished – except when I heard the drone of an aeroplane approaching.

35

Our Wonderful New Rooms

With the end of the year not too far off, Keith's long and arduous task of building the mud-brick walls of what would be our two new rooms was finally completed. The room at the western end, which would be our living room, was built on clear ground at the rear of our existing open-fronted kitchen, which occupied the space planned for our new kitchen. To enable us to still use the stove and other facilities in the old kitchen while the work was in progress, it was necessary for Keith to build the new room around it. He did this by dismantling its walls and replacing them with mud-bricks as the building progressed. During the process, he also built a proper fireplace, complete with a graceful arch supported by two halves of a steel dray-rim, over the stove.

Because the easterly entrance of the old shelter was now blocked off, it was necessary to use the space provided for the new door on the town side of the building. Another door opening connected the two rooms, but as wooden doors were not available, wheatbag curtains had to serve the purpose for a considerable time. As there was still no galvanised iron available for a new roof, the old kitchen roof of assorted sheet-iron was adjusted to suit our new kitchen.

Keith had managed to fit the window openings of both rooms with frames of pre-used sawn timber that someone had thoughtfully donated. Probably the secondhand fly-wire that covered these openings was obtained from the same source.

With no suitable material available, the back room still remained roofless. It was then that my older brothers decided that if some kind of temporary roof could be improvised, the room could be used in a number of ways that would substantially add to our comfort. After much consideration, it was decided there was only one suitable material in abundance – the room would be heavily thatched with gum tree branchlets. Without further delay a number of excursions into the nearby bush produced the required number of the most geometrically-similar saplings, to serve as rafters for the roof. After being stripped of their bark, the spars were soon set in place on the mud-brick walls. In an atmosphere of happy cooperation, us kids joined in the tedious job of carrying to the building, the fresh eucalypt coppice, which had been selectively knocked from their stumps. Although the thatching progress was slow, within a reasonable time a thick layer of leaves covered the roof, and with the subdued light from the window, a restful eucalyptus-perfumed atmosphere was created within the room.

* * *

Not long after this development, the Hardwicks, after only having had the property for about 15 months, told us they would be selling up and moving to Melbourne where, I gathered, Bill had obtained a job in an aircraft factory. Again we felt bad about losing good neighbours. Over the past year or so, due to our daily visits for water, most of us had established a friendly relationship with the Hardwicks, especially with Mrs Hardwick, for when Bill wasn't at work or tied up with his mouth-organ band, he seemed to be busy fiddling with his motorbike. Even their somewhat nasty dog Ginger, had grown to tolerate our visits without anger, although we never completely trusted him, for he still terrorised other "intruders". Perhaps Ginger's change of heart was fortunate for him, or maybe he somehow perceived that soon his future would be entwined with ours.

As far as I can remember, neither of the Hardwicks had visited our camp until just prior to their leaving, when for some forgotten reason Bill paid us a visit, during which he noticed our newly thatched roof. This prompted him to explain that he had a considerable number of good secondhand sheets of galvanised roofing-iron. He told Keith there would be sufficient to cover both our new rooms, and that we were welcome to them as a parting gift. The offer was accepted with gratitude and – sheet by sheet – the stack of iron was promptly transferred to our place.

Despite his unpleasant nature to most people, there was a strong affectionate bond between Ginger and Mrs Hardwick, so when the Hardwicks discovered that they would not be able to keep a dog in their new accommodation in Melbourne, she was devastated. In desperation she asked us if our family would look after him until they found accommodation where they would be able to keep him. They expected that would be in the not too distant future. Without hesitation my family agreed to be Ginger's guardian.

At first our faithful canine companion Caesar looked upon Ginger as being a bit of an interloper, which at times caused some hostility between them. Because of his reputation of being a bit nasty and a butcher-biter, some members of my family were a bit wary of the new dog, and I at least shared Caesar's "opinion" of him and secretly wished he would go away.

Fortunately for all concerned, Ginger soon proved to be a worthy addition to our household, and would harmoniously accompany Caesar and any of us on our bush excursions.

Although always faithful to us, on several occasions he did blot his copybook. In later years when we advanced to having the cycling butcher-boy, Bobby, call on us, at least twice he reverted to his old habits. Furthermore, he became involved with a pack of goat-mauling neighbourhood dogs. Had the offence been against sheep, there would have been no reprieve. Eventually however, against the widely accepted beliefs on this subject, after several suspected involvements over a brief time in this canine crime, Ginger completely reformed.

Over the next few years, Mrs Hardwick came to visit Ginger a number of times and on each occasion the greeting was one of mutual fond exuberance. However, as the years passed her visits became less frequent and finally ceased. It became clear that Ginger was destined to spend the rest of his long life with my family. In a state of dementia, he just disappeared in the mid-1950s.

Another friendly, easygoing young couple, Harold and Vern Williams, with their two toddlers, Graham and Lawrie, moved into the vacated house. Fortunately, our potable water supply would remain secure, for they were happy to give us all the water we required. Harold was not so engrossed in his own affairs as Bill Hardwick, for he like his wife, always seemed to enjoy having a conversation with us.

36

"Gunning" the Coolgardie and Dreary Washdays

As the end of the 1939 school year approached to our relief, the doctor's prediction seemed to be proving sound, for Dad's sudden "turns" became less frequent and severe. He also became stronger and to a limited degree was again able to resume most of his normal activities.

Some time in the first half of the year, three brothers were welcomed into my grade. Horace the youngest, was around my age, Albert was no more than a year older and Ted must have been his senior by the biological minimum. Although he wasn't as tall as me, Ted looked very solid and mature. It got around the school that none of these siblings had attended school before and that they had been virtually "press ganged" by the education authorities from a life of uninhibited freedom around their bush abode. It seems that their sudden arrival presented quite a dilemma for our school; because of their age, they could hardly put them in the "Bubs", so – in a flash of inspiration – the authorities decided to give them a kick start by putting them all in the third grade. With my track record of scholastic ability I could empathise with them: what mental torture they must have endured.

June had really enjoyed school this year; it was probably the first time since she started school that she had confidence in her scholastic potential. This was to a great degree thanks to her teacher, Miss Mitchell, who inspired June to do her best. The result was that June passed her exams with ease and was looking forward to attending the technical school the following year.

Despite Dad now receiving the Invalid Pension, financing June's further education would still be a problem. Maybe this was because Valma and Jack had also passed their exams and progressed to the eighth grade, so their books would have to be upgraded as well. Then Dad had a brain wave – that also showed just how much his health had improved over the past year or so – "I'll get Doll in and sell her", he declared.

I was delighted that June's wish to go to the "Tech" would be fulfilled, but having recently heard the tragic story of Black Beauty and seeing those poor half starved and overworked euky-horses, I couldn't help feeling concerned about Doll's future. With her free spirit, she would really suffer if she fell into the hands of a cruel owner.

Another highlight of the school year was a visit by a professional photographer, who photographed each grade, and there was no hassle about June and I buying a copy.

To top the school year off, I passed my exams – without honours – and would progress to the fourth grade.

It was still necessary for us to make the three-hundred-yard return-trip to the "spring" to get the water for washing clothes, dishes and for our personal ablutions. This was one of the reasons that ensured washday was always a day of sheer drudgery. Mostly this would be done on a Saturday, when we could help fetch the water. June and occasionally Valma, would help Auntie Mag with the washing. Auntie Mag didn't even have a proper copper in which to boil the clothes. Instead she had to use our extra-large, brass preserving pan, which was boiled on the stove. Often the preserving pan had to be supplemented with a four-gallon kerosene tin boiling on loose bricks each side of a small fire in the yard. The only suitable vessel for the actual washing was a big galvanised iron washtub, which also served as our bath. I hated the long-drawn-out weekly washdays; to me they always cast a gloom over the whole camp.

Even though our best clothes that we kept for school and special occasions, were often well past their best, after their weekly wash they would be diligently ironed by Auntie Mag. In those times most of our acquaintances used the common cast-iron flatirons with all-metal handles. These handles became very hot when the irons were heated on a stove, which necessitated holding the handle with a cloth to prevent burns. A reminder of our more prosperous times, our four streamlined, upmarket, patented irons did not have individual handles, instead there was one heat-resistant handle that easily clipped onto the irons heating on the stove. Later, as electric irons became more common, someone gave us their once valued but now superseded box-iron. Though box-irons were large with a short side-pointing chimney, they were not particularly heavy. Most of their bulk was a hollow firebox. A lid on top was easily opened so that they could be filled with hot charcoal. This negated the need to continually reheat them.

* * *

Lloyd had recently left his milk delivery job and was now working on a farm on the other side of Carisbrook. This change of jobs seemed to coincide with him beginning to engage in extended social activities – although as far as I could gather, the extent of these activities was "going to the pictures". Lloyd was always very concerned about personal hygiene and the fear of developing BO which he never did, equalled his dread of constipation.

This concern demanded that preparations for going out required at least one full bucket of spring water. Although there was normally a small supply of spring water kept in a four-gallon kerosene-tin bucket at the camp for incidental use, whenever any of us required a larger amount of water for personal use – such as a bath – each of us would walk to the spring and fetch it ourselves. After a while Lloyd, now having a few coins to spare, became reluctant to do this tedious chore himself, so he began employing June or me to fetch water, for which we received a threepenny piece. When I got the job, it took me two trips to deliver the required amount, for the same wage. Irrespective of how long we took to fetch the water, as an incentive for us innocents to do the job even faster, we were always offered the same praise on completing the task, "Gosh you were quick". As a result, his waiting time for the water became progressively shorter.

* * *

In the first warm days of summer, after much consideration about the optimum position for it, Chapman's old Coolgardie safe was installed between the big old grey box tree and the top of the sheer quarry-face just a few feet away. The deciding factors for this site were that the tree provided good shade and it was envisaged that cool air currents would rise up the rock face from the sheet of water the quarry contained. What's more, the spot was only a dozen yards from our kitchen.

At first the Coolgardie's only use was to slightly reduce the temperature of our goats' milk, meat and drinking water; even so, we considered it another big leap forward. All of us considered it was our personal obligation to attend the safe, which led to it being a bit over-serviced. This voluntary commitment included keeping the four-inch deep galvanised iron tray that completely covered the top of the safe, topped up with water, and ensuring that the numerous flannel "wicks" that fed the water down the safe's hessian sides, were kept in place and did not dry out. But I had to wait until Christmas Day to appreciate the full potential of our newest acquisition.

Christmas Day 1939 proved to be a measure of our improved circumstances. Our dinner and tea would be served in the enchanting atmosphere of our new back room with its green canopy of still fairly fresh leaves, and the various drinking vessels we had for so long called "cups" had recently been replaced with proper thick white crockery cups. We would also have two "festive delicacies" that were new additions to our celebrations, one of which I had never even seen before.

Since I first tasted that heavenly raspberry cordial at the Sunday school "do", I had often extolled its virtues and longed for the day when it would again tantalise my youthful taste buds. This may, or may not have had something to do with dear Auntie Mag making a snap decision. Not long before noon on the Saturday before Christmas, she asked Jack and I if we would like to go down to Fisher's grocery/hardware store in High Street (which was well over a mile away) to get a bottle of raspberry cordial. This was beyond my wildest dreams – how could we afford such a luxury? In those days, virtually all shops were forced by law to close at 12:30 on Saturday, so when Christmas Day fell on a Monday, as it did this year, they were not permitted to open again until the day after Boxing Day, which would be Wednesday.

There was no way we could refuse Auntie Mag's unexpected offer. There was not much more than half an hour to go before the shops closed, so without delay, we set forth in the blistering heat. We were hot and desperately thirsty by the time we returned from our successful hurried mission, but there was no way Auntie Mag would even consider letting us taste the contents of the precious bottle – it was to be a Christmas Day treat.

Except for the more luxurious venue, real cups and the cordial, Christmas was celebrated in much the same way as it had been since we moved to the bush. As usual Keith had decorated the camp with suckers freshly gathered from the bush, and a mid-morning sampling of Auntie Mag's Christmas cake with a cup of tea, again broke the busy morning of preparing our "extravagant" midday dinner. At agreed intervals throughout that thirsty day, we would assemble to be given an equal measure of delicious fruity raspberry cordial, which was sparingly mixed with the coolish water from our Coolgardie. We still didn't have drinking glasses, but as I could not remember us having such a luxury, I didn't feel the least deprived. In fact I thought we were really living it up.

After our "big blow out" – as Auntie Mag always referred to such feasts – in the cool mud brick room with its fresh green leaves, and the dreary job of washing up the dishes done, resting was the most popular pastime. Of course, during the afternoon and later in the evening after tea, considerable time was spent in what was substantially a "replay" of the enchanting reminiscing of previous years.

For tea, there was a sumptuous first course, consisting of cold meat left over from dinner, and an abundance of salad vegetables from our garden. However it was the anticipation of the sweets that aroused my taste buds most, for there was something in store that I had never seen or tasted before.

Early that morning I had watched with intense interest as Auntie Mag emptied two packets of tangy fruit-perfumed jelly crystals (one raspberry and one lime) into two of our cut crystal bowls which, like our damask tablecloth, were reserved for special occasions. When she added the recommended measure of boiling water, the increased fragrance confirmed that my anticipation of tasting something really delicious was warranted. Throughout the day we eagerly checked the jellies in the Coolgardie to see if they were setting, but the process was painfully slow. In an attempt to "gun" the safe's cooling power, we began to periodically splash the safe's hessian sides with water to supplement the supply delivered by the flannel wicks. However, our efforts were only partially successful, for when it was time for them to be served with the familiar fare of such auspicious occasions, it was still little more than slurry which fell far short of my expectations. I had no desire to ever have it again.

Despite the jelly disappointment, that Christmas Day stamped itself firmly in my memory, and as I went to bed – this time in the light of a candle – I could not help feeling smug about our new "affluence". I now realise that figuratively speaking, our fingernails had barely reached the rim of the financial chasm into which we had fallen.

Over the rest of the school holidays, Dad, with a sense of urgency, frequently mentioned, "I must see about getting Doll in".

37

Emerging Affluence

At the end of the school holidays there was still no sign of Doll and the prospects of "getting her in" seemed as remote as obtaining the school necessities for June, so her school days ended.

Even if a job had been available for her, June could not have taken it, for she was only thirteen and a half, and the legal age to start work was fourteen. Without any fuss, it was resolved that until Doll was captured, June would stay home to assist Auntie Mag and be general rouseabout. This certainly made the mornings a little less rushed for Valma, Jack and me. Although we still helped with the morning milking, if we were running a bit late, which was the case more often than not, we would leave June to happily complete the operation.

It soon became evident that even though June had shared my reluctance to be at school any earlier than necessary, she had been more diligent in this respect than me. Now that I was more-or-less a free spirit on my journeys to school, my efforts to make it before the going-in bell progressively seemed to be less important. Soon it came to the point where I habitually did not reach my classroom until precisely at the end of the ten-minute spelling bee, which was the first item of each day and the subject I hated most. At first my teacher, Miss Sears, mildly rebuked me, but accepted my believably edited and enhanced, though basically true reasons for being late. Sometimes she even kept me in for a short time after school, but missing the spelling bee made it all worthwhile. Yet, there was something else that irked me even more than the spelling bee.

Each Monday morning, before the normal procedure of marching into school to the beat of the drum played by Georgie – and after he left the school, Bobby – all the school's pupils were forced to gather under the flag high on its pole, to take the oath. Being forced to "parrot" those words was something I really disliked.

I love God and my country . . . I certainly loved Australia, even though at that time my only personal knowledge of it was Maryborough and the few square miles of bush to the southeast, plus the road to Evansford and their environs. But I had heard lots about the wide wonderful land from my elders and the moving Australian poems and stories my siblings and others had read to me. I also thought I was on pretty good terms with God. He scared me a bit, but I was grateful for all the wonderful things in nature and for the love of my family and friends. What's more, to date, my standard Christmas pudding wish was still being granted.

I honour the flag. No worries about that either – especially after the school's old red flag was replaced with a brand new one. It made me feel good whenever I saw the white stars of its Southern Cross against their blue background fluttering in a breeze.

I will serve the King and cheerfully obey my parents, teachers and the law. I certainly had no problems obeying Dad and Auntie Mag, and I did my best not to upset any teacher and I'd be too scared to break the law even if I ever had any desire to do so. It was only that bit about the King. I had nothing against the King and his family, but Dad had instilled in us that our allegiance should be to Australia, not to the head of a privileged English family.

Trouble was, I realised that I would be stretching my luck a bit by missing both the oath and the spelling bee, so on Mondays I was obliged to display my illiteracy by way of the latter.

* * *

On hearing glowing reports of the opportunities to be found grape picking in the Mildura area, Louis and one of his mates set forth for those northern vineyards.

Within a short time a communication from Louis extolled the virtues of Mildura as a fabulous place where grape picking provided plenty of work with good pay and free lodging. He implored his older brothers to join him post-haste. In response to Louis' glowing report, Lloyd and Sid Murray set forth without delay. Keith, however, was not tempted, probably it was summer and he was getting regular apiary work. He was now almost exclusively working with the partnership of Mr Rich senior ("Sticky') and his son Claude.

A short time later, to our surprise, we were informed that there was a case of grapes awaiting us at the railway station. The grape consignment consisted of two varieties, gordoes and sultanas. Although we did not know to which one we were indebted, this gift was obviously from one or perhaps both, of our brothers. It was indeed a gourmet addition to our fruit-lacking diet – I could not remember ever having grapes before. I particularly loved the seedless sultanas.

When Louis and Lloyd returned home after the picking season, it was obvious that they had both loved the somewhat rough but adventurous experience. For me, the words of their anecdotes painted an exciting picture of an environment and lifestyle of another world. But what added even more pleasure to their homecoming was that they brought home another case of grapes.

* * *

With the war now well under way, jobs were becoming more plentiful. Not long after Lloyd returned from Mildura, he met one of his former teachers from the technical school, who told him they were looking for workers at Patience & Nicholson, the local small-tools factory. Lloyd promptly applied for a job and began working there immediately.

Within a short time Keith also gained a job at the same establishment. The wages were far better than either he or Lloyd had previously received. At that time, P & N was the only manufacturer of metal-cutting drills, taps and dies in Australia. This made it a vital link in Australia's defence scheme.

Probably Louis could have obtained a job there too, but he seemed to be restless and often spoke of trying his luck in Melbourne again.

Over Easter, Jack and I made our first solo foray into community activities when we attended the opening, by our local Member George Frost, of the Simson Memorial. It was a new experience for us as we stood amid the crowd of some two thousand people watching the formalities of the occasion and listening to the many speakers extolling the virtues of our first white settlers.

* * *

It was around this time that the disappearance of our dog Caesar spread a blanket of gloom over our camp. Although it was only about three years since we got him as a pup, because of his friendly nature and dedication to our family, he was held in great affection by all of us.

This was a time when it was not uncommon for dogs to disappear. These occasions always caused an uneasy feeling in the neighbourhood, for without a scrap of evidence, the owners would often harbour suspicions of foul play from some particular person and even sensitive innocents would feel that they were under suspicion. On occasions, most male dogs would go missing and turn up several days later with severe injuries inflicted by lecherous rivals. When our dogs went missing, Dad would always say, "They have probably gone to a conference". But we knew better: we had seen packs of up to a dozen bad-tempered males around some particular house, or following a reluctant female through the streets or the bush. At first, this knowledge kept our hopes high that Caesar would return, but as the days turned to weeks, we knew in our hearts that he would never again accompany us on our excursions into the bush.

On hearing of our loss, our new neighbour, Harold Williams, explained to Jack that one of his dogs, a whippet, was in pup and that when the pups arrived he could select one. Jack eagerly, but patiently, waited for the happy event.

In those days people never used the word "pregnant": dogs were always referred to as being "in pup", cats were "having kittens" cows were "in calf", sheep "in lamb", goats "in kid" etc.

What's more, as far as the vast majority of the population was concerned, even women were never referred to as being pregnant. The most popular and polite way of referring to the condition was that so and so was "expecting" or "having a baby". Some of the old people still even used expressions such as "in the family way", or "going to bed".

Finally the whippet-staghound cross pups arrived, and Jack had the privilege of first choice. He chose a tan and white male. It was a long wait for him to be weaned but, finally with joy all around, we brought the pup home. Jack was unrelenting in his claim of ownership, but he made no attempt to restrict our access and allowed us to equally enjoy the pleasure of the lovable new pup. Finding an acceptable name for our new dog proved to be a bit of a hurdle. The ones suggested just didn't seem to suit him. Even Keith, who had a flair for thinking up unorthodox appropriate names for our goats and other pets, appeared to be stumped. In view of this, while we waited for someone's inspiration, he was simply called "The Pup". That name persisted for many years, until like our other dog, Caesar, he too disappeared.

* * *

Keith and Lloyd being in regular work substantially improved their financial positions and enabled them to chip in a bit more board than previously. Although their board was minimal, it enabled us to now regularly purchase items that were previously unknown in our household, or were only seen on special occasions. Kerosene was now considered to be well within our means and at times we even bought it in four-gallon cans. We could also afford to buy glass flues for our kerosene lamps, which certainly brightened our evenings.

In view of our emerging affluence, Dad bought a skinny old milking cow from one of the local dairies. This was done in the hope that we would be able to recommission the old family separator and once again introduce cream – the luxury that Auntie Mag seemed to miss most of all – back into our regular diet. Soon after two young heifer calves joined her in "Noor" Davies' paddock. I have a feeling that they were given to us.

"Noor's" paddock was not renowned for its grass production, besides any grass from the seed that did manage to sprout, was soon gobbled up by the goats. For that reason a subsistence quantity of food was collected from other sources. Mostly it was grass from friendly acquaintances, or a limited quantity of hay. To subsidise these meagre rations, frequently us kids would be conscripted to take the cow and calves into the bush where they were able to forage out a limited quantity of "bush-tucker". It was such a boring job; we were often distracted by more interesting things and the next thing we knew was the cows had disappeared. They were pretty smart cows; they would head straight for the town where they knew the best pickings were to be found either along the gutters and footpaths or – which was far worse anti-social behaviour – in the public and private gardens.

Although Dad always rebuked us mildly for our fall from grace, we never had to suffer the indignity of receiving the wrath of the town authorities or citizens. This onerous task was always either undertaken by Dad or, more often than not, poor Lloyd was conscripted.

Sad to say all this hassle proved to be of little avail. Possibly because of our cow's unorthodox diet, the milk and cream expectations never really came to fruition. At times we would have enough milk to be worth separating, but those occasions were few and far between and we still had to depend on our less fastidious goats for our main milk supply.

38

All Hands to an Architectural Folly

By the end of January, the eucalyptus branchlets on the roof of our new room were tinder dry and a considerable fire hazard. Worse still, the species of grub that infested and pervaded the leaf-heaps of the cutters with their silken webs, had discovered the rich environment of our thatched roof. Now the grubs, each on a silken thread, were descending on the occupants of the room, in the manner of rescuers from a helicopter. It was agreed that it was time to make use of Bill Hardwick's gift of corrugated iron. With Keith leading the operation, the work promptly got under way. This necessitated obtaining extra saplings from the bush for the framework of the new kitchen roof, and the expense of buying roofing-nails. Nevertheless, within a short time the job was completed and we were the proud owners of two spacious iron-roofed rooms.

This momentous leap forward stirred Louis' fertile imagination. He was always thinking up fanciful ideas on how our lot could be improved. Looking back, I now realise he considered himself something of a "chief". He was always trying to enthuse other members of the family to be his "Indians". Although we usually cooperated, rarely did any of his inspirations come to fruition. However, on one occasion, all his siblings embraced the idea.

His scheme was to build a much grander structure that could be used for social activities and leisure – to be precise, a family room. The most appealing aspect of his plan was the method of construction, which would enable it to be quickly built at a minimal cost.

It would be built with bush-timber and completely covered with readily available wheatbags coated with cement slurry.

The only significant expense involved in the project was for several bags of cement but in the euphoria of the occasion, that seemed of little consequence.

Without delay the older boys began constructing the framework for the – by our standards – spacious room, while we younger members of the family began opening a large number of the wheat-bags and started sewing them together with needles and twine into the enormous wagga required for its covering.

A few days later, on Saturday afternoon, the frame was completed and with the extra help from the now out-of-work "carpenters", the precisely measured wagga was completed by about noon on Sunday.

We were all anxious to see the completed fruits of our labour, so straight after dinner, with Louis as "chief engineer", the final stages of the project began.

With all hands on deck, the huge bag-blanket was stretched out on a suitable patch of flat bare ground just below the tree Dad had foreseen as ". . . an ideal hitching post for visitors' horses when our tennis court is a going concern".

Louis emphasised that because of the short time we would have before the cement started to set, it was essential that this final phase of the construction be swiftly performed.

To facilitate the procedure, the tools that would be required had been assembled at the building site. These tools consisted of a couple of rough bush ladders for those who would need to work aloft, and an ample number of slender sapling-poles for the rest of us to help hoist the saturated fabric into position.

Soon a substantial number of kerosene tins were filled with the estimated requirements of the smooth cement slurry and the sloppy job of methodically saturating the large expanse of hemp began. Then in an intense atmosphere worthy of the momentous occasion, we took up our designated positions around the huge soggy wagga, and the signal was given to lift. Instantly it was obvious there were unforeseen problems.

Even the strongest members of the workforce were only able to lift a couple of yards of its edges a few feet off the ground, while the large heavy central portion sagged and clung unrelentingly to the ground. We were somewhat shattered by this early setback, but my older brothers were far from accepting defeat and suggestions on how to overcome the problem flowed fast and strong. After a couple of hours of strenuous effort we had scarcely moved the disaster from its original position, but it was only when the cement-slurry coating began to dry and crack, that my brothers accepted defeat.

Now that it didn't matter if we damaged the material, with great difficulty we managed to drag the monstrosity into a secluded spot and fashion it into a somewhat artistic dome-shaped mound, which remained in that spot as a monument to our folly for more than twenty years.

39

Eventful Evenings

Keith and Lloyd usually worked nine or ten hours a day, alternating week about between day shift and night shift. The day-shift week carried the obligation to work overtime on Saturday, often for a full day. That didn't give them much time to carry out many of their normal duties, so Jack and I were now taking over some of their former domestic work.

One of those jobs was taking turns as honorary solo undertaker for the occasional goat that died. Jack and I had no objection to relieving them from this far-from-pleasant job. After all, we had usually attended these events, so we were well informed about the procedure. We seemed to have tacitly agreed that the departed animal should be allowed to lie in state for as long as decently possible. Usually this period endured until when the wind was from a direction where the revolting stench began to reach the camp, or less often, when one of our neighbours kindly alerted us "innocents" to the situation. Despite the fact that our delay exacerbated the onerous task of placing the maggot-infested deceased on a suitable piece of old sheet iron and dragging it to a previously selected suitable digger's-hole, we never seemed to learn. It was always a great relief, when the body was finally covered with a decent depth of earth, from the usually quite digable nearby mullock heap.

Later, when I had become the sole goat-undertaker, I had the emotional job of burying poor old Donk, who had been such a lovable family pet since before we left the house by the school. Over the years we had periodically harnessed Donk to our billycart with the harness Keith had skilfully made from bits of old discarded horse-harness, with the hope of collecting firewood or some other similar task. Unfortunately, Donk had been very poorly broken-in and invariably, more energy was expended in controlling him, than what would have been required to do the job ourselves. Nevertheless, it was always fun and we never failed to convince ourselves that it was a labour saving activity. By the time I conducted Donk's burial, I had become an avid bird-watcher. I never missed an opportunity to spend any spare time I had pursuing this healthy, outdoor hobby. When restricted to a limited time, I had discovered that the most rewarding close locality was around the local cemetery, because some of the most interesting feathered visitors to our area were to be found perching on headstones in the graveyard. This led to a genial friendship developing between the sexton and me. Often I would admire the skill of this former miner as he deftly removed flakes of the concrete-hard sandstone from the graves he was digging. At times after funerals, I would admire how artistically he had fashioned the neat heap of earth atop the grave. I decided that Donk's grave was worthy of such a mound. Instead of just finding a suitable digger's-hole, I selected a peaceful spot on the top of the hill between Louis' old mine and our place and began the gruelling task of digging Donk's grave in the hard hilltop earth. Contrary to the practice in some human societies, where eminent persons are allowed to lie in state for long periods, because of his prominence and my affection for him, I decided he should be promptly buried. After the interment, I completed the job with a mound that my sexton friend, Peter, would have been proud of.

All went well for several weeks; worthy Donk reposed in peace. Then one night around 10 o'clock, just as we were all thinking about going to bed, our attention was drawn to the sound of several muffled voices and torches coming across the quarry bank towards our place. Louis approached them to ask the reason for their intrusion at such a late hour. He was quite startled when he realised the party consisted of our local detective, three constables and one of our nearest neighbours. Very much annoyed, the officious detective explained that the now embarrassed neighbour had noticed a grave on top of the hill, and in the spirit of a responsible citizen had reported it to the police, who in turn arranged the moonlight dig.

I assume that at the first sighting of Donk's grey hair, they thought that they were on the verge of revealing a dreadful crime. That may sound fanciful, but the fact that they continued to completely exhume poor old Donk's remains and scatter them in a wide area around the grave, seemed to indicate that they suspected it might have been used as a ruse to conceal some ghastly deed hidden below. After unpleasantly endeavouring to transfer their own stupidity to us, they left the scene. The thing that upset me most though, was that they didn't have the decency to return the remains to their resting place and refill the grave, that putrid job was left for me to do next day. It was some weeks before I was free of the guilt and embarrassment for causing our normally affable law enforcers so much manual work and failure to bring a bit of excitement into their jobs. Now when I look back, I realise that this episode was a compliment to Peter's unintentional teaching.

After celebrating her fifteenth birthday in May, Dad agreed that Valma could fulfil her wish and apply for a job at MKM, the local knitting mill. At that time, it was by far the biggest employer of females in the town, employing over 300 workers. There appeared to be a demand for more labour in most factories: this was required to meet the production demands of the war, so it was no surprise that Valma was asked if she could start the next day. On her fourteenth birthday a week later, June also applied for a job at the same establishment, and as a result started work next day. Like Keith and Lloyd they were also expected to work overtime, although not to the same extent. They would start work at 7:45am and knock off in the evening at 5:45pm. These hours included an hour break for dinner, which enabled them to come home.

With the winter upon us, it was quite dark at 5:45, and both my sisters were scared of the dark, so someone was always on hand to meet them at Harrop's corner. This job which was usually a pleasant task, was mostly allocated to Jack and me. At times Dad would carry out the duty. On rare occasions when either Jack or I was unavailable to fulfil this obligation, the other would perform the guard duty solo. I can't speak for Jack – he would never have admitted it even if he was – but the trip down to the corner alone, always scared me stiff, and I am sure that I was far more relieved to see our sisters than they were to see me.

This left only Jack and I attending school. We were once again committed to not only milk all the goats, but each morning to trudge over to Williams' place with our billycart, to fetch our daily requirements of two four-gallon tins of potable water. Sometimes, if we were running late and because Jack had further to go to school, I would make the trip alone and more rarely Jack would have to go alone. On my own, I could only manage one tin of water at a time, so we would suffer water restrictions until someone was available to collect more.

Valma and June, with their own personal income, seemed to blossom. Although they were not expected to pay any board, their being to a limited degree self-sufficient, certainly further relieved our financial position. Within a short time, my sisters decided to buy a new bike each on time-payment. The cost of the bikes was sixteen pound each. They signed up to pay this off at ten shillings a week. Because they were only earning sixteen shillings and sixpence a week, Dad was quite concerned at them burdening themselves with such a debt. But after some persuasion, he consented and signed the agreement. As was the case with Lloyd, they would often hire Jack or me to do little jobs for them and at times – which was always the case with Keith – they would give us a modest donation.

* * *

In 1937, the main shopping street of Maryborough was dramatically transformed when G. J. Coles opened a "grand" chain store, the likes of which had never been seen in the town before. They proudly boasted that nothing in the shop cost more than two-and-six. For that reason, it was commonly known as the half-crown shop.

This new business certainly out-shone the town's only other chain store. This new challenge to their supremacy evidently stirred the O. Gilpin establishment into upgrading their now humbled shop. As a result, they shifted into a fine big building, just a few shops down from Coles, in 1938.

Each Friday night the shops in the main business centre stayed open until 9 pm. In the atmosphere of togetherness that the war had created in our community, this event was virtually looked upon as a social occasion that was not to be missed by the young at heart, for the atmosphere in High Street always seemed to be jubilant. With a few disposable shillings to spare, my sisters began to enjoy the pleasures of late night shopping and soon made it a weekly event. For their protection, Dad encouraged Jack and

I to accompany them, which caused no pain at all. Even Jack and I could now jingle a few coins in our pockets, although our combined wealth would have rarely reached "two bob", but as was the case with most of the others that roamed through the shops, the main attraction was window-shopping, not buying. When Jack and I did buy anything we always spent our money wisely, mostly at Coles, or O. Gilpin's.

A few months after the start of our enchantment with Coles, we were sorely disillusioned by a very nasty event. At the time, I still retained my penchant of earlier years for heavy, oversized overcoats. One night while we were innocently browsing over the display of mind-boggling items that we could never hope to possess, two despicable floorwalkers approached us and in front of the other people that crowded the shop, ordered us to accompany them to the manager's office. On noticing our plight, faithful Valma and June followed us. Without any preamble, the haughty manager instantly accused us of shoplifting and ordered us both to turn out our pockets and then remove our coats. My certainty of our innocence did not ease the sheer terror that I felt. After much humiliation and a thorough search of all our pockets and not even finding as much as a pin, without the slightest apology we were escorted to the front door and told not to return.

When we told Dad of the event he was ropeable and swore that he would speak to the manager about his outrageous behaviour towards us. Dad visited the shop early on the following morning, and severely berated the manager, who cowered before Dad's verbal assault as he apologetically offered weak excuses.

That was my last visit to a Coles chain store until I was well into my 20s. Jack was even less forgiving than I was, for he never again entered a single G. J. Coles shop. Treat the young well, for the chances are they will have a long time to remember.

40

Socialising and Shopping Sprees

Our new kitchen and living rooms, with their door and screened windows, did wonders to reduce the fly problem in those areas. In the kitchen at meal times, the amount of waving required to ward off determined competition for our food was greatly reduced.

However, these improvements did nothing to reduce the problem in our tents, for the Council rubbish tip was still operating within a few hundred yards from our home. During the warmer months, each night the flies continued to cluster in thousands on the ridge-poles of the tents and Dad was still doing his morning round with his firebrand of poker and kerosene soaked rag. Although this was a big improvement on the flaming rolled up paper, it was still a pretty crude piece of equipment. Its worst aspect was that once it was lit, there was no way of controlling the flame; it just blazed dangerously, not only while it was singeing wings in the highly flammable tents, but also during its journeys between them.

The high danger of this procedure worried me, but I was aware that for our health and sanity, the job had to be done. That problem aroused my imagination into trying to think of a safer device. Possibly owing to Dad's influence, or perhaps through the genes he had passed on to me, from the time I first learned to reason I was always daydreaming up new and "wonderful" things to make. Unfortunately, at this time, not even one of those "fabulous" ideas had been tested; they only ever had form in my imagination, for there was no way I could have made them myself and I resisted mentioning these inspirations to anyone, because of an unfounded fear of being ridiculed. Eventually an idea dawned on me, it would be simple to make and I felt sure it would be a winner. Yet, even with the conviction that it would be a goer, I would never have dared to proceed with the project alone. I mustered the courage to mention the concept to Jack and I was amazed at his enthusiasm.

As I have previously mentioned, discarded working fly spray pumps could be readily found at the rubbish tip and at any time we would have several on hand – but never any fly spray. The quantity of spray we would have needed to kill all our flies, made that option still far beyond our means. Kerosene though, was now a different matter. Without delay, we assembled the several fly sprays in our possession and filled each one with water to test them for leaks and suitability. There were two distinct types: one kind had a small siphon tube, which could only send out a slender column of vapour not much more than a foot in length. The other brand had a siphon pipe of a much larger diameter. This one produced a cone of vapour about eighteen inches long, and at its furthest point it covered an area more than a foot across. That was the type we selected for our project.

Within minutes we had the tank of one filled with lighting kerosene. Although we had often heard this oil was very unlikely to explode, it was with considerable trepidation that we advanced to the next step. I took the box of matches from my pocket and held a match at the ready. With synchronised timing, Jack pushed the pump handle home as I held the match flame at the edge of the vapour cone. With the sound of a mild explosion, a large, scary cone of red flame burst out before us. We repeated the experiment several times with equal success.

The only drawback was that it was a two-person job and rather extravagant with matches. Suddenly, Jack solved the problem with a simple idea that had not even crossed my mind – we would wire a short piece of candle to the spray's fuel tank, so that the flame from the candle would be just in front of the opening of the siphon tube. The problem was solved. But there was still a major obstacle – we would have to present it to Dad for approval.

To me, Dad's adjudications on potential dangers never seemed consistent. For example: he would severely berate us for placing any object too close to a path where it might trip someone; or for leaving a shovel turned up the wrong way because if stood on, it could fly up and cause injury. Yet he allowed us to have bows and arrows, shanghais and carry matches. In view of this, what he would think of our flamethrower was completely unpredictable.

To our amazement, he was instantly impressed by our invention and was obviously proud of our ingenuity. What's more, every member of the family shared his enthusiasm and flamethrowers quickly became our standard method of fly control and were even used in our two new rooms when a few flies came in. Strangely, they produced a very low-temperature flame, it was quite useless to try and heat up any object with them, and it even took several bursts to set paper alight.

* * *

The evening visits from Harry and Lil Williamson were becoming more regular since the two rooms were completed and illuminated. They would often stay well into the evening, playing euchre with various members of our clan. Within a short time the Williamsons introduced Valma and June to the card game of crib, to which they soon became addicted and played at every opportunity.

For as long as I can remember, Auntie Mag loved playing cards and if she could spare the time, she was always pleased when we asked her to join in our games. We played a variety of games, ranging from grab to euchre. Auntie Mag had taught me the simplest of these games in two-handed "bouts" back in the house by the school. Although Auntie Mag knew all about crib and at times would reminisce, "We played crib at home, when we were young", it seemed strange that she had not taught us the game. My only interest in crib was the intriguing ornate counting board and its pins. I have no doubt that not having such a board was the reason why our devoted aunt failed to teach us that particular game.

When they came before dark, on pleasant evenings, the Williamsons still preferred to sit outside and chat with various members of our family. With the war news daily becoming graver, it was always a significant proportion of the conversation. Harry was by no means a fool, yet his high esteem for Dad, resulted in him making an exaggerated assessment of my father's ingenuity and inventive powers. Persistently he would make it known to Dad that he should be putting his mind to discovering something that would help the war effort.

Rarely would a visit pass without Harry asking Dad, "What invention are you working on now, Courtney?" Dad would give some vague non-committal reply, into which Harry would read a hint of it being something of great national significance. Although fully aware of the many matchbox messages of those days, about the dangers of idle talk, for example: "Loose lips sink ships", Harry could not subdue his curiosity: from time to time he would "fish" for a clue as to the nature of Dad's endeavours. One evening when Dad was evidently feeling a bit "loose lipped", he "confessed" that he was working on a gun that would shoot around corners. For moments Harry was silent, he seemed stunned by the concept, then the mere absurdity of such a thing suddenly sent the sound of his hearty laughter through the camp. Yet, when the laughter ceased, it was clear that Harry wasn't quite sure how to handle the information, but the fact that on every visit he would furtively ask Dad "How's the invention coming on?" showed that Harry had not dismissed Dad's answer out of hand.

While Harry was still engrossed in this atmosphere of mystery, one of Jack's new technical school friends gave him a breeding pair of domestic white doves. The doves were to be free ranging, so to cater for their roosting and nesting needs, a specially made nesting-box was placed high in the grey box at the edge of the small quarry. By the time Harry and Lil arrived each evening, the doves were "tucked up" in their new home, thus obscuring the box's purpose. But it didn't take Harry long to spot the box and conclude that it had to be part of Dad's "secret project". On following visits Harry would furtively view the box and on noticing the lack of change, he always seemed disappointed at Dad's tardiness. We were sorry when Harry and Lil shifted to Talbot and their visits came to an end.

Around this time Mrs Keith, with her son and daughter Courtney and Barbara, began to visit us on a regular basis. Courtney was my age; Barbara was a couple of years younger. Mrs Keith was the wife of Hughie, a major shareholder and director in the Goeben Wheel Company and I had been told that before the death of our mother, they were both close friends of my parents. The Keiths had four children, three girls and one boy. I gathered that a few years before this time, the Keiths had legally separated and the father had custody of the two oldest girls and had taken them to live on his farm in the Boort area. The two youngest children lived with their mother in Park Road. I think we all enjoyed their visits, although I admit I was a bit envious of Courtney's pump-up wheeled scooter and the sparkling new bikes that Barbara and he rode. To me they appeared to ooze with affluence.

Before long members of my family, including us four youngest, began to return their visits and were regularly invited down for tea, after which we would play cards and other games I had never seen before. I particularly enjoyed the game of Bobs. During these visits, I could not help admiring the plant with beautiful strange waxy looking leaves and flowers that grew in a square cement pot on their back veranda. This plant covered much of the house's back wall to which it clung. It appeared to be very old. When Mrs Keith died many years later and the house was being cleared for sale, I became the proud owner of the plant that I had admired for so long. Almost seventy years after I first saw it, that hoya still thrives, in that very same pot, at our front door.

* * *

Owing to our increased prosperity and his greatly improved health, Dad had been able to make several trips to Melbourne on business to do with his dormant Goeben Wheel Company. He was usually away for two or three days and would either stay at the home of an old company friend, or at the Melbourne Coffee Palace which I gathered, offered very reasonably priced accommodation. His reports on these Melbourne visits indicated that they followed the same agenda: he visited the Patents Office and a number of his lapsed company's shareholders, and a visit to Parliament House to see our State Member, George Frost, seemed to be obligatory.

Although Valma and June were now working and slowly changing into young women, my three youngest siblings and I still retained a special bond of trust and affectionate understanding. However, a few things were changing. The competition between June and Jack simply faded away, and they were less interested in joining Jack and me in our recreational activities and began to find their own interests. They (especially Valma) began to make new friends and acquaintances. Valma always seemed to have some girl whom she proclaimed to be her "best friend", but it proved to be a fleeting honour, for they were always changing. Dad soon realised this habit and after each change became obvious, he would tease her by solemnly asking, "How's so and so?" to which would come the standard reply, "Oooor heeer!"

Near the end of spring, Valma and June joined the Knitting Mill's

Ladies Cricket Team and began to play in local competitions. On one occasion, a match was arranged to play a game against a team in Ararat. Dad was very reluctant to let them go by themselves, so Lloyd obligingly agreed to accompany them as their chaperone. This necessitated Lloyd borrowing Louis' suit for what proved to be for him a momentous occasion, for it was during this trip that he met Evelyn – another member of our sisters' team – who in due course, became his wife.

Not long after that occasion, Valma and June made a train trip to Talbot, to spend a weekend with the Williamsons. The girls enjoyed the visit so much that they decided to shout Jack and I on a similar train trip, with the added pleasure of spending a day with Harry and Lil.

The four of us turned up at the station at the appropriate time, for what we anticipated would be a great adventure, for it would be Jack's and my first train ride. But there was a problem. When our sisters fronted the ticket box, they discovered that the price was more than it had been on their previous trip and they were a few pence short. We stood bewildered and disappointed, as the departure of the train was imminent. Then without hesitation, June insisted that we three go without her. There was just time to get the tickets and without thinking, we were off. I will never forget the sight of our unselfish youngest sister standing forlornly on the platform as we slowly moved away. The train trip was a wonderful experience and Harry and Lil were delighted by our unexpected visit, but sadly, that wonderful day was severely blighted by guilt for deserting June.

* * *

Now that Keith and Lloyd were earning reasonable incomes, they both – as Louis had always done – began to lead more active social lives. Lloyd still seemed to prefer going to the pictures, not only on Saturday, but when he was not on nightshift he would often go on Wednesday night as well. He also began to go out more with his friends during daylight hours. Keith also started going to the pictures on occasions, but he preferred dancing, so he began to attend the regular Saturday night dances, which were held at the Workers Hall.

These activities called for an upgrade to their wardrobes and the trendiest male attire for socialising – especially ballroom dancing – at that time, was a double-breasted suit. Louis, of course, had been in possession of such a suit for as long as I could remember. Although such suits were available "off the rack", in Maryborough, on one of his frequent visits home from Melbourne, Louis convinced our brothers that he could get them a better deal in Melbourne, so they readily accepted his offer. After taking their precise measurements, he set forth on his mission and shortly after, each became the proud possessor of a pinstriped navy-blue double-breasted suit. Keith could now also attend the balls that were periodically held in our town.

Because we still lacked wardrobes, storage remained a problem, so the practical thing to do was to keep the suits in the large flat cardboard boxes in which they came. Lloyd decided that the best place to store his box was on the converted washstand table in his tent. Even there, space was also at a premium so it was necessary to place the suit-box on top of a number of other items that occupied some half of the tabletop. Unfortunately, the suit-box was far bigger than the things on which it rested and overhung them like a veranda.

One evening a few days later, Valma had some reason to go into Lloyd's tent and unconsciously placed a burning candle on the table with its flame several inches below the overhanging box. Suddenly, to her horror, she smelt smoke and then saw that it was emanating from beneath the suit-box. Despite immediately taking appropriate action the candle had burnt through the thick box and had scorched a small hole in the suit. I can only imagine the terror Valma must have felt having to face up to our brother, especially as it was Lloyd, and to admit having caused such a disaster.

Possibly because the loss was so devastating for him and because he knew he had the heartfelt sympathy of us all, his reaction to the accident was quite subdued – for Lloyd. We all felt dreadful about the event, not only for Lloyd, but even more so for our guilt-distressed sister. Thankfully the skill of a local tailor saved the day with an unbelievably-excellent example of invisible mending. Even the closest directed scrutiny could scarcely detect where the hole had been and the "life" of the suit was not reduced by a single day.

* * *

Good rains during 1939 had eased the water shortage for Maryborough so, with a false sense of security, the local water authorities had dismantled the "life-saving" Princess Royal Mine pipeline that they had constructed only a couple of years before. The foolishness of this action soon became apparent, for 1940 proved to be the driest year on record for Maryborough. The low rainfall also had a bad effect on our household. By Christmas the quarry was little more than a very dirty puddle. To make things worse, the "spring" which we had depended on for washing water since we moved to this camp was completely dry, and the water from the quarry was totally unfit for the purpose.

Since we first met Mr Chester, he had often remarked to various members of my family, that the quarry was originally many feet deeper, but in past years it had been one of the regular dumps for the town's rubbish. Now in our hour of need, this knowledge stirred our imagination. As a result, a "well" a few feet in depth was dug a few yards from the edge of the muddy duck puddle. To our delight, the hole rapidly filled with water that had been filtered by the sediment to a clear odourless state. In some ways it was superior to the "spring" water. For instance, it was completely free from pond life such as wrigglers, the tiny semi-transparent water fleas and at times, even boaties. However, it failed one test, the rainwater from the stone-walled "spring" was soft, that from the quarry's seep-hole was quite hard, which was inclined to combine with the home made soap into a curd-like scum. Despite this drawback, it served our needs. Even when substantial rain in January filled the "spring" and substantially raised the water level in the quarry, another well was dug some distance from the quarry's high-water mark. For it was generally agreed that, except for special purposes, such as washing hair, the diminished effort required to climb the short distance down and up the quarry bank, compared with the long trek to the "spring", more than compensated for the hardness of the water.

Throughout 1940, the citizens of Maryborough were eagerly anticipating the opening of our new Olympic swimming pool in the coming summer. Work on the pool had begun in 1939. To a degree, this project was considered financially feasible, because much of the construction could be performed by the town's numerous "susso-workers". I imagine the pool would have been completed earlier, had it not been for the outbreak of war, which created a desperate demand for manpower and quickly dried up that source of cheap labour.

Unfortunately, the seventh of December proved to be a day of mixed emotions: more than 2,000 people gathered at the pool to see the highly-respected former Olympic Games swimmer and current Lord Mayor of Melbourne, Sir Frank Beaurepaire, perform the opening ceremony. Sadly, within a short time, the exuberance of the opening was dashed by a grievous event.

After the celebrations, the body of a seven-year-old boy was found on the bottom of the pool. How this tragic drowning could happen while there were so many spectators and people swimming in the pool seemed incredible. The sorrow and disbelief that swept through our community quickly diminished the earlier excitement of the pool's opening ceremony.

* * *

As the end of the school year approached, it was a huge relief for all concerned to learn that my scholastic efforts were again to be rewarded, I would be promoted to grade five the following year. Jack had effortlessly romped through his school year, for which he was rewarded with the Merit Certificate.

The start of the school holidays again filled us with anticipation of the somewhat exaggerated joys those weeks of freedom would bring.

Although Jack and I now avoided Coles like the plague, we continued to look forward to our Friday-evening visits to the town's shopping centre. What's more, through the generosity of various members of our family, we would always have a few pence to spend and at times we could have as much as a couple of shillings.

With Christmas approaching, the Friday night street gatherings took on an even more festive atmosphere. There were various stalls and forms of entertainment to be found in High and Nolan Streets. One night Jack and I were particularly attracted to a spinning wheel that was operating in Nolan Street, which was repeatedly conducting a series of spins. There were consecutive numbers around the wheel, which were being sold at threepence each and once the numbers were all sold, a spin of the wheel would decide the winner, who would be invited to choose his prize from a nearby crate.

After consultation, Jack and I decided to try our luck in what would be our first adventure into gambling. One unusual thing about the set-up was that the patrons could select their favoured number; Jack and I agreed our number would be 16. We patiently waited as the remaining numbers were sold to a somewhat slow market. Finally the operator gave the wheel a hefty spin and we watched as the blurred numbers sped past the pointer. After what seemed to be an eternity to me, the wheel's momentum began to sluggishly expire, and my heart missed a beat as our number crept towards the pointer, then with an uncertain rock, it came to rest on 16. In a state of jubilation we accompanied an attendant to the nearby crate and selected one of the fine large white Muscovy ducks that served as the exclusive prizes. That spin was not only lucky for us, perhaps that duck was even luckier. With Christmas approaching, I feel that instead of spending many happy years of cruising our quarry until it died of old age, it would have been part of someone's yuletide celebration.

Our Christmas Day celebrations more or less followed the well-tried format of previous years, but our improved prosperity enabled us to indulge ourselves with even more special things than we had enjoyed the previous year.

It was hard for me to imagine any greater cause for exuberance than those Christmas celebrations, but a day or so later a long awaited and unexpected event lifted our family to a state of sheer ecstasy. We received word from Yvonne, who was now working, that she was coming alone by train, to spend a short holiday with us over the New Year, and she specified the time of her expected arrival. As we stood in the spacious ornate entrance-hall of our imposing railway station and waited for the train that would bridge what seemed to me an eternity of separation from our eldest sister, our excitement was tinged with a hint of uncertainty. As we waited, I visualised – as I had done so often before – departing Yvonne waving from Uncle Will's car as it crested the hill on the town side of our first camp.

I look back over the scores of years that have slipped so quickly by since then, slightly less than six years seems so brief, but at that time much more than half my conscious life had passed since I last saw Yvonne. Valma and June would be together with their sister for the first time in over eight years.

As the train approached the station, we presented our obligatory platform tickets and passed onto what our town proudly boasted was the longest railway platform in country Victoria. A few minutes later, in a flood of emotion, we greeted our long-lost sister. Despite the years of separation and the profoundly different lifestyles we had known, it soon became clear that the bond of kinship and affection had endured.

Yvonne's homecoming created an atmosphere of warmth and elation throughout our camp, the likes of which I had never known before. The joy of the occasion was further enhanced by her thoughtful generosity of having brought a small present for each member of our household. During her increasingly frequent and longer visits over the next few years, Yvonne never failed to bring a small gift for each of us.

Nineteen forty-one arrived with great jubilation from the large crowd that traditionally gathered in the precinct of the splendid buildings of our civic square. Maryborough was very proud of the strong Scottish traditions that seemed to imbue the descendants of the multitude of nationalities that formed our close community.

For us, New Year's dinner was again a special treat concluding with a generous helping of the second Christmas pudding.

Yvonne was keen to go to Maryborough's prestigious New Year's Day Highland Gathering, and earlier that day had asked June to accompany her that afternoon. In preparation, Yvonne had spent much of the morning grooming June for the occasion and adorned her in one of her own good frocks and the appropriate accessories – including stockings. Lipstick and mak-up completed the "dollying up". June's transformation was impressive. Auntie Mag proudly pronounced that it showed that with the right clothes, our girls could hold their own anywhere. We all agreed. My sisters had a wonderful afternoon, more so June, for she had never been to such an outing before.

Sadly, all too soon with a flood of emotion, we had to say farewell to our sister at the station. She assured us all that she would be coming home again during her next holidays. Yvonne proved to be true to her word. She spent many other wonderful holidays, of various lengths, with us whenever her work permitted. It was surprising how strong the bond remained after all those years of separation. She accepted us with the same loving exuberance as we accepted her.

Soon after that first visit from Yvonne, we again had the traditional visits from the usual members of our southern relations. Thankfully these visits were now quite agreeable: Auntie Tot was becoming more affable with the passing of time and my older brothers all had jobs.

* * *

Since Jack started going to the technical school, he had been introduced to practical lessons in the various manual trades and he immediately developed a passion for woodwork. He was also developing a strong desire to make things at home, but our family's collection of tools at that time was limited to an axe, shovels, picks, crowbar and various articles of mining equipment such as gads. The only woodworking tools we had were an old hand saw and a couple of claw hammers, so naturally he was keen to get a few more tools that would help him make things.

One night when we were well cashed up, while browsing in O. Gilpin's chain store – to which we felt some affiliation because Yvonne worked for them – Jack set his eyes on a brace-and-bit at what seemed to be a reasonable price of one shilling and threepence. With a smug sense of achievement we invested our combined financial resources and purchased – to us – that fine implement and we were still left with a few pence to buy a couple of extra bits of different sizes. Over the next few days we spent much of our spare time boring various-sized holes in any piece of timber at our disposal as we glowed in the aura of our newfound power. Soon Jack became more adventurous, and with the aid of our old saw, hammers and "six-penn'th" of mixed-nails, he began to make little things at home. In doing so, he took his first step on the path of his chosen trade.

Soon after that episode, when we were again "cashed up", we invested in a bright copper soldering iron, spirits of salts and a bargain priced pair of new tinsnips. Dad seemed very pleased with our purchase of the soldering iron: perhaps that was because as Uncle Jack had told us many times, "Your father was a great solderer". This statement was supported when Dad showed us his superb method of "tinning" the soldering iron on the bottom of a jam tin. The soldering iron proved to be very useful. We were now able to make use of some of the solder that Lloyd had gathered over the years, to mend and make various things. For instance, we proudly soldered handles on condensed milk tins to make pannikins like some of our slightly more posh acquaintances had used, while we were using just the empty tins held in newspaper. I found this type of work far more interesting and less strenuous than woodwork and it was this that kindled my future love and affiliation for working with metal. Over the next few months, pliers, screwdrivers, pincers and a couple of wood chisels were added to our tool collection.

Once again, restless Louis had found employment in Melbourne, and although his departure was cordial, for many months we heard little and saw even less of him.

41

Gings and Other Things

Our meagre trickle of pocket money also enabled us to significantly upgrade our shanghais. The two local newsagencies stocked strong, high-quality six-inch diameter elastic rubber bands, which were considered rather expensive at sixpence each. I never discovered what their legitimate use was, but when most youngsters purchased them, they would innocently ask for shanghai-rubbers. This was because when they were cut into equal halves they were spectacularly superior to those cut from old car-tubes. From memory, these yellowish light brown translucent bands were about nine-sixteenths of an inch wide and just under an eighth of an inch thick.

This technological step forward came at a very opportune time, for our goat flock now exceeded a hundred and although they still regarded the precinct of our camp as home, most of them were just short of being feral. With our sisters now working long hours, Jack and I were left with the day-to-day care of the goats. It would have been completely impossible for us to manage this task on our own without our gings, which we had learned to use with astonishing skill.

Prior to each mustering of the goats for milking, or any other purpose, each of us would spend some minutes filling our left-hand trouser pocket with carefully selected roundish marble sized stones from the countless thousands of quartz fragments that covered the bare ground under the ironbarks of the surrounding hills. On locating the goats, by buzzing these stones along the ground with uncanny precision either around or through the flock, we could prevent breakaways and draft out the goats we required. Such was our aim, a stone rarely hit a goat, and not a single one ever suffered any detectable injury from this action.

It was almost certainly due to those new rubbers and the rapid firing of the several stones we had learned to hold in our left hands, that was essential to control the unruly flock, that gave us unusual ability with these instruments. Contests were often held over any large stretch of water – especially our quarry and the Carisbrook reservoir – to see who could shoot the furthest and how many stones anyone could keep in the air at once. I received extravagant praise from Jack, who widely proclaimed my ability to consistently repeat the feat of having four stones in the air at once. This resulted in frequent challenges from others who thought they could better my performance, but none of them – including Jack – ever succeeded. Being "champion" for the first time at anything, made me feel good, but what meant much more to me was Jack's obvious pride in my prowess. For the first time in our lives Jack considered my endeavours were worthy of wide praise.

Strange as it may seem, despite this almost obsessive attachment to our shanghais and our efficiency in their use, we never attempted to shoot a single bird. Jack however, would occasionally shoot a rabbit, which was still welcome fare, but I was too soft-hearted – or squeamish – to even try. Nevertheless, we would efficiently dispatch the white cabbage moths that invaded our vegetable garden, and to my everlasting shame, at times shoot down the beautiful dragonflies, as they gracefully skimmed a couple of feet above the quarry's water, hunting for insects. To salve our guilt for this ghastly deed, we convinced ourselves that we were protecting Keith's bees, which indeed were among their favourite prey.

With string at four pence a ball, it was now considered to be an extravagance within our reach, so kite making rocketed in popularity with us. We were now making them bigger than any I had seen before and by using several balls of string tied together, they would rise to considerable heights. Under ideal conditions, the tether-string could be attached to a secure anchorage and left unattended for hours. At times we would leave them flying hundreds of feet up all night and find them in a similar state next morning, but mostly, the string would have broken and the kite and string were gone.

To overcome this problem, we decided to experiment with the idea of replacing the string with the bright fine super-strong steel wire that Keith used for the strengthening cross wires in the honeycomb frames of his beehives. This increased the kites' performances to an astonishing degree; they attained incredible heights and at times they would stay aloft weaving around in the gentle breezes completely unattended for a couple of days. It was not uncommon for these high-flying kites to attract the attention of birds of prey, including wedge-tailed eagles.

Spasmodically, over the next few years when weather conditions were suitable, we would practise this seemingly harmless pastime without any problems. Then one morning after an unexpected gusty night, we were alarmed to discover that a kite's tether-wire had broken away from its anchorage.

Realising the gravity of the situation, we began a desperate search through the bush to the southwest of our place. Eventually we located the several hundred yards of the shiny fine wire stretched over the forest canopy. Unfortunately for me, I was the only one who could spare the time to retrieve the potentially dangerous thread. Slowly, but with considerable hustle, I began to retrieve the wire from well beyond Louis' old mine, to just past an old double-storey stone house on the Majorca road. It was there that I literally got a bit of a shock. High in a tree on the other side of the road hung the battered remains of our kite, with its trailing wire luckily held high above the road by the roadside telephone lines. With the long stick I was carrying for the purpose, I managed to hook the wire and drag it down to within reach. Then, without thinking I grasped the wire. Instantly I felt a terrifying sensation as the non-lethal current from the telephone lines tingled through my body. We never tempted fate again by using wire anchor lines.

* * *

Nineteen forty-one brought me a new scholastic experience, for the first time I would have a male teacher, Mr Campbell. To my surprise, generally speaking, I found him to be quite likeable and a good teacher. He was a returned soldier from World War I, and was totally imbued with the notion that it was glorious to fight and die for our King and the British Empire. This view, he relentlessly endeavoured to pass to the somewhat-doubtful young male members of his class. Each morning he would report on the progress of the war and the news was getting worse each day. His reports about the death and destruction wrought by the London blitz, which had been bad over our holidays, chilled my whole being. My heart went out to those involved – especially the children – as I silently thanked God for being so far from it all. I shuddered with horror when he spoke of the terrible battles raging in Europe and North Africa and of ships being torpedoed at night, thousands of miles from anywhere.

In the latter part of autumn, our teacher gave us frightening daily reports on the siege of Tobruk. Mid-year, we heard of the terrible events that were occurring as Hitler invaded the USSR. However, I sensed that the hopes of the community were somewhat lifted by our side having another powerful ally and their leader, Joe Stalin, was soon widely referred to with grateful affection, as "Uncle Joe". Knowing that all this horror was so far away did offer some solace – but before the end of the year, the comfort of that knowledge would vanish as the threat of war came closer to Australia.

In December 1941, a chilling event engulfed me with an even greater terror than I had felt the day the war with Germany was declared. Japan had escalated the war by stealthily bombing Pearl Harbor, the American naval base in the Pacific. That action brought these two previously neutral countries into the war, for Japan joined Germany by declaring war on Britain and America pitched its lot in with Britain and her allies, which included Australia. Japan's action brought the war even closer to Australia and the probability of us being invaded was generally accepted. To me, the gravity of this situation seemed to create an atmosphere of goodwill in the community.

Whereas in pre-war times when the occasional aeroplane flew over, it was regarded as something of a treat, now the first sound of a plane approaching would fill me with a cold dread. One plane was bad enough, but at times more than a dozen would fly over and – to me – threateningly circle the town for many terrifying minutes. After a while I was told that the commonest of these planes were our own Whirraways, which were probably on training flights, so as soon as I verified that they were that type, I would relax. But when some other type of plane flew over, with bated breath, I would fearfully watch it intently as I strained my eyes to make sure it wasn't dropping bombs.

It was about this time that working bees dug a number of slit trench air-raid shelters on the bush side of my school. This action – together with blackout regulations – only confirmed my fears that air raids were imminent.

* * *

Jack seemed to be increasingly enjoying his time at the technical school and from time to time he would proudly bring home things he had made in the various trade classes. Things I particularly remember are a candlestick made from sheet metal and a wooden clotheshorse, a beautifully made wooden form (a long seat) and a new Coolgardie safe, complete with a galvanised water-tray. Especially the latter two proved to be valuable contributions to my family's comfort.

Dad continued to make his visits to Melbourne at irregular intervals. One of these visits coincided with the onset of the chilly nights of late autumn. This particular trip extended over most of the week, during which – as was usual – there was no communication with home. During his absence, we received notice that there was a large parcel for us at the local railway station. In an air of mystery, the parcel was promptly collected, and on its opening the mystery deepened, for it contained a pair of high quality fluffy creamy-white woollen blankets for each of our beds. The event remained a total mystery and a subject of much conjecture, until Dad returned home.

In hindsight it seems ridiculous that it hadn't occurred to any of us that Dad may have purchased the blankets during his stay in the city. This was because we didn't dream he would have had the cash to make such a major purchase. Even if we had, the idea would have been dismissed, for we would never have imagined him buying cream blankets for our humble camp. I never learned how he happened to be flush enough to make the purchase; I can only conclude that Dad, unbeknown to any of us, must have planned to buy them well in advance and began slowly saving the necessary cash.

After accepting our coat, wagga and paper bedclothes for so long, even the luxury of having any kind of real blanket would have been reason for elation for Jack and me, but the thought of having luxurious fluffy ones would have been beyond our wildest dreams. The "tiles" of overcoats and the newspaper of our bed were promptly discarded, although we still retained our wagga as a bedspread. Being still without sheets, skin contact with the fluffy blankets over us, enhanced their sensuousness, and without the need to frequently rearrange overcoats and paper, we at last knew the glory of restful winter sleeps.

Unfortunately, because of the shortage of building materials due to the war, and because my brothers were working long hours – frequently twelve-hour shifts and all day Saturday – it was not practical to do much about our lowly accommodation.

Most of our acquaintances now had a wireless, but there was still no suggestion that we should obtain one, I gathered because of their cost and the licence fee they were still considered to be something we could do without. However, Jack had made a new friend at school who was considered to be a technical whiz kid in the field of making crystal sets. He lived in the double-storey house on the Majorca Road, and on a number of occasions he invited Jack and me to his upstairs bedroom/workshop, where he made major alterations to the old crystal set that Keith had brought home from Melbourne a few years before. Much to our delight, his modifications worked wonders and we were thereafter able to receive not only 3AR Melbourne, but also – under good atmospheric conditions – 3BA Ballarat and 3BO Bendigo.

At times after sunset on "good nights", we would intently turn the dial and glow with a sense of self-satisfaction when we picked up virtually inaudible murmurs from distant and mostly unidentified stations. Our improved crystal set was an enlightening breakthrough; it enabled us to more promptly keep abreast of world events by way of the news broadcasts.

* * *

Over the previous few months, the seven pence admittance fee was available for us to occasionally "go to the pictures" at our local Paramount Theatre. The theatre had picture-shows each Wednesday and Saturday night, as well as a matinee on Saturday afternoon. As an extra inducement for people – mostly kids – to regularly attend the matinee, as well as the normal two films, a serial of about a quarter of an hour duration, was also shown. In time, those occasional visits had increased. We were now able to go almost once a week, and at times when something "special" was on a Wednesday, we could manage that too. For the night sessions, we mostly went with Valma and June. On the infrequent occasions when we went to the matinee, Jack and I would usually go by ourselves. However, the serial bait didn't work with us, for I doubt if we ever saw more than one episode of any of those serials.

Occasionally, at half-time we were still cashed up enough to buy Buffalo Snow ice blocks at Marty's across the road. These were no ordinary ice blocks: they were more like frozen whipped cream and in our town Marty's had exclusive rights to the secret recipe. Sometimes after the pictures on cold nights we even had the money to buy a hot pie at four pence each, from one of the three nearby cafes, which we would slowly eat on the long, cold walk home. On such nights we would often stop and warm our hands on the square, hot-steam exhaust pipes that ran down the outer wall of the knitting mill.

Dad was never completely at ease about us going to the pictures. He seemed a bit concerned about us being culturally contaminated by the American way of life, but that was certainly not his main concern. One of our acquaintances, a very reputable builder, who had played a major part in the building of the theatre, was adamant that the method in which the roof was attached to the walls was extremely questionable. He fervently predicted that it was inevitable that it could at any time crash down into the body of the theatre. For that reason he insisted that members of his family only sit under the balcony of the elite dress circle at the rear of the hall. Our seven-penny children's tickets were only valid for the first few rows from the screen at the front of the theatre. Dad saw this area as being very vulnerable in the event of a roof fall. However, at this stage of our economic rise, Dad allowed our desire to go to the pictures to outweigh his fear for our safety. Even though we were still entitled to children's tickets, as soon as it was financially viable Dad insisted we buy the one-and-threepenny front-stall tickets. The rear of those seats enabled us to access the shelter of the balcony. Back stalls were entirely covered by the balcony, but they were one shilling and nine pence. The dress circle, or "upstairs" as it was commonly called, despite being closer to the roof was even more expensive.

To my young, country eyes the theatre looked grand. The spacious foyer with its ticket windows and sensational posters seemed to reflect the glamour of Hollywood. Midway between the foyer and the actual theatre, a wide, spectacular, carpeted stairway ascended to the dress circle. Entrance to downstairs, was by way of double doors on each side of the stairway and the projection room that divided the back stalls. The seat closest to both these doors was always reserved for a fireman in full uniform, who guarded a sand-filled red bucket with FIRE boldly painted in white on its side. The same precaution would have occurred upstairs. Because we were told the firemen did not have to pay, we thought they had a pretty good job.

42

New Horizons

Unlike the previous year, we had received excellent rains during 1941; as a result by late spring the quarry was brimming. Viewed from its cliff top, near the kitchen, as it gracefully curved behind the mound of overburden along the eastern rim, the body of water looked soothingly picturesque against its background of trees. This enchanting sight evidently stirred Keith's latent "nautical" aspirations, for he began to make a small boat.

The trouble was there were only a limited variety of materials around for such a purpose. He decided that the only suitable thing at hand for the basic body of the boat, would be one of the 10-foot sheets of corrugated iron that had previously served us so well, but was at that time redundant. True to his nature of always considering the rest of his family, he decided to make his boat large enough for three people. To achieve this, after folding the sheet and fastening each end in a watertight join, it was necessary to extensively extend the sides further to provide sufficient freeboard. After the structure was made watertight with rag and coal tar, it was fitted with a keel, wooden floor and seats. The boat proved to be very popular and many delightful hours were shared cruising the length and breadth of our "river". However, it was a bit cumbersome and not capable of achieving many knots. Jack was a bit critical of this factor, so some time later he decided to build one to his own design with the other sheet of iron. Jack's boat was much sleeker. More like a canoe, it catered for only one person at a time, but was more sophisticated, having a rudder controlled by foot pedals and cables. It could be paddled at what seemed to me, an astounding speed and was extremely manoeuvrable. Over the next several years those boats played a major part in our family's summer recreation.

* * *

With the ever-increasing threat of invasion constantly lurking to various degrees in the back of my mind, it was hard to get enthusiastic about anything, but as Christmas approached, Jack and I received an undreamt of surprise that for a while lifted our spirits above the war gloom.

Earlier that year in its final months, the Menzies Government had introduced universal child endowment. The endowment was paid to the mother for all but her first child under sixteen, at the rate of five shillings per week. This condition excluded fifteen-year-old June, but Jack and I were eligible. In our case the money was paid to Dad, who said he would set the money aside for our exclusive benefit.

Dad proved to be true to his word, for out of the blue just prior to Christmas, we were told that we were each going to get a new suit. Shortly after Valma and June escorted us to Lucas', the town's most prominent drapery shop, where we were each fitted for a suitable suit from stock. After serious consideration of several options, pinstriped, navy-blue double-breasted suits – with long pants – were selected. The long pants were a special milestone for Jack and me, for they were the first pair we had ever owned. But that wasn't all: suitable shirts, ties, hankies and socks that would do the suits justice, were selected. It was a moving moment as I watched our cash with the relevant documentation being loaded into the small ornate brass container prior to it being shot by a strong rubber-propelled device along a wire that led to the raised office in the centre of the spacious shop. A few minutes later the container carrying our change and receipt returned with a clunk to its station above the counter where we were being served, then the four of us proudly left the emporium. Despite our big spend up in that shop, there was still sufficient to purchase shoes to complete our outfits. Once more our guiding sisters escorted us to what they considered was the town's most appropriate shoe shop, where after much consideration our quest was completed. I felt really smug about my new suit and for the first time in my life I knew the sin of pride.

Christmas again reflected our ever-increasing prosperity and as always, was celebrated as a special occasion. Yvonne again spent a good part of her annual holidays with us, but by now this was not such a novelty, for she had made a number of short visits to see us during the past year. Nevertheless, her visits were always times of great joy.

Items that were considered luxuries just a couple of years before were now taken for granted. Although candles were still a major component, a brand new lamp, with a glass hexagonal kerosene – bowl and similar nine-inch high stand boosted our nightly illumination. With dedication, Dad took it upon himself to keep the lamp in tiptop condition by frequently trimming its wick and daily cleaning the glass flue to a spotless condition with newspaper and table salt, which resulted in it emitting its optimum of bright yellow light. This lamp was usually reserved for our main communal area, where it enabled us to further extend our evening activities.

Our meals now included some things I had not indulged in before. Auntie Mag's baking now included various cakes and puddings that contained ingredients that had previously been – as Auntie Mag always put it – beyond our means. These indicators of our improved circumstances included frequent batches of delicious date scones, a wide range of cakes, sponges and slices, as well as a variety of baked and boiled puddings, many of which were from her long-treasured cookbooks. Her favourite cookbooks seemed to be Lucy Drake's and the P.W.M.U., but she also tried recipes from other sources and many of the hand-written recipes that she had collected over the years when the idea of ever being able to afford to make them was just a dream.

A week or so into the New Year, Jack and I received another unexpected surprise. Dad announced he was taking us to Melbourne for a few days, to show us its highlights. Neither Jack nor I had ever been to Bendigo, Ballarat, Castlemaine, or even to Dunolly, which was only 14 miles away, let alone Melbourne. Even though I was exaggeratedly concerned about the risk of it being bombed by the Japanese while we were there, being ecstatic in anticipation of the exciting experience to come outweighed my fears. Although it was done discreetly without desire for acclaim from him, many years later I learned that Keith was the instigator and major – if not the only – sponsor of this special adventure for his two youngest brothers.

With Jack and I a picture of sartorial splendour in our new suits, which we proudly wore exclusively for the duration of our holiday, we boarded the train early one Monday morning. Even though I secretly considered myself something of a seasoned train-traveller after that trip to Talbot, the prospect of over a hundred-mile trip to Melbourne sent tingles up my spine. After all these years, in moments of reflection, I relive the adventure and joy of that more than three-hour trip. Dad drew our attention to features of the changing landscape, including as I perceived it, the grandeur of Mt Macedon and other highlights along the line. My world expanded as we stopped at the numerous stations, some in towns I had never even heard of and others that were until then just vague meaningless names.

As we neared Melbourne, I was fascinated by the electric trains and by the frequency that they flashed past, and bewildered by the maze of rails and the multitude of signals that determined each train's progress.

When we alighted at Spencer Street Station, I was disoriented by its size and complexity. I was never far from that mental state for the whole duration of our stay in Melbourne.

Before leaving the station – after a wide-eyed extensive guided tour – Dad said, "This is a great place for meals, so we'll have one before we leave". Because I had never eaten at a restaurant before, I felt quite strange as we sat at one of the many tables, with complete strangers all around us. At first I found it quite intimidating. But when the waitress came to take our order, it kindled the latent snobbery that was never far below the surface in the males of my kin – even when we were in the most diabolical circumstances – and I felt at ease, in fact, even a bit proud. It seemed that cost was not a consideration, for Dad ordered a sumptuous three-course meal for each of us. All I can remember about the soup and main course is that they were a gastronomic delight. In contrast, the mental picture of the sweet is still as vivid as it was the moment the waitress placed it before me. On the plate was a large "solid" block of really cold raspberry jelly in a sea of fruit salad and cream. It was indeed a taste sensation, especially the jelly. It tasted even better than I had imagined it would on that Christmas Day when I was nine, before my expectations were so cruelly dashed with the half-set sickly slurry that was dished up for tea.

On leaving the station, I was even more astounded by the thousands of bustling people that were everywhere and by the noisy trams and other traffic that flooded the streets. Our first destination was the Melbourne Coffee Palace, where Dad booked us a room for four nights. This new experience was also somewhat unsettling for me, so much so, that during our entire stay there, I could not help but feel like an interloper. With our anchor point settled, without delay we set forth on a hectic tour of the city's highlights that Dad had planned for our gratification and enlightenment, which – except for sleep – did not end until we boarded the train for home on Friday evening.

We spent that first day at the zoo. Although I could not expel the lingering sadness I felt at seeing the animals being denied their freedom – especially for those in small cages – I was fascinated by this wonderful window on the world, through which I could experience visual contact with so many of the earth's diverse creatures. As one might expect, I experienced my greatest delight from the antics of the various monkeys and apes. I felt a primitive kinship with the orang-utans. Their human-like behaviour intrigued me, as we watched them carry buckets and handle various other items with great dexterity. At times when we saw them lie down and endeavour to cover themselves with the several wheatbags they possessed, with a deep sense of affinity I relived the torment of those winter nights that Jack and I had spent repeatedly arranging the coats and bags of our blanketless bed.

We spent the next couple of intriguing days exploring the wonders of the Melbourne Museum, Art Gallery and State Library. I was amazed at the massiveness of this cluster of institutions, and even more so by their contents.

While I was completely overwhelmed by them all, it was the Museum that stirred my interest and imagination the most. First we stood and gazed at the exquisitely reconstructed Phar Lap, so amazingly lifelike in his glass case, while Dad admiringly related his great racing achievements and the suspicious circumstances surrounding his untimely death in America. For me though, there were far more interesting things to be seen in the multitude of other exhibits. Of particular interest to me were the towering skeletons of long-extinct dinosaurs and other animals of bygone ages. I spent hours scrutinising the multitude of stuffed and mounted skins of Australian birds and animals and was still keenly perusing the other countless exhibits when it was time to move on. The wonders of the science section were equally intriguing, but we only had time to skim over the exciting exhibits. I reluctantly left dreaming of the time when I could return to this wonderful place soon, but more than six years would pass before I visited Melbourne again.

For me, the Art Gallery was a place of extreme emotions. I was embarrassed by the paintings and statues depicting the naked human form: I had never seen anything like this "brazen" display before and I didn't know which way to turn to hide my glowing red face. In other galleries, however, I was emotionally moved by the splendour of the many paintings – especially those of Australia. We stood before *Gippsland Sunday Night*, which depicted an image of the disastrous bushfires in 1898. It was of such grandeur that the lump in my throat deprived me of speech. Because of his years in Gippsland, this painting seemed to have a special appeal for Dad, as with a hint of nostalgia, he quietly pointed out different aspects of the "captured" event.

There was only time for a cursory visit to the State Library with its impressive reading room, but the vast number of books, which Dad explained encompassed so much of human knowledge made me feel insignificant.

We also visited the fascinating old Aquarium. Here Jack and I were as much intrigued by the building's gloomy, unearthly interior – which was lined with something that looked like wet cork – as we were with the marine creatures on display.

We also visited the Melbourne Botanic Gardens and saw Government House and what I considered was the ugliest building I had ever seen – the Shrine of Remembrance. We walked around and scrutinised the Exhibition Building, as Dad told its history. We also mounted the steps of Parliament House, and the "home ground" of Wirth's Circus was brought to our attention.

It was clear that at this point, Dad considered he had fulfilled the trip's main objective of showing us the major elements of Melbourne's culture, so we could now spend the remaining time on more trivial pursuits.

We slotted in a visit to a palatial picture theatre – I forget its name. I was astounded to discover that a particular film, or films, would be repeatedly re-shown all day and into the late evening, which allowed patrons to enter the theatre at any time and sit through until you reached the point of entry. Even more, if they so desired, they could sit there all day.

Dad decided he would take us to the pictures again, and I gathered it was more to do with seeing the theatre than the films that were showing. This time I can remember the theatre's name, it was called "The Regent". Jack and I were overwhelmed by its magnificence, but the thing that fascinated us most was the imposing theatre organ.

The remainder of our stay consisted of a whirlwind tour of lesser Melbourne features. Dad took us to see the part of Collingwood where he spent his childhood. I think it was there that we saw a shot tower. Dad explained the principle of making shot, and instructed us that it was "A great land mark, if you happen to be in the area by yourselves".

We had glimpsed the sea and some ships tied up at a dock from the train as we approached Melbourne, but Jack and I made our first actual contact with the sea when we visited Brighton beach. The sand, shells and waves were fascinating. I was puzzled at how the waves were coming in when the prevailing wind was blowing out to sea – this would never happen on a country dam. Even Dad, my fountain of knowledge could not answer that one.

I was amazed how Dad with the most nonchalant demeanour, effortlessly navigated his way through what seemed to me to be a hopeless jumble of buildings, streets and roads and how he unfailingly selected the right train or tram to take us to our destination. By contrast as the days passed, I became increasingly disoriented and lost all sense of direction. It was all so different from the country environment that I knew and loved.

It had been five days of relentless activity for us all. From the time we arrived in Melbourne, we had not wasted a single minute. It had been the most stimulating and exhausting time of my life. I am sure we all gave a sigh of relief, as we boarded the train that Friday evening, for the journey home. The outing had expanded my little world and the exciting memories of that adventure have lingered throughout the intervening years.

Notwithstanding the city's wonders, I felt a lingering sadness for the children condemned to spending their childhoods in such a place, without ever knowing the freedom and wonders of "my" bush. On the happy journey back to our humble town, I made the silent vow that nothing on earth would ever induce me to live in such a city.

That visit to Melbourne confirmed that the final remnants of the severe deprivations that had plagued our family for most of my life had passed, thus ending these recollections from the Great Depression years of my childhood. However, I feel that a brief sketch of how we fared over the next few years is obligatory.

Postscript

Because of the great demands the war was making on Australia's resources, the government, under the leadership of John Curtin, was compelled to progressively introduce rationing for a number of items.

Petrol had been rationed since October 1940, at the rate of enough fuel to allow the type of car involved to travel 16 miles per week. As a result of that severe restriction, many motor vehicles were now piggybacking – or sometimes trailing on separate wheels – cumbersome ungainly contraptions known as gas-producers. These, in a way I never quite understood, made gas to fuel the engine from charcoal. I concluded from their crude appearance, that most, if not all were the product of backyard workshops. They seemed to be reasonably efficient, and by the time petrol rationing ended they were almost in plague proportions.

Of course we had no use for petrol, so its rationing didn't bother us at all. By mid 1942, ration books were issued, with designated coupons for:

Clothing: 112 coupons per year.

Tea: Half a pound per person every five weeks.

Sugar: Two pounds per person per fortnight.

Butter: 8 ounces per person per week. Later this was reduced to 6 ounces.

Meat: 2 pound 4 ounces per person per week, with some meat being exempt.

Looking back, the rationing didn't have a big effect on my family.

We were used to not having butter, and our plentiful supply of honey was a good substitute for sugar.

Tea was the only thing that seriously altered our normal way of life. Although the pot was always drained of its last dregs to avoid waste, we never seemed to have sufficient supplies to satisfy our needs – even after we were given coupons from relations and friends who were less addicted to the beverage. Not being able to make a "cuppa" when it was desired was a deprivation we had not even known in the darkest days of our poverty.

Fortunately, that situation was relieved to some degree when we obtained the recipe for SWS, which I gathered was promoted by the rationing authorities as a substitute for tea. The name was an abbreviation for sugar, wheat and salt. The appropriate proportions of these ingredients were mixed in a baking dish and roasted in the oven until they congealed into a dark brown slab. To make the brew – that tasted more like coffee than tea – a required proportion of the slab was broken off and boiled for some twenty minutes. It was a poor substitute for tea, but it did relieve the situation.

Rationing ceased for sugar in 1947, clothing and meat in 1948 and butter and petrol in 1950.

Identity Cards for all people over 16 had been introduced early in March 1942. Dad considered this requirement an infringement on his birthright and refused to register for one. Strangely, the authorities ignored this act of defiance for some months, but when rationing was introduced it was necessary to produce the card to procure ration books. Dad felt bad about depriving the family of his entitlements, but stubbornly stood his ground until the local detective, Fred Coppick, approached Jack and me one afternoon in High Street. In what could only be described as a pleading tone, he asked Jack to persuade Dad to apply for an Identity Card. Dad was a bit outraged that he had approached Jack and not himself, but without further ado he obliged the detective.

From the beginning of 1942, it was obvious that the war was an ever-increasing threat to Australia, as the Japanese wave of terror swept down through the islands to our north. Soon after our visit to Melbourne, the Japanese planes made their first raid on Darwin, and shortly after Broome and Wyndham were also bombed. Three midget submarines entered Sydney Harbour and sank a ferry, killing 19 people. To many, it seemed that widespread invasion of Australia was inevitable.

About this time, it was announced that the widely-acclaimed American, General Douglas MacArthur, the Chief Commander of the Allied Pacific Forces, was to establish his headquarters in Melbourne. This news lifted our spirits, for it offered a hint of salvation.

Nevertheless, things seemed to be becoming even more serious as the year progressed. Each daily paper contained the names of Australians who had been killed in New Guinea and other islands to our north, and news that the Germans were still rampaging through Europe and the USSR, with reports that the slaughter was horrific.

Regulations required the windows of buildings to be blacked out and for motor vehicle lights to be fitted with masks of horizontal slots with veranda-like covers. Streetlights were not switched on and outside lighting was forbidden.

My school joined in to help the war effort. The boys in the older grades began making camouflage nets, out of brownish hemp-twine on Wednesday afternoons and during the recreation breaks. I really threw my weight into the net-making and the many hours I spent engaged in that project were the most fulfilling period of my primary-school years. But I'm ashamed to admit that the main driving force for me was that I loved the job. Girls also put their talents to the test by knitting small items for the troops.

It was now common to see servicemen in their various uniforms around the town. It had become something of a ritual for crowds to gather around midnight on Saturdays at the railway station after the pictures or dances to meet the Mildura express, when it stayed for a meal-break of about twenty minutes. There were always lots of servicemen to be seen in the crowd, most of them on leave to their home here, and in towns further along the line. We would frequently tag along after the pictures just to experience the friendly, somewhat surreal atmosphere of people crowding shoulder to shoulder, on the station's entrance hall and platform.

Towards the end of 1942, a tremendous sea battle between the Pacific War's opposing fleets at Guadalcanal resulted in a decisive victory for the Americans and seriously depleted Japan's sea power. That seemed to be the turning point in the Pacific War, although there were still terrible conflicts and difficult times to come before peace was declared.

Jack left school in 1944, and obtained a carpenter and joiner apprenticeship at the town's biggest woodworking factory, W. Phelan and Sons. As one would expect from his previously displayed aptitude for such work, Jack excelled at the trade.

Near the end of the war, Lloyd purchased a house on five acres of land, near the cemetery. This coincided with Yvonne - now a manageress - being transferred at her request, to the Maryborough branch of the chain store she had worked for since leaving school. In accordance with our strong family spirit, Lloyd offered her accommodation in his house, which she accepted on the understanding that she would have her meals with the rest of us at home. This proved to be a satisfactory arrangement, which continued for several years, until she moved to Melbourne.

After the war, Louis and Keith went into free-range chook-farming. As would be expected, Dad appointed himself as adviser. On leaving school I was employed as general rouseabout for a couple of years. With Dad's passion for adopting unorthodox procedures, it did not take long for the venture to become hilarious, as thousands of chooks free-ranged through the surrounding bush. It was no surprise that three or four years later the business folded.

By the time Jack finished his apprenticeship, materials were becoming more accessible, so he and Keith decided to build a mud-brick house at the site near the quarry. They both made the bricks, Keith laid them and Jack did the carpentry, joinery, cabinet making and plumbing, with Keith as his competent assistant.

In the second half of the 1940s the goat flock, then numbering about 120, had become superfluous to our needs. Something had to be done to end their ever expanding range of marauding and the problem of the flock's ever-growing numbers. I suggested that we deprive the flock of *all* its billy goats. This suggestion was adopted, and within just a few years — with the undoubted help of unknown poachers — the flock dwindled out of existence. Sarah was one of the last survivors and she died peacefully, close to our home.

After the poultry farming fiasco, Louis obtained a job as a dragline-operator with State Rivers working on the construction of Cairn Curran Reservoir. He loved that job, and was deflated when the project was completed. After that, he began working as a machine-operator at the P&N tool factory. He remained there until his death, after an operation to remove a pituitary gland tumour, in January 1961.

After Lloyd lost his job with many others at P&N, during a slack period in the early 1950s, he managed to get a job demolishing an old part of the local hospital, where he was seriously injured when a brick wall fell on him and another worker, who was tragically killed. Lloyd suffered serious back injuries and was unable to work for almost a year. He then spent a short stint working for the Country Roads Board. Finally he obtained a job as storeman, at Phelan's joinery factory, where he remained until he retired. After enduring many years of debilitating ill health, caused mainly by arthritis which began to develop after his accident, Lloyd passed away in 2009. Lloyd and Evelyn had five daughters and one son.

Keith loved working with bees, and Jack was developing an ever-increasing interest in those insects. As a result, Jack left Phelan's in the early 1960s, and he and Keith formed a partnership and became successful apiarists, which kept them busy until they retired.

Unfortunately a short time after Jack's retirement, his health began to deteriorate. After suffering years of painful crippling ill health due to heart problems and arthritis – despite dedicated 24 hour care by Keith – Jack died in November 2003.

Dad's inventive genes were not completely lost to his offspring, which resulted in the manufacture of numerous mechanical innovations that were put to practical use. These included a double bladed circular saw; capable of breaking down logs up to three feet in diameter. The timber was mostly used to produce thousands of bee-boxes and hive-frames of the highest quality. The saw also provided the timber for three of our family houses. Those, with other machines we made, enabled them to produce virtually all the equipment their apiarist business required.

After Yvonne went to live in Melbourne, she worked at various jobs both before and after she married George Stanley. After the birth of her own children, two sons and one daughter, Yvonne soon acquired the nickname, "The Pied Piper". This was due to her habit of rounding up her neighbourhood kids, to take them on treats.

Despite being parted from the rest of the family in her childhood, a strong bond between Yvonne and the rest of us persisted. We exchanged frequent visits, and her family spent a lot of their holidays in Maryborough, which enabled us to watch their children growing up, and they in return got to know their Maryborough kin. They lived in Melbourne until they moved to Cobram, after George retired.

Between leaving the knitting mill and marrying Alan Iskov, Valma spent time working in a local café. Being a "people person", she loved that job. After her marriage Valma moved to Alan's family farm in Strathlea, in the vicinity of Newstead. Under the influence of her gracious mother-in-law, she became involved with a number of the small town's community activities. Valma and Alan both retained their passion for ballroom dancing well into their advanced years. Over the years they organised lots of district Debutante Balls, which included many training sessions to prepare the "debs" for their big event. Alan eventually inherited his family's dairy-shorthorn stud farm, which they ran for the rest of their married life. Valma passed away shortly after a heart attack in 2008. Valma and Alan had one daughter and one son.

Near the end of the war, after lots of friction between her and the head of her section, June left the mill and remained at home for some time helping with the housework, until she received a letter from the government Manpower Authority, directing her to a job in a canning factory at Leeton in NSW. Neither Dad nor June was happy about this direction. To resolve the situation June managed to get a job at O. Gilpin's shop in Maryborough. Sadly June's career as a shop assistant only lasted about two weeks. Soon after, our prosperous cousin, Hazel Phelan, offered her a job as a domestic and childminder. She remained at that job until some three months before she was due to marry Johnnie Shepherd, when she decided to return to the knitting mill for that period – because the pay was better. June and Johnnie had three sons and three daughters.

Louis and I also established lifelong marriages but did not have any children.

Keith and Jack never married and remained in the house they had built near the quarry. Until their deaths many years later, Dad and Auntie Mag were respected, well cared-for members of that household.

With the exception of Yvonne and Valma, the rest of my siblings and I established our homes within half a mile radius of our old camp. Being in close proximity to each other enabled us to cooperate in our endeavours and over the years support each other in times of crisis.

After my part in the poultry-farming "disaster", and the previously mentioned bout of ill health, I spent my working life as a maintenance fitter, at the local firm of Patience & Nicholson, a producer of small engineering tools. I took full advantage of the opportunity the management gave me to invent many original machine-parts to solve problems and improve efficiency. In spite of only receiving fitter's pay, I really loved that part of my job, especially when I saw my visualisations actually working.

In 1955 I responded to a newspaper call from the Commonwealth Serum Laboratories, for red-back spiders they needed to produce an antivenin. As a result, I supplied the spiders they required for over forty-three years. Approximately 50,000 spiders later, which were caught in all states of Australia, I officially gave up this time-consuming hobby in 1998. For this activity I was the recipient of an Order of Australia Medal in January 2001 and later a Centenary of Federation Medal.

My only claim to fame is that I have almost certainly seen more red-back spiders – for each one I sent away, at least ten were rejected because they were under-size – than any other person in the history of mankind.

I now live in retirement with my wife Eileen, on an acre bush block – where we built our house when we married in 1965 – situated half way between the house where I was born and my family's first bush camp.

The hard conditions and our diet seemed to have had little effect on our growth. All the boys attained a height of at least six feet, which was considered above average for those times.

* * *

Dad's greatly improved health, allowed him to live a long and happy life in close contact with his family and his grandchildren, to whom he was devoted.

He marvelled at the wonder of television and knew the enjoyment of the many normal household conveniences and comforts of those times. He died suddenly at the age of 85. Virtually until the last, he retained faith in the concept of his "Wonder Wheel" and would crouch down and study the undercarriage of any new car that came around the place to see if they had caught on to his ideas.

Eventually Auntie Mag delighted in the luxury of running hot and cold water, a washing machine, refrigerator, and her numerous other electrical appliances. She again knew the comforts of carpets, comfortable lounge chairs and good electric lights which enabled her to read late into the night, the romantic tales from the generous supply of women's magazines or novels, purchased for or passed on to her. As our situation improved, Auntie Mag's strong sense of humour again blossomed. She smiled a lot, and often something amusing caused such laughter that it brought happy teardrops.

Auntie Mag instinctively "adopted" the spouses we brought home and extended to their offspring, her mantle of loyalty and affection. She formed a special bond with some of her older great nieces and nephews — especially the ones that lived close by — and always had some treat from her oven for them when they visited. One nephew, Melville, from the toddling stage, became little short of being addicted to her "dripping buns". Although they were now made with butter, we all continued to still call them that. With the same loving dedication that I had known in my early years, happily she endeavoured to always have them especially available for him, on the frequent visits from his home just down the road.

Sadly, Auntie Mag's deafness had progressively become worse with the passing years. Now even June and I — who previously she had always found easier to understand — found it increasingly difficult to communicate. She did consult a specialist and obtained a hearing aid, but technology had not advanced enough to overcome her problem.

Over her last few years to communicate any but the simplest exchanges, it was necessary to write your part of the conversation on a writing pad she kept at hand. Most of us nearby, would usually visit "up home" on a daily basis, and would spend considerable time with her exchanging our news and thoughts. Auntie Mag often kept some of the communications written by her very young great nieces and nephews, so she could later discreetly share with other members of the family, the emotions stirred by those lovely quaint notes that the children had written.

Fortunately, from the time I first introduced Eileen to Auntie Mag, there was a strong mutual rapport between them.

Prior to our marriage, Auntie Mag would keep written communications from our bigoted Presbyterian spinster Auntie Alice, in which she derided the Catholic Church and Catholics in the most unflattering words. At the first opportunity, with bubbling laughter that brought tears to her eyes, Auntie Mag and Eileen would mutually share the mind-tickling humour of those outrageous dossiers.

One particular tirade ended with Auntie Alice expressing her abhorrence at Auntie Mag "permitting" me to marry a Catholic and stated, "He wouldn't be marrying her if I had brought him up". When Eileen mirthfully replied, "If she had brought him up, I'm sure I wouldn't want to marry him", Auntie Mag's laughter reached new heights.

Thankfully, the episode had a happy ending. Auntie Alice humbly attended our wedding, and thoroughly enjoyed the event, even while expressing, "I never thought I would ever go into a Catholic Church". What's more, from that point, all animosity towards Eileen ceased. She gratefully accepted meal invitations to our place, and regular trips with us to see her relations in Evansford. She also felt free to ask Eileen for any other help she needed. Even more astounding was the fact that later when she introduced her new Presbyterian Minister to Eileen, she said, "This is my niece Eileen" – then with an air somewhere between pride and disbelief, she added – "and she's a Catholic".

Eileen began to buy a particular weekly magazine for Auntie Mag, because she knew it was one of her favourites. However, at first Eileen did not perceive that the gift included an obligation to read the magazine's short stories and weekly serials, so that on our near-daily visits, they could discuss the stories' plots and the adventures of their various characters. These reviews resulted in numerous pages of Eileen's replies to Auntie Mag's views on various aspects of the stories. Our aunt would often express exasperation at the foolish actions of the heroines and the caddish behaviour of some of the male heroes.

June, as did I, spent lots of time with Auntie Mag and wrote reams on family matters and general discussion. On baking days, June often became Auntie Mag's honorary kitchen maid, who would do most of the actual work under strict supervision. This was particularly so in regard to the several Christmas cakes and puddings produced prior to the festive season. When Auntie Mag eventually needed to go to the doctor June would invariably accompany her. June also did most of her personal shopping, which included buying her clothes.

When Auntie Mag thought she had the house to herself, she would often pass the time sitting at her piano, softly singing her favourites from Sankey's *Book of Sacred Songs*. In later years, if Eileen chanced to come along the solo would become a duet.

Auntie Mag loved her chooks and to the last she would scurry the 50 yards to the chook house several times a day to either feed them or to collect their eggs.

Before Auntie Mag came to live with us, she had made a will. Although she had little financial wealth and had few worldly possessions, because of her changed circumstances, the will was totally opposed to her wishes and its existence worried her. For more than 20 years, at frequent intervals she would say to me, "I must get rid of that will of mine, Lyle, and I want you to be here when I burn it". On one of my normal evening visits to see her, as we sat alone, she suddenly sprang to her feet with some urgency saying, "I'm going to get that will and we'll burn it now". I procrastinated and wrote "Don't bother now, we'll do it another day". But Auntie Mag persisted and hurried to her room. A few minutes later she returned to the lounge where, with appropriate solemnity, she ceremoniously burnt the aged document.

The next day Auntie Mag was feeling a bit unwell and had spent the day in bed. That evening June and I went to see her, and as we talked after the doctor had made a home visit, there seemed no particular reason for concern. She had had lots of such days over recent years. After the three of us had an extended chat, I returned to the lounge to talk to Jack and Keith. Within a few minutes we heard June desperately calling. We all rushed in to find Auntie Mag had collapsed, with her eyes open but unable to speak or move. As I looked into the seemingly pleading eyes of the person I loved so much, I was filled with dread. Moments later she slipped into unconsciousness. June accompanied her in the ambulance to the hospital and was with her when she passed away from the result of a stroke soon after, at the age of 82.

Auntie Mag is buried in the Courtney plot in the Maryborough cemetery close to my mother, for whom she so selflessly accepted the burden of her children. Those who casually read her tombstone as they pass could not know how appropriate, yet so inadequate, are these words in her inscription, "Loving Aunt of the Courtney Family".